IMAGES
of America

ARKADELPHIA AND CLARK COUNTY

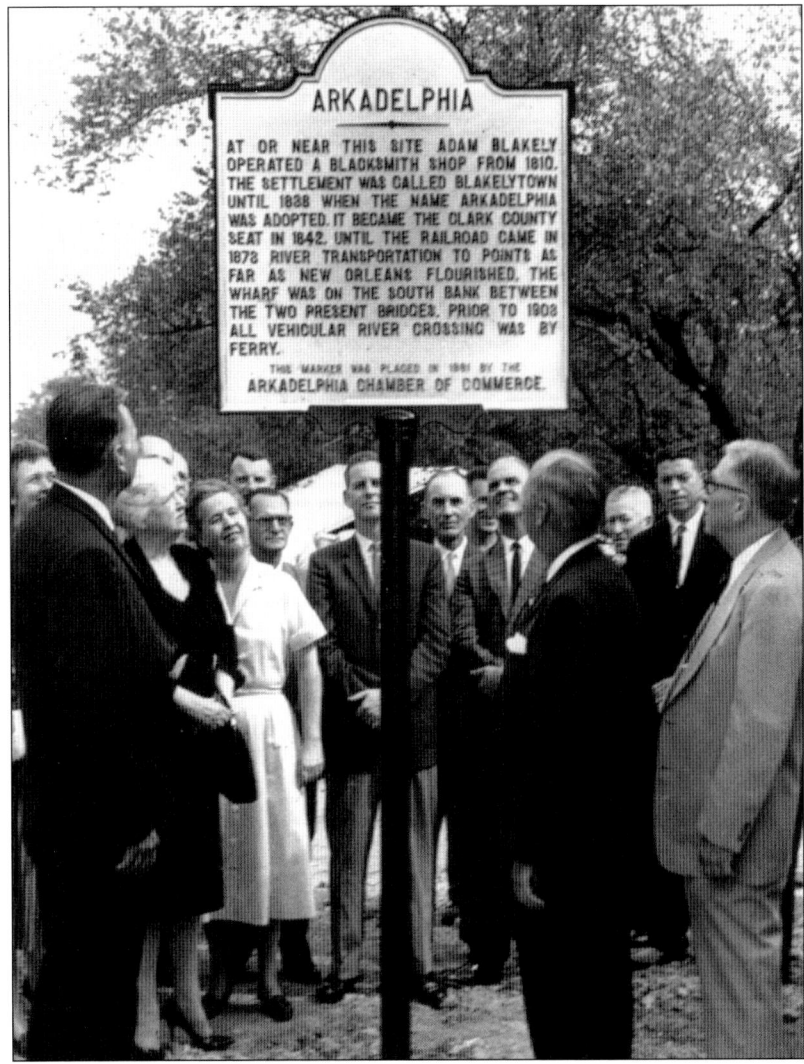

Members of the Arkadelphia Chamber of Commerce attend an installation ceremony on October 10, 1961, commemorating the town's settlement. The original settlement on the bluff above the Ouachita River was called Blakelytown after early settler and blacksmith Adam Blakely. The name was changed to Arkadelphia in 1842 when the county seat relocated from Greenville. Facing away from the camera are, from left to right, chamber president Dr. H.D. Luck, Mayor Louis Crow, and historian Farrar Newberry. (Courtesy of Henderson State University.)

ON THE COVER: The timber industry has played a major role in the economy of Clark County since the late 19th century. The town of Gurdon, incorporated in 1880, was an important railroad juncture and center of timber operations. First settled around 1818, Gurdon experienced a significant population increase in the 1870s after the construction of the Cairo & Fulton Railroad. Strategically located at the intersection of several key rail lines, Gurdon's timber industry prospered, with 10 mills in operation by the late 19th century. The Georgia-Pacific Corporation, located in Gurdon, is today one of Clark County's largest employers. The Gurdon public school's athletic teams, the Go-Devils, are named for a type of equipment used to drag heavy logs. (Courtesy of Ouachita Baptist University Archives.)

IMAGES
of America

ARKADELPHIA AND
CLARK COUNTY

Dr. Lisa Speer

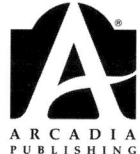

ARCADIA
PUBLISHING

Published by Arcadia Publishing
Charleston, South Carolina

Printed in the United States of America

Library of Congress Control Number: 2025932437

For all general information, please contact Arcadia Publishing:
Telephone 843-853-2070
Fax 843-853-0044
E-mail sales@arcadiapublishing.com

Visit us on the Internet at www.arcadiapublishing.com

For my Dad, Clyde Speer, for sharing his love of history with me.

And in memory of Abigail Bryant, John Christman, DeMorris Ann Christman, Reita Coffey, Donna DeBoise, and Michael Lumpkin.

CONTENTS

ACKNOWLEDGMENTS

In compiling this volume, I received support from a number of people. I am indebted especially to Ken Angell, archivist, and Natalie Scrimshire, library director, at Henderson State University for providing a large part of the images that make up this volume. Additionally, I am grateful to the Clark County Museum and the Clark County Historical Association, which house their archives at Ouachita Baptist University. Their collecting efforts made this book possible. I would be remiss to not acknowledge the scholarship that facilitated my research. In particular, I am indebted to several chroniclers of local history, W.H. Halliburton; Farrar Newberry; Dr. Wendy Richter, compiler and author of the tome *Clark County: Past and Present* (1992); and Steve Fellers, for his compelling photographic documentation of the 1997 tornado. While this volume draws on their work, any errors or omissions are my own. Carolyn Halliburton Linton and Caroline Luck provided invaluable assistance in identifying and dating images, and Willie Ross and Annie Tate were particularly helpful in identifying individuals in Peake High School photographs. Taylor Lawson, an archival assistant at Ouachita Baptist University, was a vital part of this project, giving me the flexibility to balance work on the book with my duties as a university archivist. Dr. Lewis Shepherd, vice president for community and intercultural engagement at Ouachita Baptist University, also provided helpful information and reached out to community members on my behalf. As with all projects I have undertaken in my life, I owe the deepest gratitude to my parents, Clyde and Katie Speer, who loved and believed in me at every turn.

The images in this volume appear courtesy of the archives at Ouachita Baptist University (OBU) and Henderson State University (HSU).

INTRODUCTION

Clark County was created as a part of the Missouri Territory on December 15, 1818, eighteen years before Arkansas became a state. Named for the Missouri Territorial governor, William Clark, also of the Lewis and Clark expedition, Clark County was one of the first five counties created in what became Arkansas Territory in 1819. Initially, Clark County encompassed all or parts of 15 counties in present-day Arkansas and parts of six counties in present-day Oklahoma.

Clark County is situated in two of the state's five distinct geographic regions—the Ouachita Mountains and the West Gulf Coastal Plain. The presence of two rivers—the Caddo and the Ouachita—shaped the region's settlement patterns and development for millennia. Prior to the arrival of the first Europeans, Native Americans inhabited the region as early as 14,000 years ago. Archeological evidence documents the presence of the Caddo tribe, one of the four main groups who lived in what is now Arkansas.

The Caddo lived in the Red and Ouachita River Valleys of southwest Arkansas and used these arteries for trade and interaction. They were the first documented people to engage in the production and trade of salt from the area's briny springs as early as AD 1200–1300. Spanish explorers, the first Europeans to arrive in 1542–1543, recorded the presence of an active Caddo population in the area. The Caddo continued to inhabit the area until around AD 1700, at which time a number of factors caused them to move south to join other Caddo communities near the Red River.

The first detailed European exploration of the area occurred shortly after the 1803 Louisiana Purchase. In 1804–1805, George Hunter and William Dunbar set off from Natchez, Mississippi, to explore the Ouachita River. This expedition was one of four commissioned by Pres. Thomas Jefferson to explore the new territory. While the Hunter-Dunbar expedition is not as well-known as the later Lewis and Clark northwest exploration, it provided the fledgling United States with the first scientific study of the land, animals, and plants in early southern Arkansas and northern Louisiana.

The first European settlers to arrive came in the years immediately following the federal government's publication of the Hunter-Dunbar report. Adam Blakely erected the first building, a blacksmith shop, in what is now Arkadelphia in 1808, and subsequently, the settlement was named Blakelytown after him. By 1811, John Hemphill and Jacob Barkman, pioneers in manufacturing and trade, had also arrived.

Hemphill secured the area's salt wells and opened a refinery, alleged to be the first industry in Arkansas. The salt refinery continued to operate for over 50 years. Barkman, often referred to as the "Father of Clark County," was an influential planter and merchant who opened the Ouachita River from Clark County to New Orleans for steamboat traffic in the second decade of the 19th century. Until the coming of the railroad in 1873, Clark County was dependent on the river as one of the few sources of transportation and commerce. Barkman built his home not far from the other main regional travel hub, a trail later known as the Southwest Trail or the Military Road. His home served as a stagecoach stop as well as the first seat of government in Clark County.

Settlement in Clark County increased significantly after 1830 as the result of military bounty land grant claims by soldiers who had fought in the War of 1812 and through federal land sales. From 1820 to 1860, the population increased from 1,040 to 9,735, with new settlers drawn to the region's rich agricultural lands. In 1840, Blakelytown was renamed Arkadelphia, and the county seat moved there from Greenville in 1842.

From the 1840s on, Arkadelphia grew as the county's center of government, commerce, and education. The first county courthouse was constructed in 1844. Churches and schools were priorities for early settlers. By 1859, three churches—Baptist, Methodist, and Presbyterian—operated in Arkadelphia, along with several private academies. That same year, a Baptist minister, the Reverend Haucke, opened the Institute for the Blind in Arkadelphia on a bluff overlooking the Ouachita River. That campus functioned as the state's only blind school until 1868, when it moved to Little Rock. By 1860, Arkadelphia had the seventh largest population in Arkansas.

The American Civil War (1861–1865) had minimal impact on Arkadelphia and Clark County. The county supplied troops, and Arkadelphia served as a medical and munitions depot. Arkadelphian Harris Flanagin became the state's wartime governor and briefly operated from the town until the Confederate capital relocated to Washington in nearby Hempstead County. Small skirmishes occurred in and around Arkadelphia, and Union general Frederick Steele's troops came through the county during the Red River Campaign. Following the Civil War, the Freedmen's Bureau operated an office in Arkadelphia, assisting the county's roughly 3,500 formerly enslaved men, women, and children as they adjusted to life as free people.

In the years immediately following the Civil War and Reconstruction, two primary forces shaped the growth of Arkadelphia and Clark County—the railroad and education. In 1873, the Cairo & Fulton Railroad was completed through Arkadelphia, providing passenger service from Little Rock and points north and spurring the growth of a new industry based on forest products. Short spur lines spread out from the Cairo & Fulton (later the St. Louis, Iron Mountain & Southern Railway), connecting to local sawmills and mill towns.

Across the Ouachita River from Arkadelphia, the Arkadelphia Lumber Company began operations of a large mill at Daleville in 1886. By 1902, the company produced more than 150,000 board feet a day. In 1912, after depleting local timber supplies, the mill moved to western Clark County. Operating as the Grayson Lumber Company, the mill was one of the largest producers in the South for a time. The mill prospered between 1915 and 1920, largely due to the high lumber demand brought on by World War I. As the mill grew, so did the mill town of Graysonia, which boasted a large commissary, movie theater, and three hotels as well as its own water system and electric services.

In 1880, the town of Gurdon, located on the main branch of the St. Louis & Iron Mountain Railway, was incorporated. Located at the intersection of several rail lines connecting surrounding counties, Gurdon had 10 mills operating at its peak in the late 19th century. The Concatenated Order of the Hoo-Hoo, a fraternal organization for lumbermen, was founded in Gurdon in 1892. The Hoo-Hoo still exists with chapters across the world, including one in Gurdon. Gurdon is also now the home of the International Hoo-Hoo Museum. Paper goods giant Georgia-Pacific maintains a plywood and lumber operation at Gurdon even today.

The coming of the railroad also fostered the growth of Arkadelphia as a center of education. State-supported public education did not become a reality in Arkansas until after the Civil War and, even then, lagged significantly behind other parts of the country until well into the 20th century. The earliest educational endeavors in Clark County were pre–Civil War private academies. Arkansas's first steps toward public education came in 1868 when the new state constitution established a framework for the system. Public education in Arkansas from the late 19th century through the mid-1960s was characterized by a dual system in which White and Black students received separate and inherently unequal educations. In the early years of public education, small community schools were the norm. Compulsory consolidation after 1948 led to the closure of many rural schools, but they remained segregated along racial lines until the mid-1950s. Even then, integration did not happen quickly in some communities. Arkadelphia schools were integrated in 1969.

Between 1886 and 1896, four institutions of higher learning were established in Arkadelphia, earning the town the nickname "the Athens of Arkansas." Ouachita Baptist College was the first of the four, opening in 1886 on the site of the former Institute for the Blind. Arkadelphia Methodist College, now Henderson State University, opened four years later in 1890, just across the road from Ouachita. In that same year, F.L. Jones organized the Arkadelphia Industrial College for African American students. The school was renamed Arkadelphia Academy in 1892 and was affiliated with Arkansas Baptist College in Little Rock. The academy continued to operate until the 1940s. In 1891, Bethel Institute, affiliated with the African Methodist Episcopal Church, moved its location from Little Rock to Arkadelphia. Soon after, the institute was renamed Shorter College. The college operated in Arkadelphia until 1898, one year after the main campus relocated back to North Little Rock. Henderson and Ouachita have operated continuously since the late 1800s, and education continues to play an important role in Clark County in the 21st century.

In the 20th century, the county's development was heavily influenced by changes in transportation and by one particular hydroelectric project—the damming of the Caddo River to create DeGray Lake. Since settlement, Clark County has occupied a key spot on important trade and travel routes. With the automotive revolution of the 20th century and the development of paved roads in Arkansas and across the nation, Clark County again benefitted from its location on key transportation routes.

In 1916, the Bankhead Highway Association organized to promote a cross-country automobile route running from Washington, DC, to San Diego, California. The Bankhead Highway was considered an "all-weather" driving route, as it passed through southern and southwestern states, skirting mountains, and was largely free from snow and ice year-round. The highway had both main and branch routes running through 14 states, including Arkansas.

In Arkansas, the main route ran from the Tennessee border at Memphis to Little Rock, where it diverged into two routes, both running in a southwesterly direction. The branch route ran from Hot Springs to Oklahoma, while the main route passed through Arkadelphia on its way to Texas. Along the highway, new forms of commerce serving motorists—gasoline stations, garages, restaurants, tourist courts, and hotels—boomed.

Construction of the highway received an enthusiastic response from Clark County citizens, who had lobbied hard with the Bankhead Highway Association. Securing the main route of the highway was a windfall for the county, placing towns like Arkadelphia, Gurdon, and later, Caddo Valley on the state's main transportation artery. In 1923, when the Arkansas state highway system was formed, and later, in 1925, when the US Highway System was established, the route from Little Rock to Texarkana followed the main route of the Bankhead Highway. US Highway 67 became a primary route connecting the central United States from its northern terminus on the border of Iowa and Illinois to southwest Texas.

Newspaper advertisements and postcards from the era reflect the importance of these travel routes to towns along the way. Among the many local hotels and tourist courts that opened were Madden's Café and Tourist Court and the Terra Cotta Tourist Court, both located at the junction of Highways 7 and 67 in Caddo Valley, and the Carlson Motel, between Arkadelphia and Gurdon. In Arkadelphia, motorists had their pick of tourist courts and hotels that included the Colonial Tourist Hotel; Pete's Court and Café; George's Court and Café; Mrs. Ward's Tourist Home, which advertised its location on the "Broadway of America;" and several others. Garages and service stations, like Johnson's, Peoples, and the Bankhead Service Station, also opened during this time.

Following World War II, another development in the nation's transportation infrastructure brought changes and challenges to Clark County. In 1956, Pres. Dwight D. Eisenhower signed the Federal Aid Highway Act, an effort to improve the nation's automobile routes by establishing standards for road construction and signage. In some places, this meant constructing entirely new roads, while in others, existing stretches of highway were incorporated. Interstates 30 and 40 traversed Arkansas, with Interstate 30 passing through Clark County at Caddo Valley but several miles from the downtowns of Arkadelphia and Gurdon.

As was the case with many towns located near the interstate, downtowns began drying up, while existing and new commerce relocated in proximity to the interstate. In Clark County, this change resulted in growth for places like Caddo Valley, while towns like Arkadelphia had to shift patterns of commercial growth toward the interstate. This change continues to influence economic growth today, although many small towns have benefitted from revitalization efforts to create downtowns that appeal to residents and travelers wishing to support local businesses and explore local history and culture.

The other major development of the 20th century that impacted Clark County was a project that took over 50 years to accomplish—the construction of DeGray Dam and Lake. In 1909, Arkansas Power & Light founder Harvey Couch allegedly suggested the idea of a dam in the area. Parts of Clark County were prone to flooding from the Caddo, Ouachita, and Little Missouri Rivers. Beginning in the 1930s, the federal government carried out geological studies of the area, but nothing came of these efforts.

The idea for the dam had support in Clark County and in adjacent Hot Spring County. Sen. John McClellan and Congressman Oren Harris, both of Arkansas, provided influential support for the project. Locally, the Ouachita Valley Association (OVA) had worked to raise support for the project since the late 1930s. The dam, once built, would impound water from the Caddo River, creating a 13,400-acre lake that would provide hydroelectric power and a recreational outlet and improve the arability of the surrounding land, only about five percent of which had been cultivated due to periodic flooding.

After several false starts between 1950 and 1960, Congress finally appropriated funding for the dam in 1961. Construction began in 1962 and took seven years to complete. The gate was closed on DeGray Dam on August 8, 1969, and the dam was dedicated on May 20, 1972. In all, the project cost approximately $64 million and required the movement of seven million yards of earth. DeGray Lake and its subsequent incorporation into the Arkansas State Parks system and the construction of a lodge and conference center, camping and picnicking areas, a marina, and a golf course created and continues to provide a recreational tourism industry in Clark County.

Despite the changes of the preceding decades, Clark County maintained a small-town, community-focused atmosphere. However, an event that occurred in 1997 tested the county's resilience. On March 1-2, 1997, the central and southern United States experienced a major tornado outbreak, affecting areas from Arkansas to Kentucky. The outbreak produced 58 tornadoes, with 16 of them in Arkansas. Twenty-seven people died, with all but two of the deaths occurring in Arkansas. One of the cells that spawned multiple tornadoes was the "Interstate 30 Supercell," which tracked through towns lying along the interstate in southern and central Arkansas.

Mid-afternoon on March 1, an F-4 tornado cut a 51-mile swath through Clark and adjacent Hot Spring Counties. Crossing the interstate at Gum Springs, the tornado blew vehicles off the road—killing one motorist—overturning a tractor-trailer rig and destroying a truck stop. Touching down again on the southwestern edge of Arkadelphia, the tornado, which stretched three-quarters of a mile wide, destroyed or severely damaged over 60 city blocks, including much of downtown. The tornado destroyed approximately 120 residences and damaged another 256. In a mobile home park, the tornado destroyed 56 of the 57 homes. Sixty-one commercial or public buildings, including a nursing home and the county courthouse, were destroyed or damaged. Gov. Mike Huckabee, who toured the area soon after, called the scene "apocalyptic."

In the wake of the deadly tornado, which was responsible for the deaths of six people in Clark County, the community pulled together to support those who had lost their homes and businesses. Relief centers opened at local churches, and residents helped their friends and neighbors salvage what they could from the rubble of their homes, cleared away fallen trees and limbs, and assisted in countless other ways. Students from the town's two universities, which weathered the storm unscathed, also assisted in recovery and cleanup efforts. While the look of Arkadelphia was changed forever, as were many lives, the spirit of the community was unbroken. Clark County remains, as the motto on Arkadelphia's water town proclaims, "a great place to call home."

One

A COUNTY TAKES SHAPE

This pre–Civil War building near Fourth and Main Streets in Arkadelphia was at different times used as a harness shop, grocery store, barbershop, saloon, and private residence. After the Civil War, federal authorities seized the building and converted it into a Freedmen's Bureau, where all formerly enslaved persons in the area were registered as citizens. The Arkadelphia Bureau was one of 36 locations in the state where civilians and Army officers labored from 1865 to 1869 to assist an estimated 110,000 Arkansans to adjust to freedom. Among other services, the bureau provided education, legalized marriages, reunited families, and helped negotiate fair contracts between planters and freedmen. Unfortunately, this historic structure was demolished in 1972. An historical marker erected by the Arkadelphia Chamber of Commerce in 1963 preserves the memory of the important work done here. (OBU.)

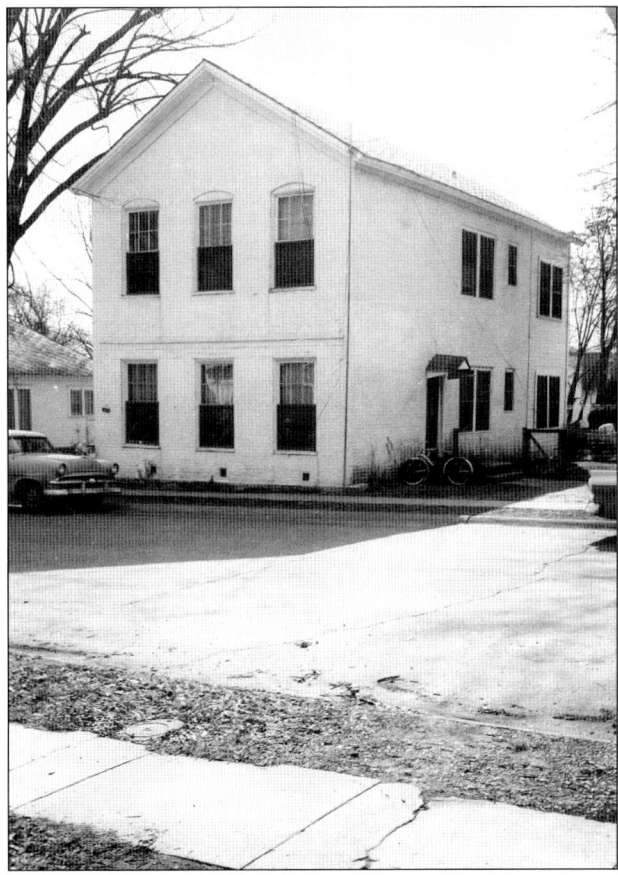

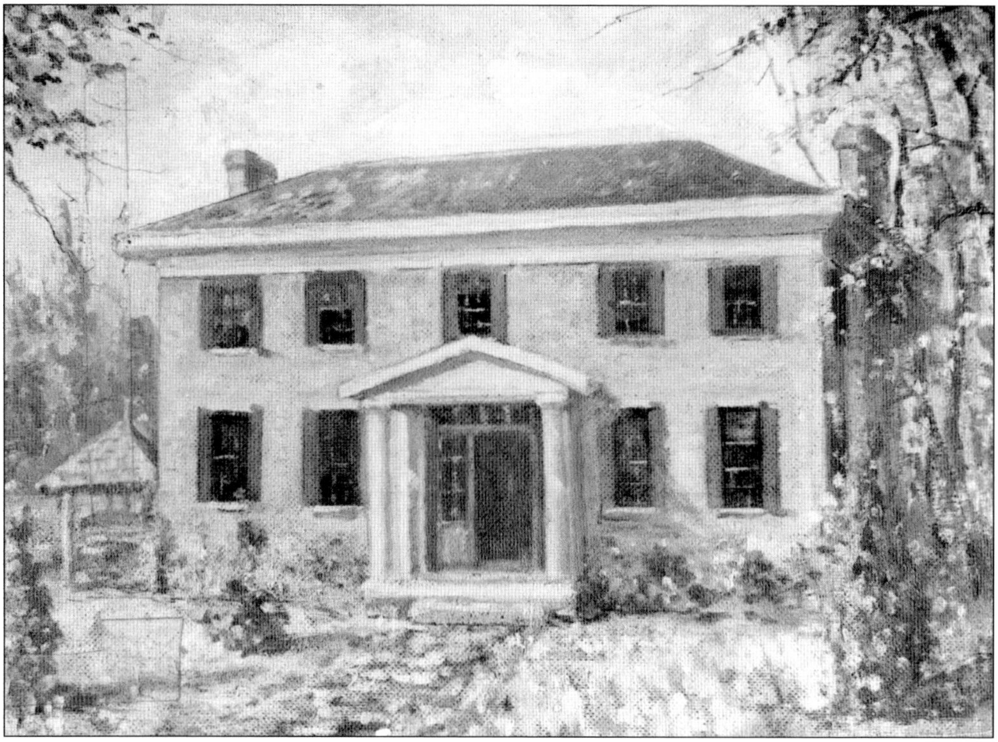

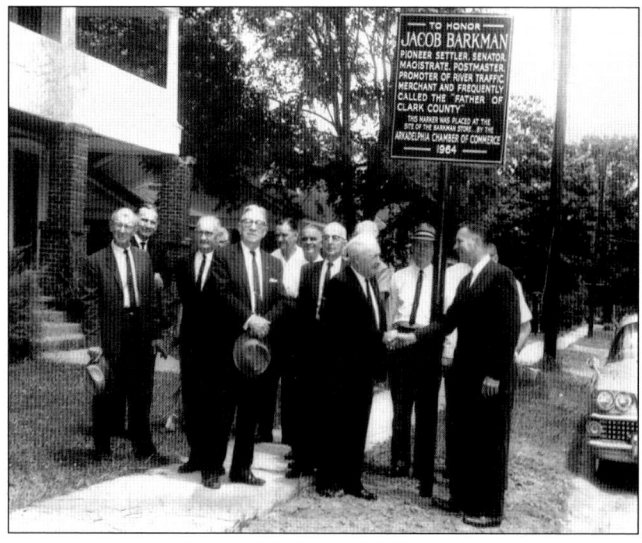

This artist's rendition (above) shows how the Jacob Barkman house, constructed in 1815 near the Caddo River, may have looked. Barkman was a Kentuckian who came to Clark County with his wife and brother around 1811. The Barkman "mansion" was constructed of bricks made on the property. It served as the first seat of government in Clark County in 1819, the first post office, a stop on the Southwest Trail stage, and the first county jail. Barkman was one of Clark County's most successful early entrepreneurs. He also introduced the sport of horse racing to Clark County, using the large field in front of his house as a track. In May 1964, the Arkadelphia Chamber of Commerce dedicated a marker (below) commemorating his significance to the county. (Above, OBU; below, HSU.)

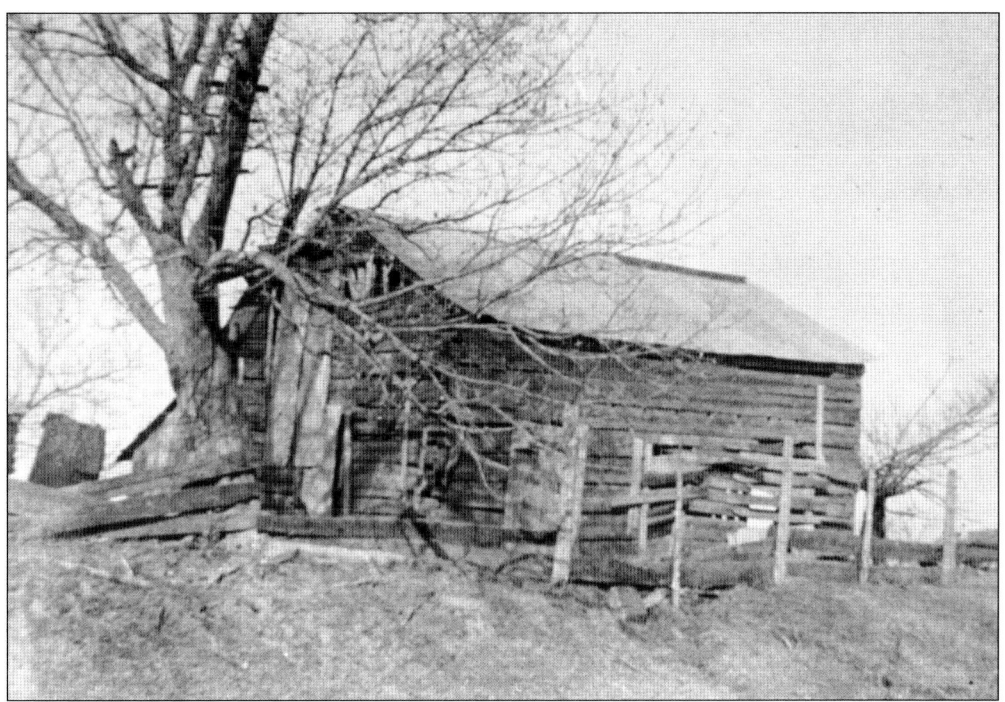

The cabin belonging to Abner Hignight represents the home of one of the county's earliest White settlers. Born in Tennessee around 1790, Hignight allegedly traveled from Missouri into Arkansas, following the path later called the Southwest Trail. In 1810, Hignight settled along this road about two miles from Hollywood. Hignight died in 1857. While his burial location is not known, a marker of him stands near Highway 26 and Terre Noire Creek. (OBU.)

The gravesite of Meriwether Lewis Randolph, grandson of Thomas Jefferson and protégé of Andrew Jackson, is located on private land southeast of Gurdon. Randolph came to Arkansas as secretary of the Arkansas Territory in 1835. Following his term in office, Randolph decided to stay in Arkansas and worked as a land agent. Commissions from the sales of thousands of acres allowed him to purchase over 10,000 acres for himself in southeastern Clark County. His plans to build a great house, patterned after Monticello, were foiled in 1837 when he died of malaria following a trip down the Ouachita River to purchase supplies. (OBU.)

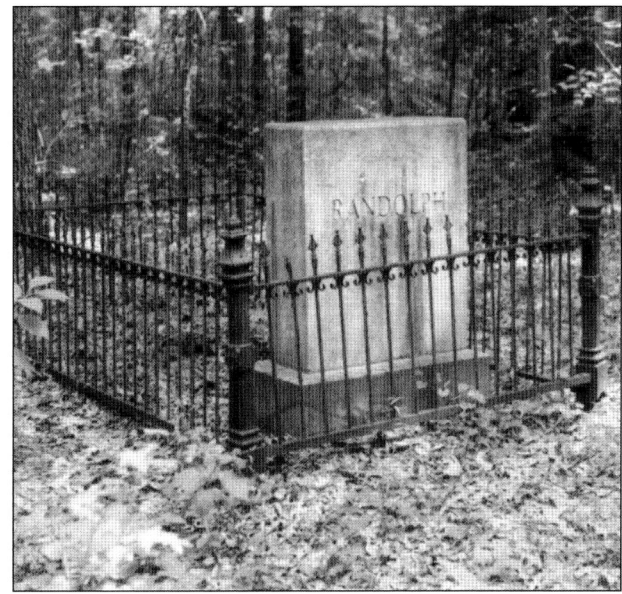

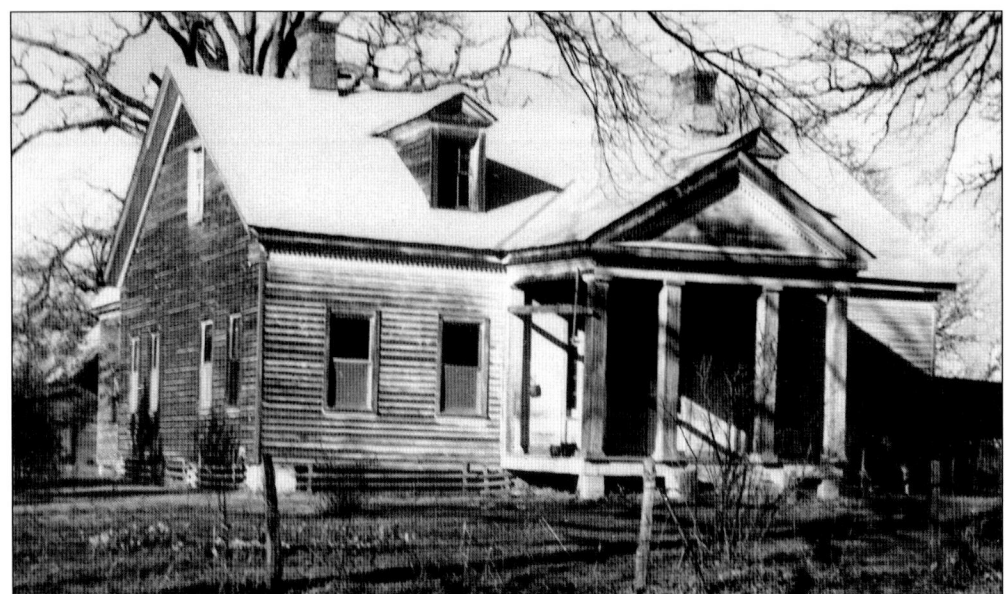

The Bozeman House, situated about eight miles southwest of Arkadelphia on Highway 51, is one of the oldest surviving structures in Clark County. The Greek Revival home, shown here prior to restoration, was built at a cost of $1,500 in 1847 by Michael Bozeman, a Georgian who moved to the Arkansas Territory in 1835. Bozeman's wealth came from owning one of the most successful farming operations in antebellum Clark County. Bozeman died in 1883 and is buried in the cemetery behind the house, both of which are privately owned today. The house was added to the National Register of Historic Places in 1978. (OBU.)

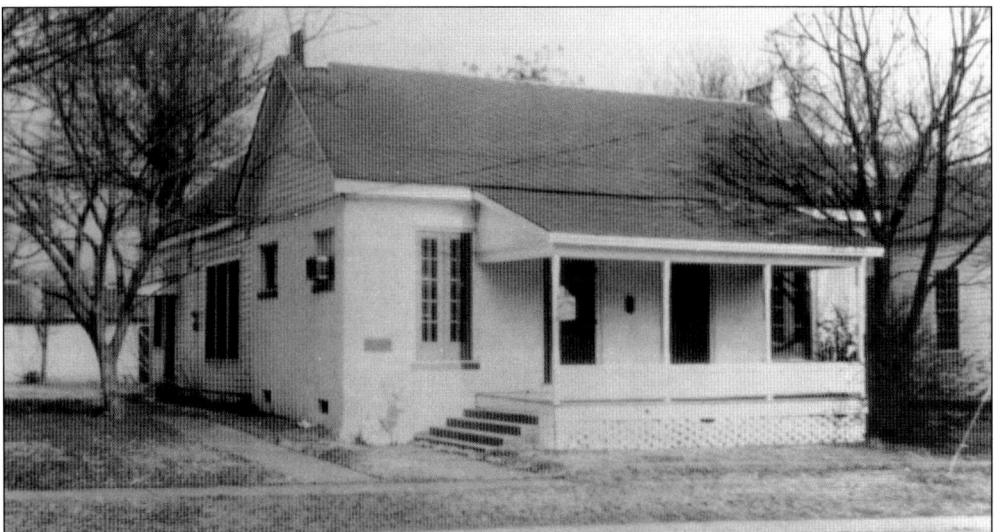

This brick-stucco building at 320 Clay Street in Arkadelphia has served as a law office for several Arkansas lawyers and politicians since the 1850s. The structure first served as a law office for J.L. Witherspoon and Harris Flanagin. Flanagin came to Arkansas from New Jersey in 1839 to practice law. After serving two terms in the Arkansas legislature, Flanagin became the Confederate governor of Arkansas in 1862. After a brief use as a residence in the late 19th century, in 1903, a local judge purchased the property, which since has been used as a law office. In 1977, the Flanagin Law Office was added to the National Register of Historic Places. (OBU.)

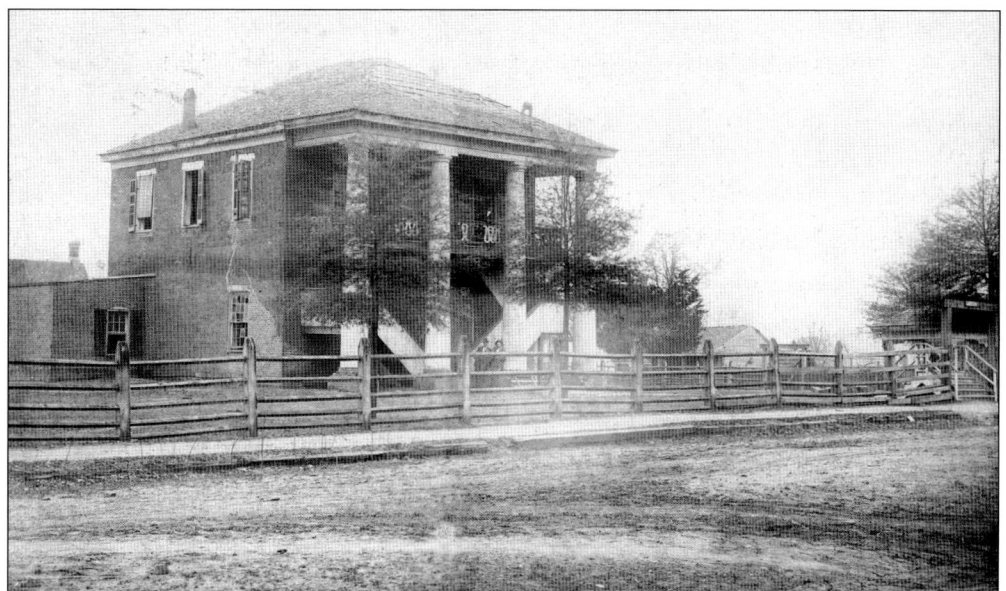

When Clark County was created in 1818, it encompassed roughly all of five present-day Arkansas counties, including Saline, Garland, Hot Spring, and Pike, and parts of southeastern Oklahoma. Early county seats included Hollywood, Biscoeville, and Greenville. In 1842, the county seat moved to Arkadelphia, and a courthouse was constructed in 1844. This edifice served the county until 1899, when the current courthouse was constructed near the same site on Clay Street. (OBU.)

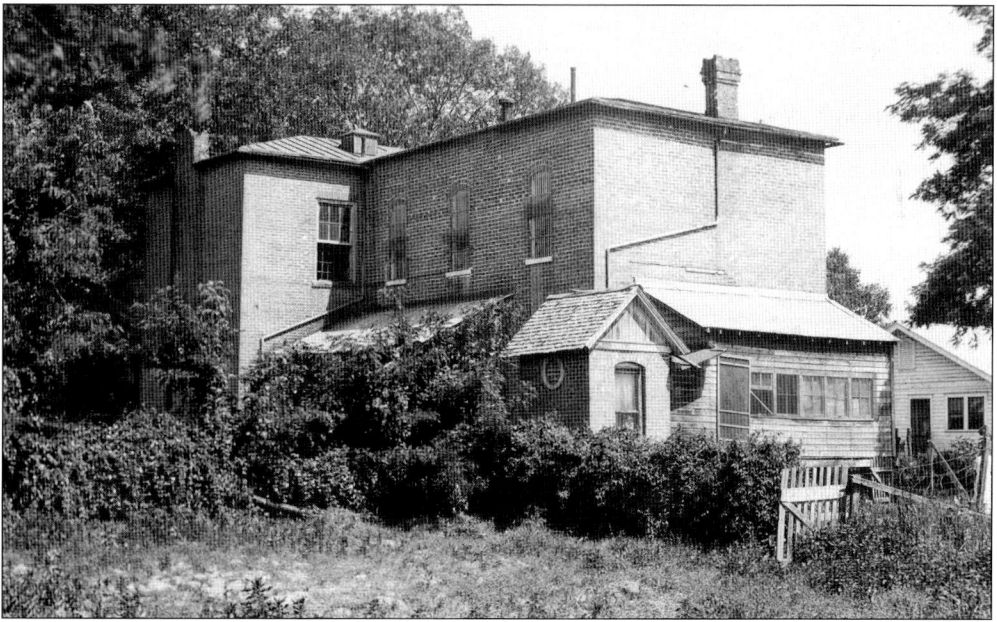

This building served as the county jail between 1861 and 1931, replacing an earlier log structure. The county's new facility for prisoners, located across from the courthouse, featured 16-inch reinforced walls of brick and concrete, hot and cold running water, and saw-proof steel cells. J.H. Obaugh manufactured the brick for the jail. Obaugh served as Arkadelphia's first mayor when the city was incorporated in 1857 and was responsible for brickwork on the first courthouse built in Arkadelphia. (OBU.)

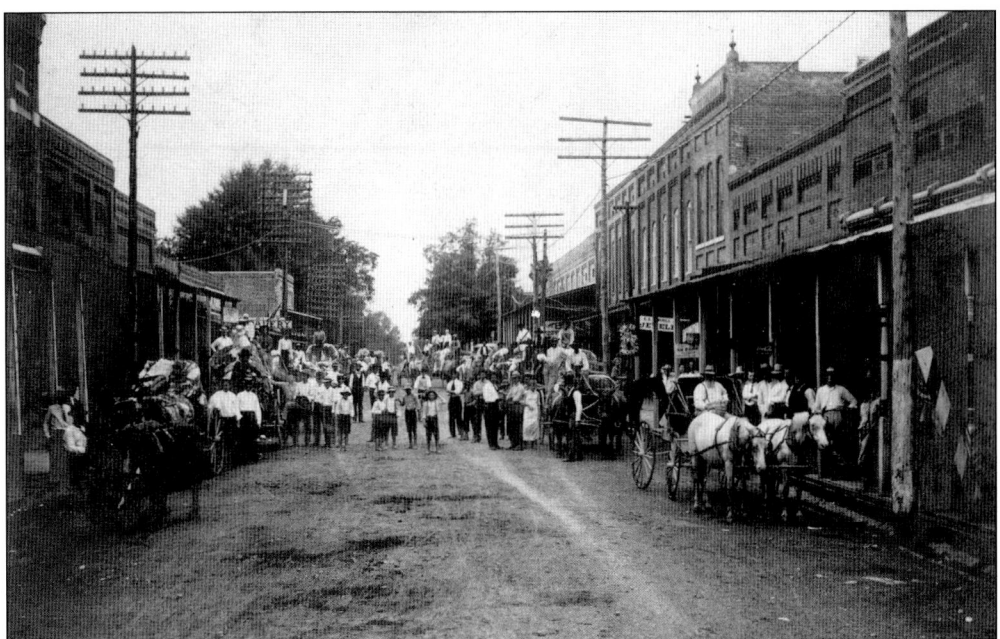

These two postcard images show Main Street in Arkadelphia around 1908. The above image looks west from about the intersection of Main and Maddox (now Sixth Street). Some of the businesses on this block of Main Street included S.A. Rudisill's Jewelry Store, a Singer sewing machine dealer, the City Bakery, and J.A. Finger's Jewelry as well as a moving picture theater, an undertaker, three drugstores, a harness maker, a grocery, and a meat shop. Among the businesses in the image below are the Famous Racket Store; Clark, Sloan & Company; Cox Brothers Tailors; and Heard's Drug Store. Dentist offices resided on the upper floors of both corners. Telephone and electrical services reached parts of the city by 1891, but the streets remained unpaved several decades into the 20th century. (Both, OBU.)

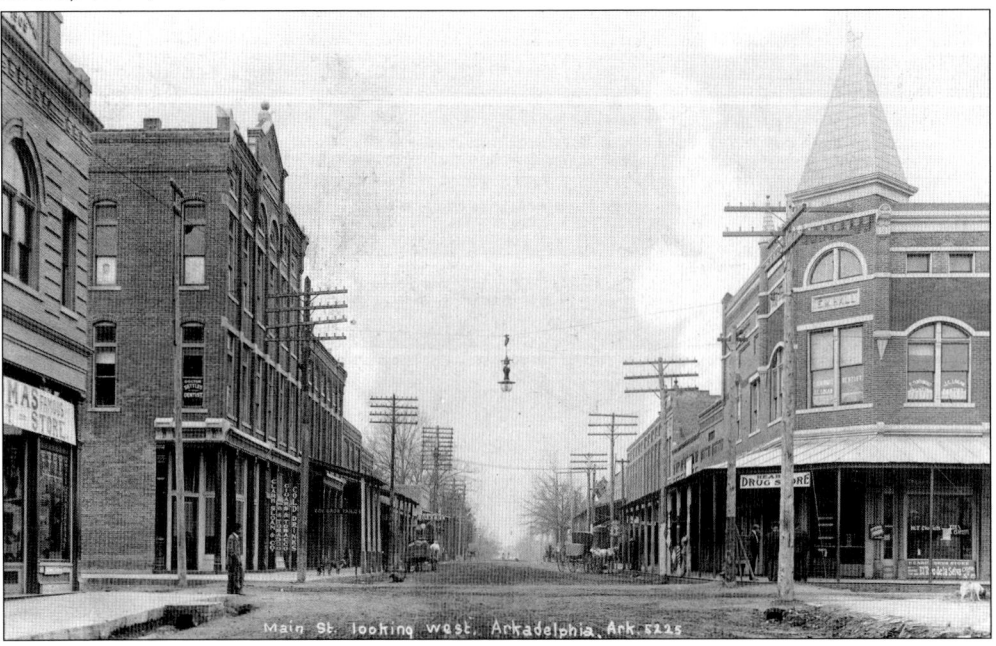

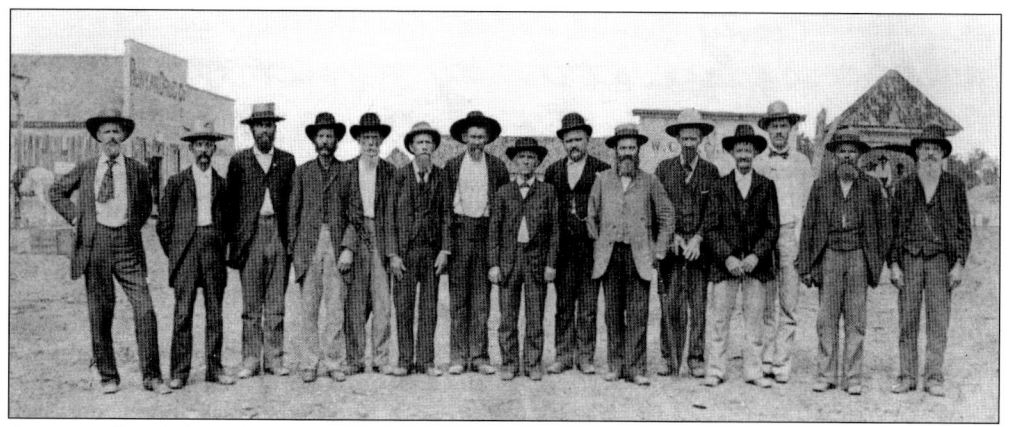

A group of candidates for office pose for a photograph at Amity's town square, with Runyan's Drug Company visible in the background around 1902. Among those identified in the photograph are James H. Abraham, who served 24 years as county sheriff and tax collector; Alex McKnight, an Arkadelphia merchant who unsuccessfully ran for Arkansas governor in 1898; Thomas Franklin Callaway, who served as county constable in 1880 and county clerk in 1898; Paul Davidson, Hollywood merchant and city councilman; Lawrence C. Newberry, county clerk in 1898; and Marion Telemicus "Mack" Shackelford, who ran for state representative in 1910. (HSU.)

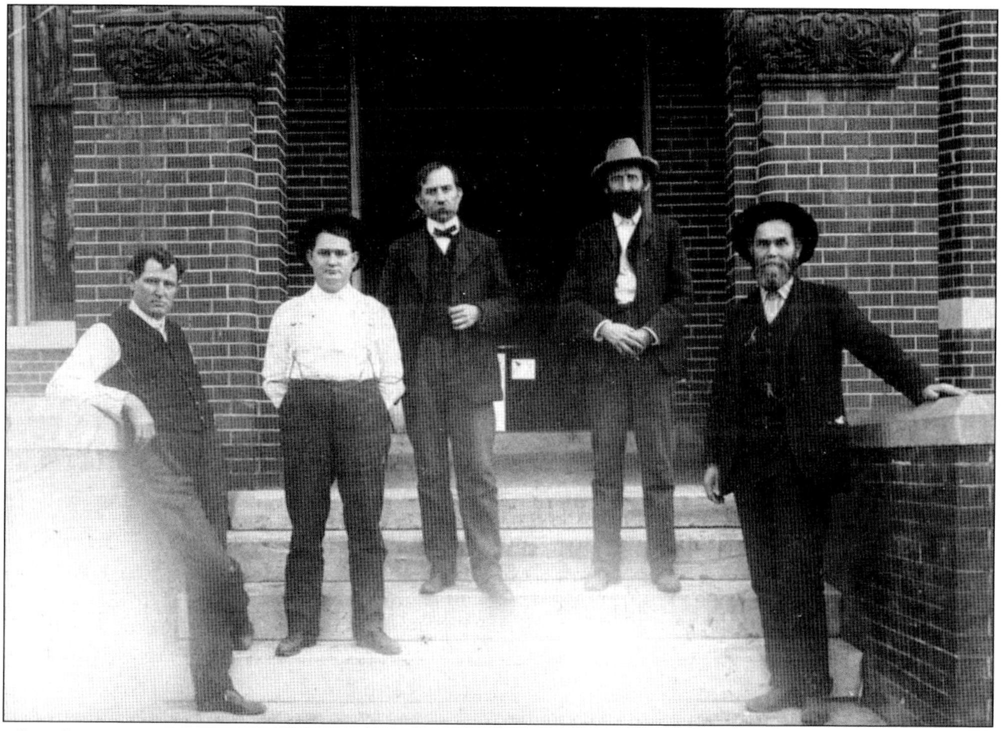

This distinguished group of men standing on the steps of the courthouse in 1902 were county officials John Allen, clerk; Alec Allen, circuit clerk; Winn Singleton, deputy sheriff; James Abraham, sheriff and collector; and Claude V. Murry, circuit judge. (HSU.)

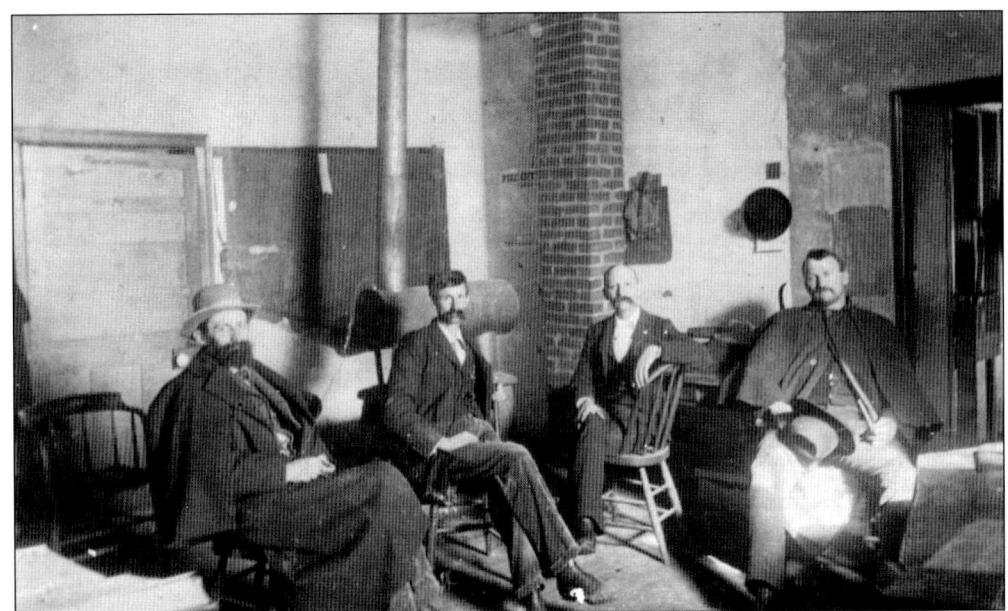

Arkadelphia and county officials assemble around the stove in the county clerk's office in the old courthouse in 1897. The men are identified as Winn Singleton, deputy sheriff; Charlie Wilson, deputy clerk; Tom F. Callahan, county clerk; and James Franklin Hart, city marshal. Hart later served as chief of police for Arkadelphia. (HSU.)

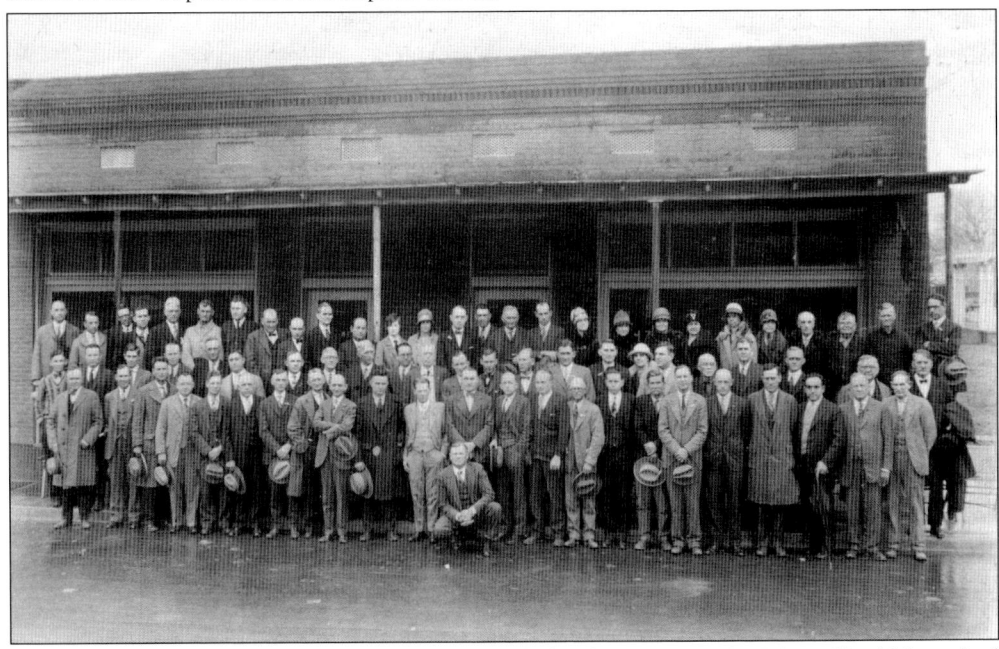

In 1921, several local merchants and the editors of the local newspaper, the *Siftings Herald*, launched a campaign to form an organization to promote commerce in Arkadelphia. A sizeable crowd of interested men and a few women attended a planning meeting on December 12. The chamber of commerce was formally organized on January 12, 1922. Through the years, the chamber has been active in securing business and industry for the region, including the Oberman Manufacturing Company, the Tectum Corporation, Reynolds Metals, and DeGray Dam and Lake. (OBU.)

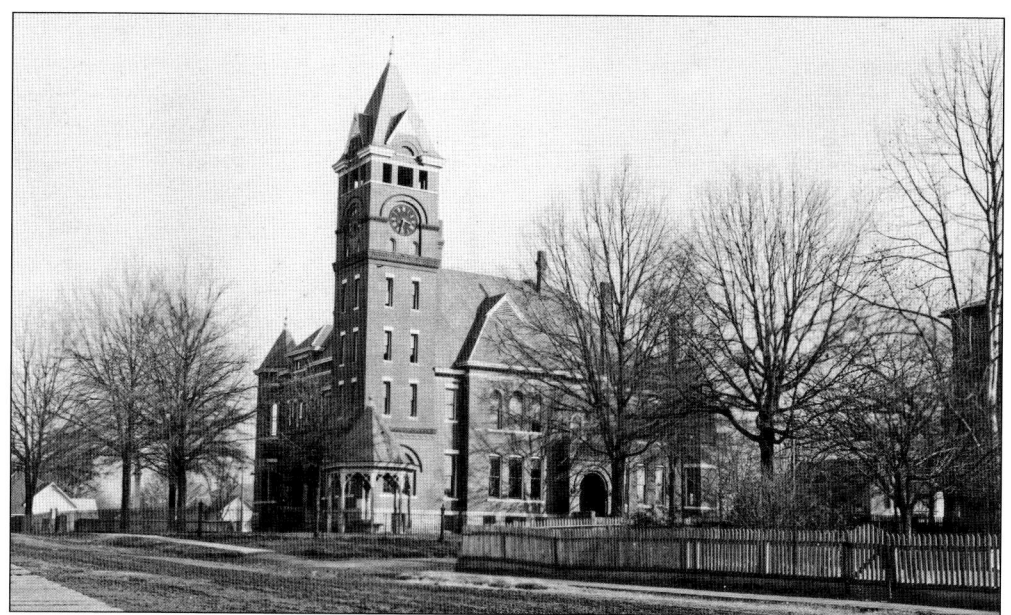

The Romanesque-style courthouse at Fourth and Clay Streets in Arkadelphia was constructed in 1899 to replace the 1844 courthouse. Except for a brief period during restoration following the 1997 tornado, the building has operated continuously as the seat of county government. The original building featured a six-story conical clock tower. In 1931, after experiencing several lightning strikes, the county removed the V-shaped roof. This feature was restored in the late 1990s remodeling. The courthouse was added to the National Register of Historic Places in 1978. (HSU.)

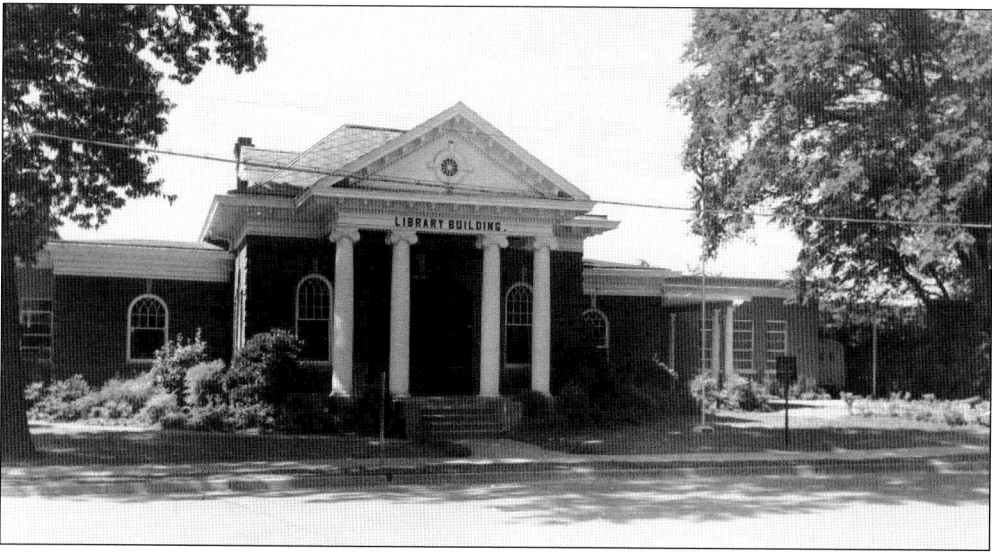

Referred to in its early years as "the Ladies Library," the public library in Arkadelphia owes its existence to a determined group of local women. The building was constructed in 1903 with funds raised by the Women's Library Association (WLA), which had been working on a library for the city since 1897. The WLA operated the library from 1903 to 1939, at which time it donated the facility to the city. The library was added to the National Register of Historic Places in 1974, the same year it became part of the Clark County Library System. It continues to serve as the public library. (HSU.)

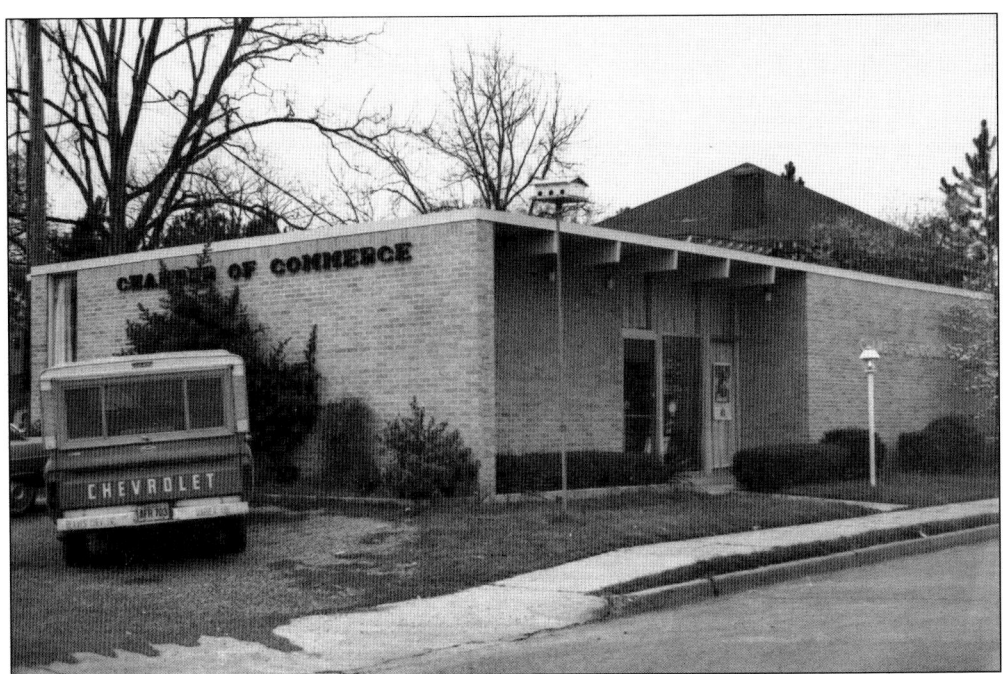

The Arkadelphia Chamber of Commerce building on North Sixth Street served various functions through the years, including the office of physician Dr. Eli B. Gary and the headquarters of Clark County's Democratic Party. The building was razed in December 2021 to provide additional space for the Arkadelphia Fire Department at the nearby intersection of Sixth and Caddo Streets. (OBU.)

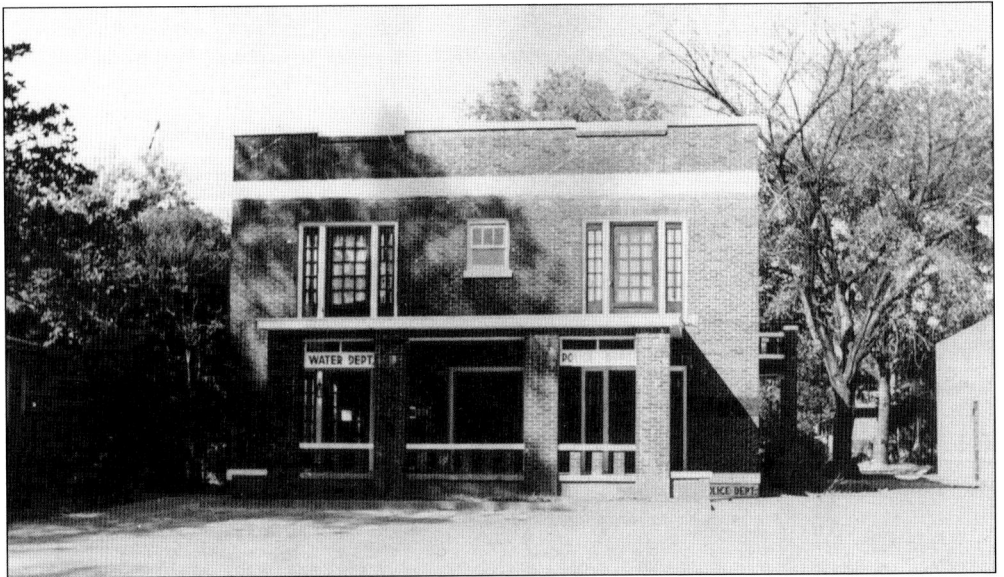

The building that served as Arkadelphia City Hall and police station at 610 Caddo Street was originally constructed around 1920. Prior to housing city hall, the building served as a hospital until the opening of the Clark County Memorial Hospital on Pine Street in 1950. Built by Drs. Noble R. and Charles K. Townsend, father and son, the younger Townsend sold the hospital to Drs. Joe Winston Reid and James Russell Barnett, who ran their practices here until the hospital opened. (HSU.)

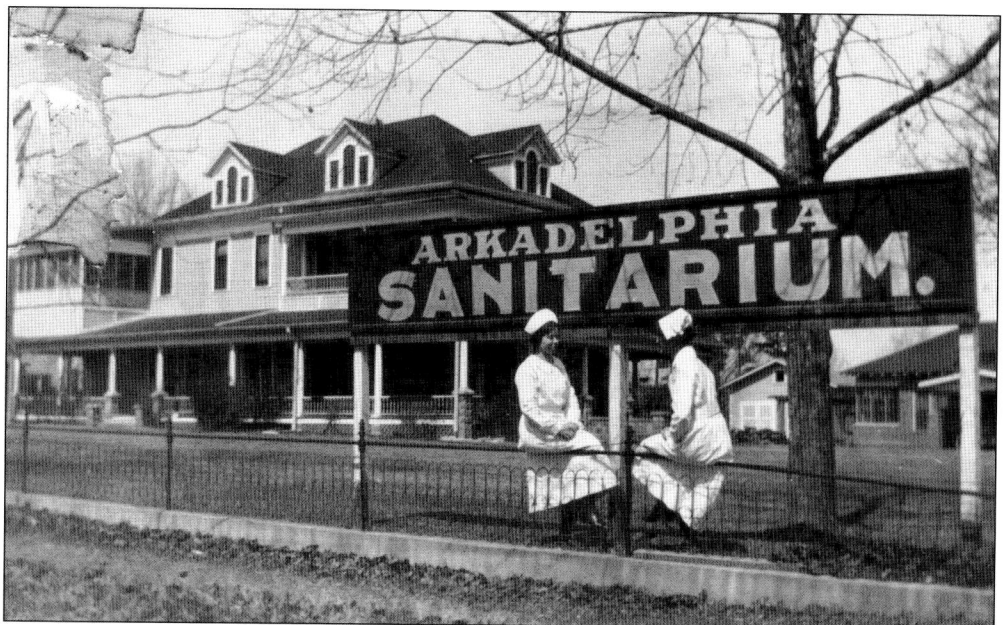

The Arkadelphia Sanitarium served as a medical facility and hospital for the first half of the 20th century. Established as the Bell Sanitarium on Main Street by Dr. J.H. Bell, the practice transferred hands after Bell left for service in the US Army Medical Corps in 1916. From 1916 to 1924, the practice operated as the Rowland & Doane Sanitarium or the Arkadelphia Sanitarium, although local newspapers continued to refer to it as the "Bell Sanitarium." (OBU.)

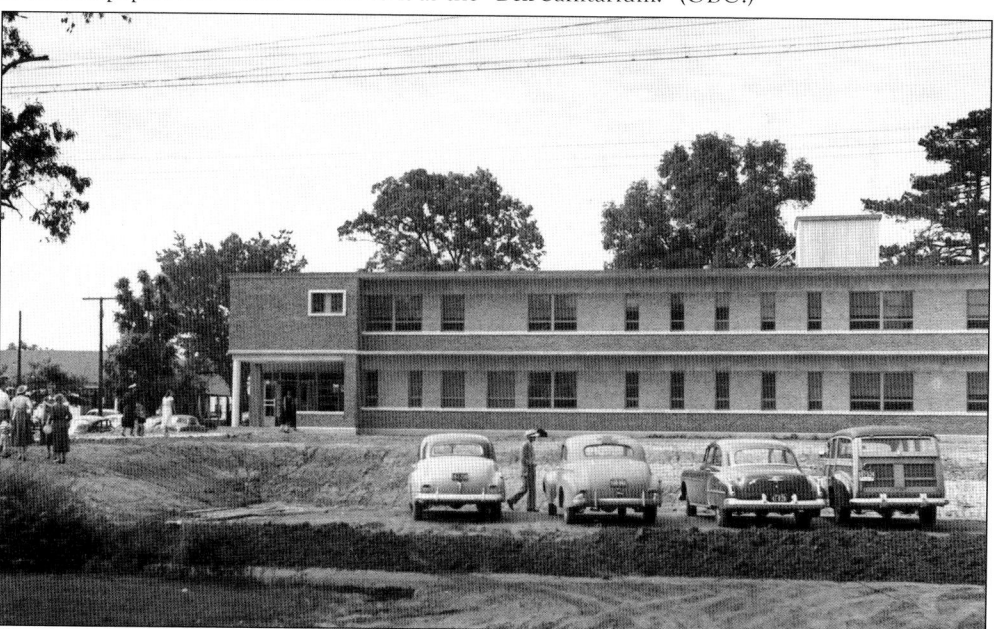

Over 1,500 visitors turned out to tour the new Clark County Memorial Hospital on June 4, 1950. The 100-bed facility once sat on the corner of Fifteenth and Pine Streets, the current site of the anticipated Martin Luther King Jr. Park. The hospital served patients until the Baptist Health Medical Center, originally the Twin Rivers Medical Center, opened on Professional Park Drive in 1981. (OBU.)

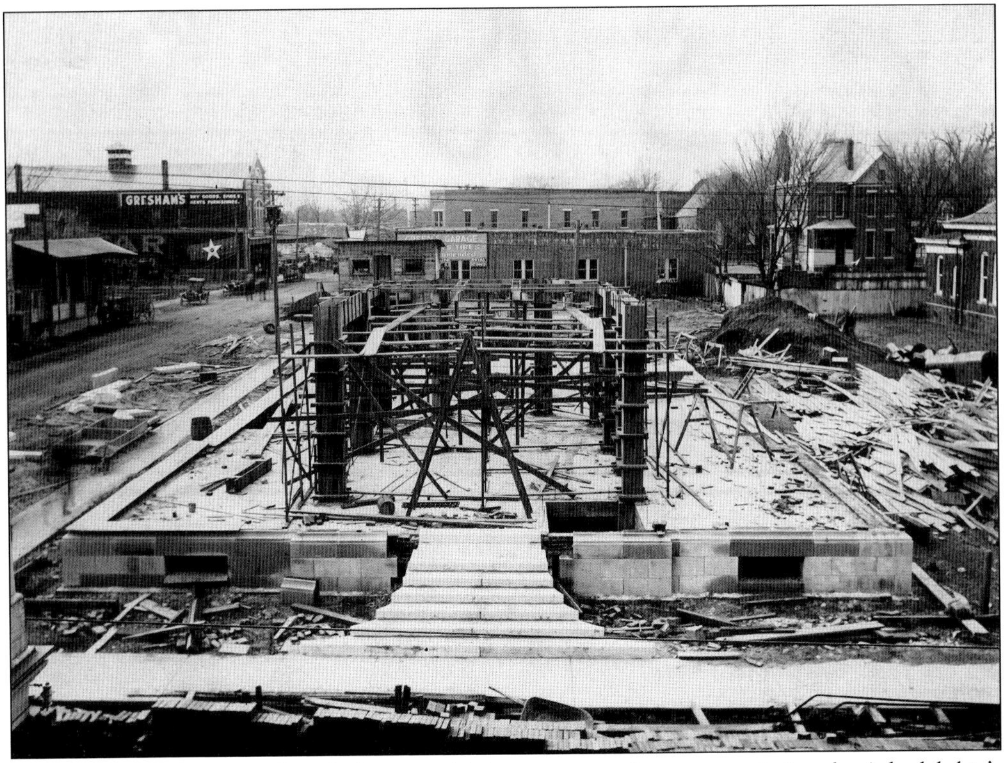

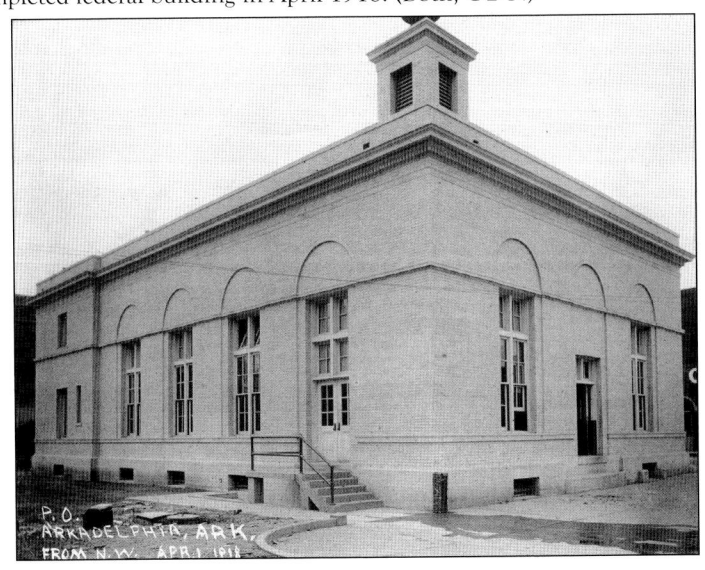

In 1915, US senator Joseph T. Robinson of Arkansas secured an appropriation for Arkadelphia's first federal building and post office. H.F. Doyle, a contractor from Cotton Plant, Arkansas, secured the contract with his bid of $44,800. The project at the corner of Sixth and Clinton Streets took two years—from April 1916 to April 1918—to complete. The above photograph, from January 1917, shows the foundation and part of the frame. Also visible, at right, is a corner of the Arkadelphia Public Library and the First Christian Church; at center, Green's Garage; and, at left, Gresham's Mercantile. Today, the building houses Southwest Sporting Goods. The image below shows the completed federal building in April 1918. (Both, OBU.)

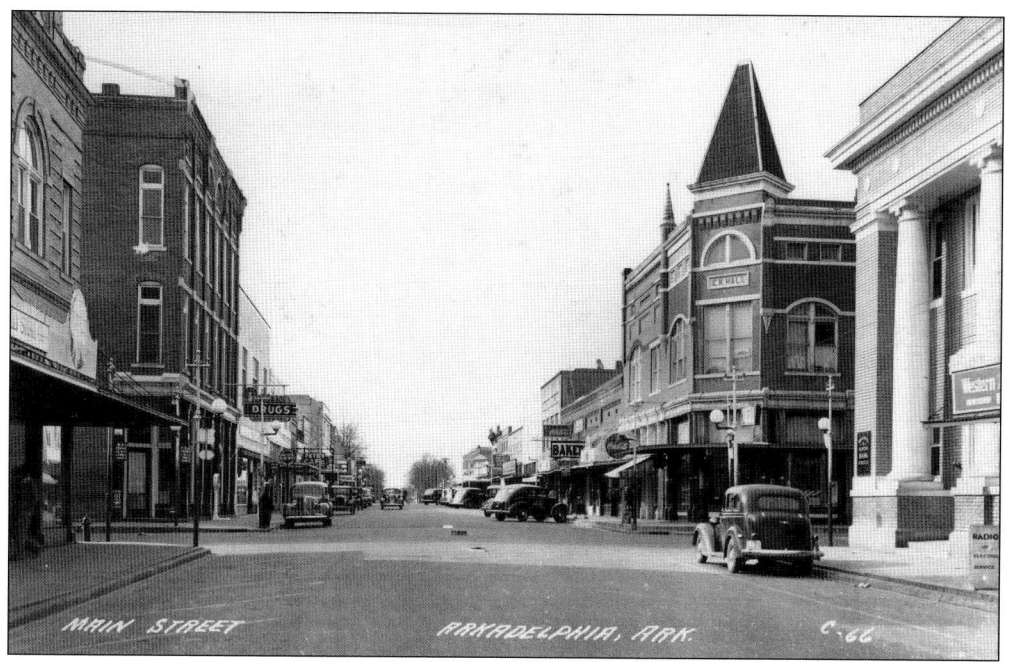

Two postcard views show Arkadelphia's Main Street in the 1940s (above) and 1950s (below). The above image shows Main Street near the intersection with Sixth Street. Visible, at left, are Elk Horn Bank, Sloan's Drugs, Pete's Café, and the Royal Theatre and, at right, Merchants and Planters Bank. Dr. J.M. Pate's office was located on the second floor of the E.M. Hall building. In the image below are businesses that include, on the left side, from the front toward the back, Gem Jewelry Store, Whipple's Grill, Heard's Drug Store, Merchants and Planters Bank, Western Auto, the Radio Theatre and, at right, from the front toward the back, Aud's Café, Ben Franklin, J.C. Penney Company, and the Fuller Boyle Walgreen Agency. (Both, OBU.)

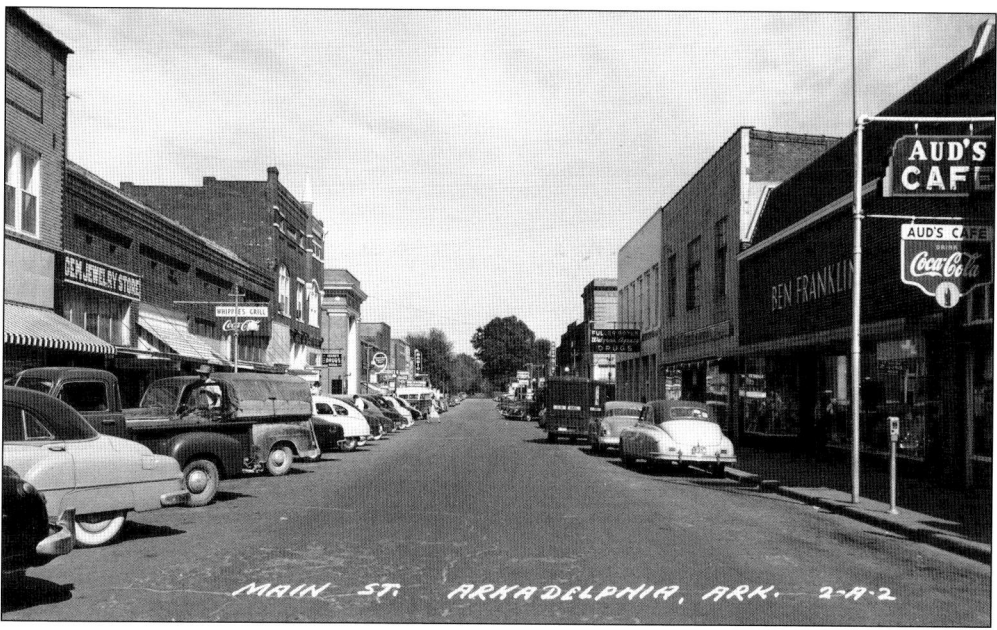

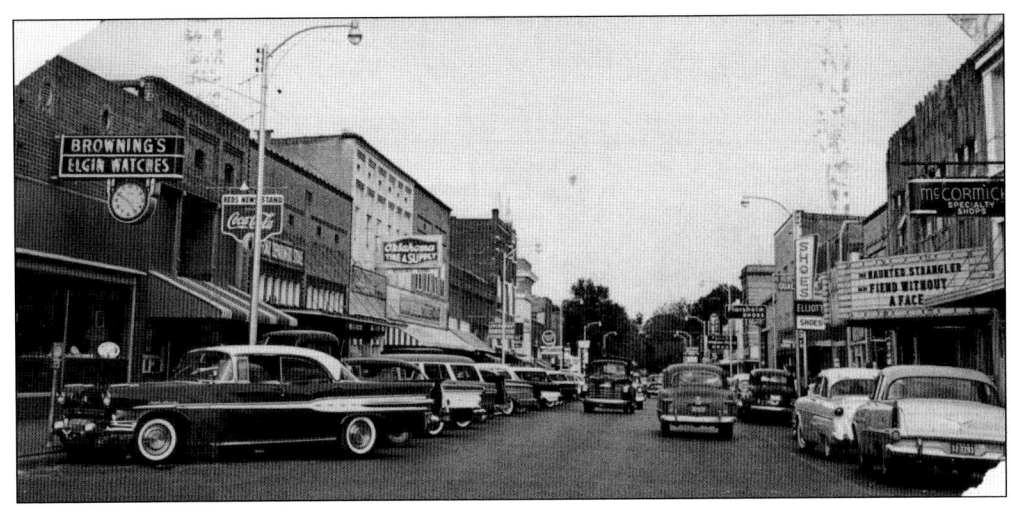

Two postcard images show Arkadelphia's busy Main Street in 1958 (above) and in the 1960s (below). Businesses visible in the above image include, at left, from the front toward the back, Browning's Jewelers, Red's Newsstand, Orr Department Store, Oklahoma Tire & Supply, Sterling Store, and Heard's Drug Store and, at right, from the front toward the back, McCormick's, the Royal Theatre, Quality Shoe Store, and Fuller Drug. In the image below are businesses that include, at left, from the front toward the back, Western Auto and West Brother's Department Store and, at right, Citizens Bank. (Both, OBU.)

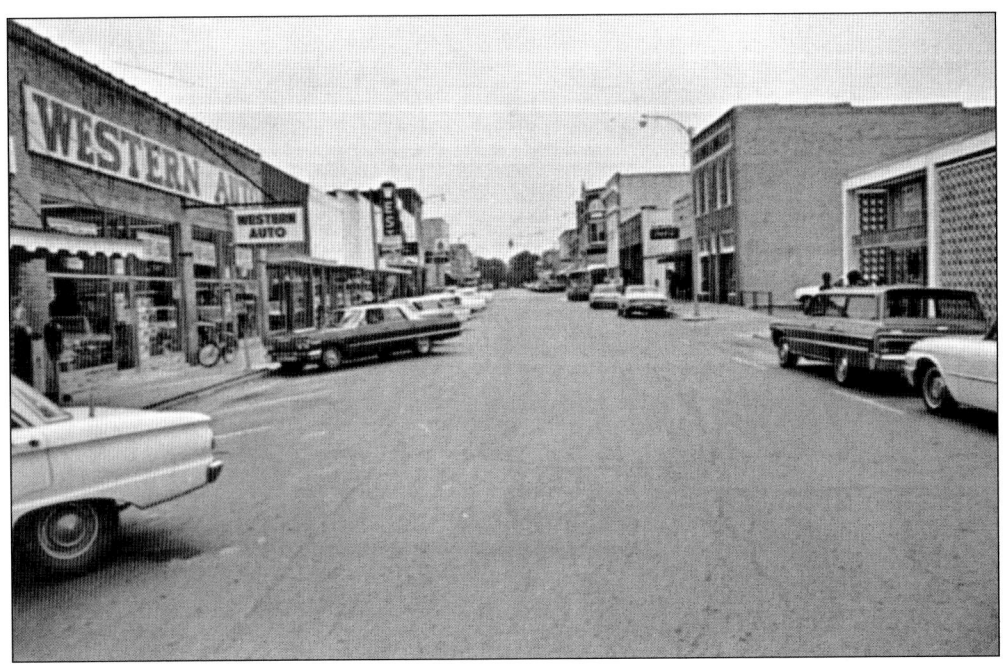

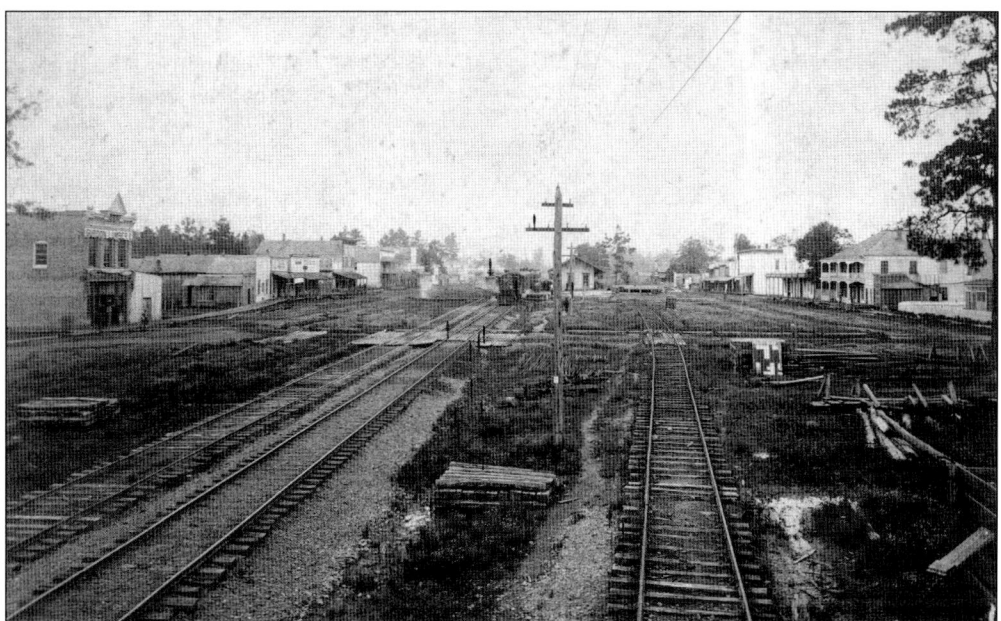

This c. 1890s view of downtown Gurdon looks south down the railroad tracks toward the train depot. The Gurdon Lumber Company is the first building on the left. By 1875, Gurdon had a post office, and by 1880, the date of its incorporation, the settlement had a depot, and the town had been laid out. (HSU.)

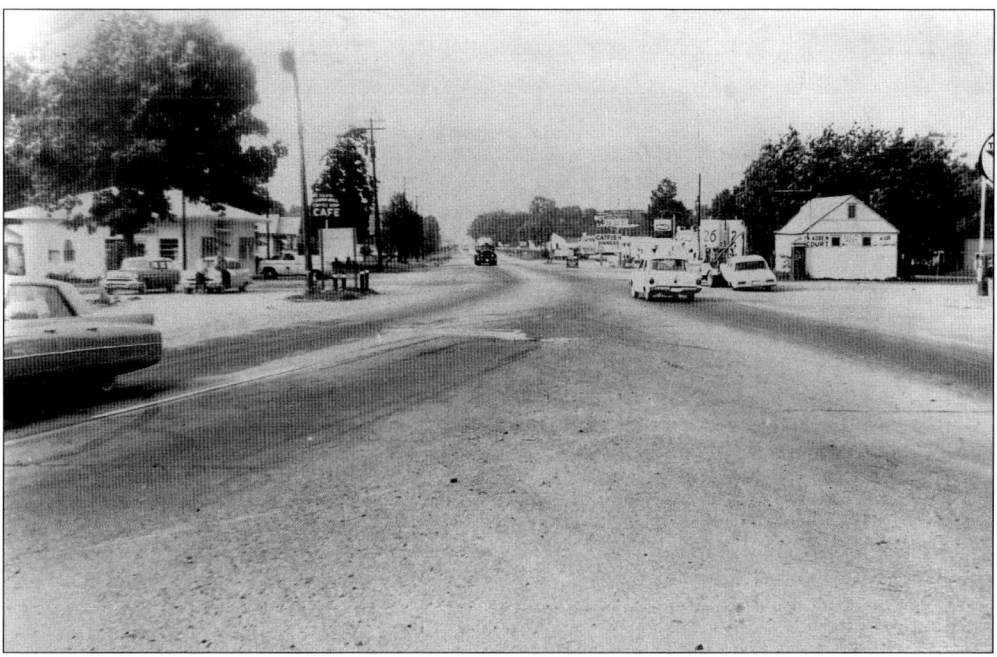

Caddo Valley, on the north side of the Caddo River, has been a crossroads for travelers since the earliest days of the county. The Southwest Trail and the Military Road passed through the area. Today, Caddo Valley is a busy intersection for travelers motoring on Interstate 30 and US Highway 67—part of the original Bankhead Highway—and scenic Highway 7, just as it was here around the 1960s. The Madden Tourist Court is visible at right. (OBU.)

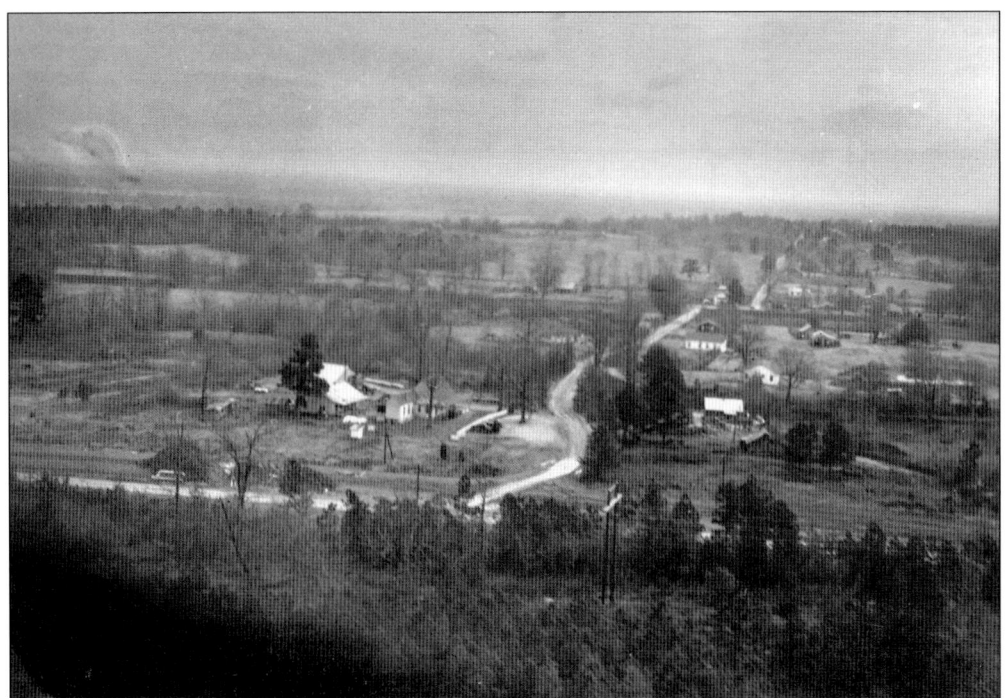

This undated aerial view shows the small community of Gum Springs, located five miles south-southwest of Arkadelphia. The county's poor farm was located at Gum Springs in 1887, near the eventual townsite, and a post office was established there in early 1889. The town was established along the Missouri Pacific Railroad, but the depot later closed. Although still a small community, Gum Springs's population grew during the time the Reynolds Metals Company plant produced aluminum there from 1943 to 1984. Since 1979, Gum Springs has been home to Clark County's Industrial Park. (OBU.)

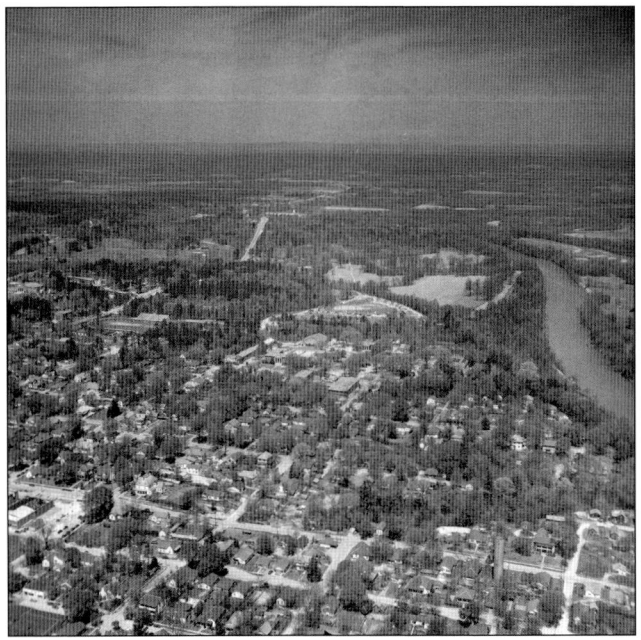

This aerial view of Arkadelphia, taken April 10, 1961, shows several blocks of residential streets west of the Ouachita River, the campus of Ouachita Baptist University, the edge of Henderson State University, and Highway 67 running north toward Caddy Valley. (OBU.)

Two

HANDS AT WORK

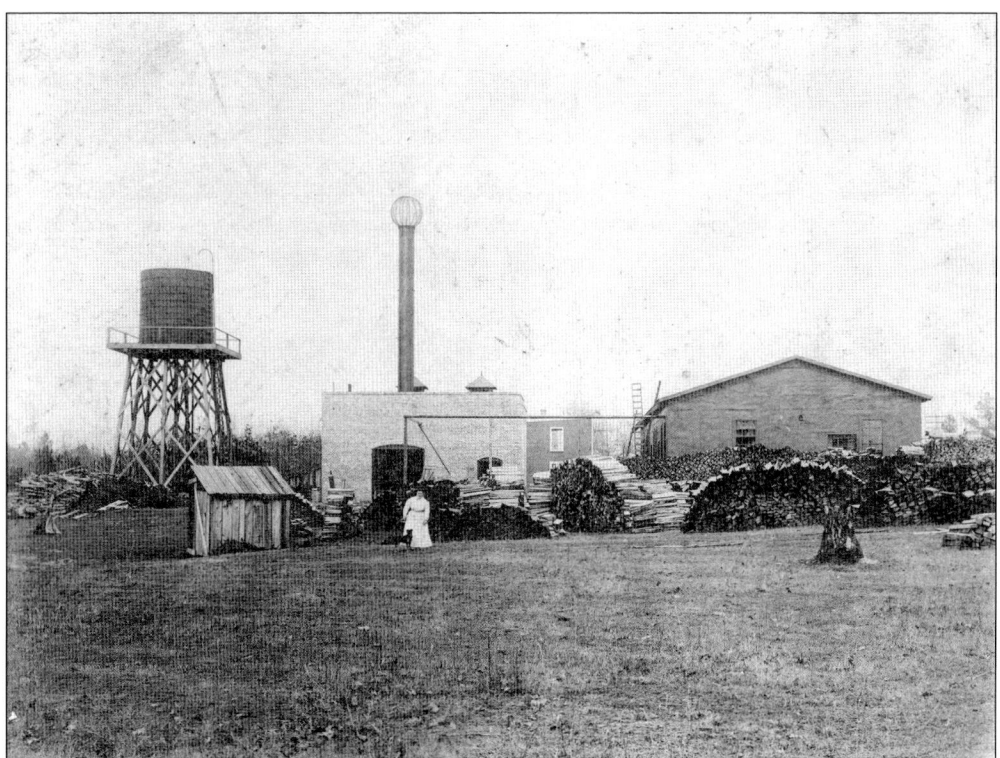

A woman identified only as "Mrs. Miller" stands in front of a stave mill at Gurdon with her dog in 1908. Stave mills produced strips of wood used in the production of barrels. Gurdon was a hub for mills sending lumber and wood materials to larger markets. Two of the most successful lumber mills that operated in Gurdon in the 19th and 20th centuries were the Barringer Mill and the Gurdon Lumber Company, both of which were purchased by International Paper Company in the 1970s. (OBU.)

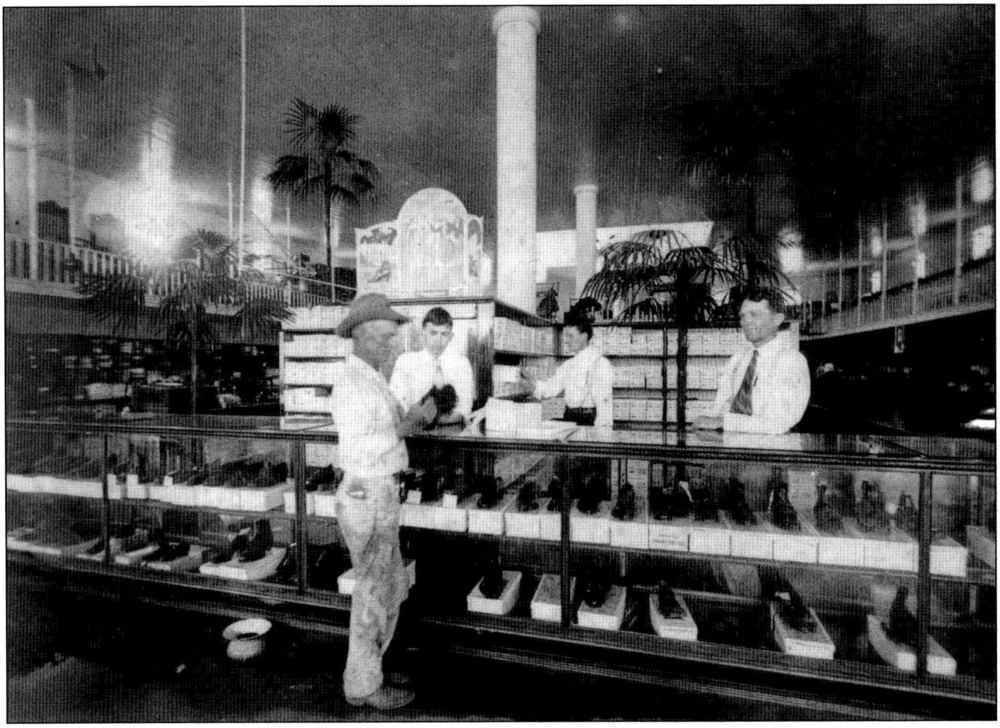

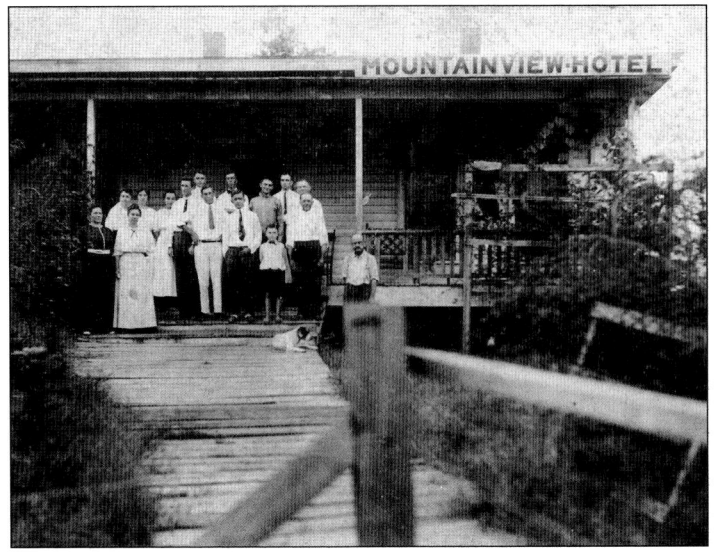

These scenes show two of the businesses that operated in the mill town of Graysonia—the commissary (above) and the Mountain View Hotel (below). Founded by the Grayson Lumber Company in 1907, Graysonia was home to nearly 1,000 residents at its peak. In addition to three hotels and a large commissary, the town also boasted a pool hall, a "cold temperance drinks" hall, a barbershop, a school, a church, a post office, and an outdoor movie theater. Residents enjoyed free electricity powered by the sawmill generators. While the mill was among the largest lumber producers of its day in the southern United States, by 1931, it had fallen on hard times due in part to clear-cutting practices. By 1950, Graysonia had emptied of its residents, leaving a ghost town in the wake. (Both, OBU.)

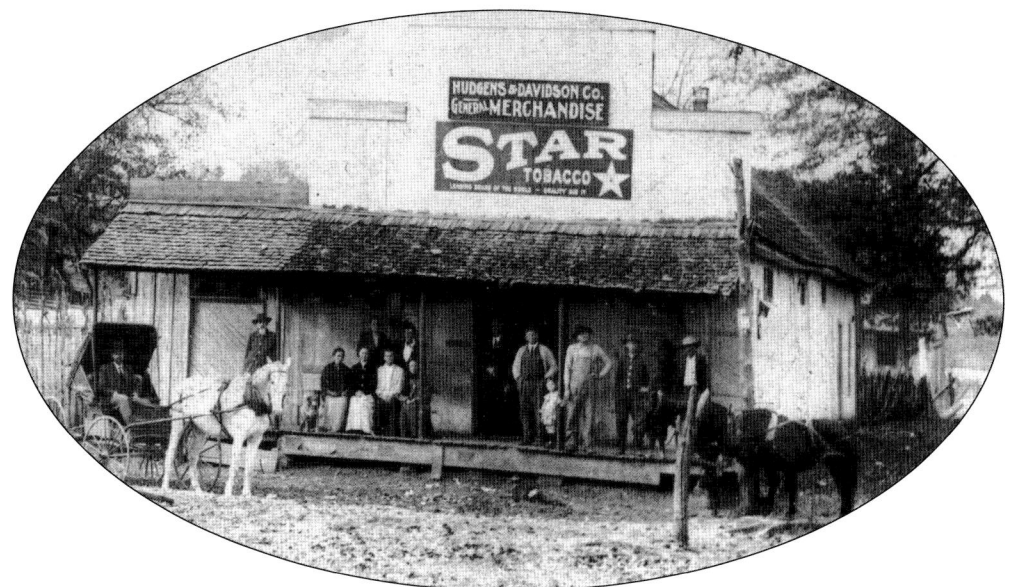

Samuel Robert Hudgens and Paul Thomas Davidson started this mercantile store in the Hollywood community sometime around the turn of the 20th century. In 1911, their success led them to open a second store in Arkadelphia in the Dr. J.H. Bell building at 629 Main Street. (OBU.)

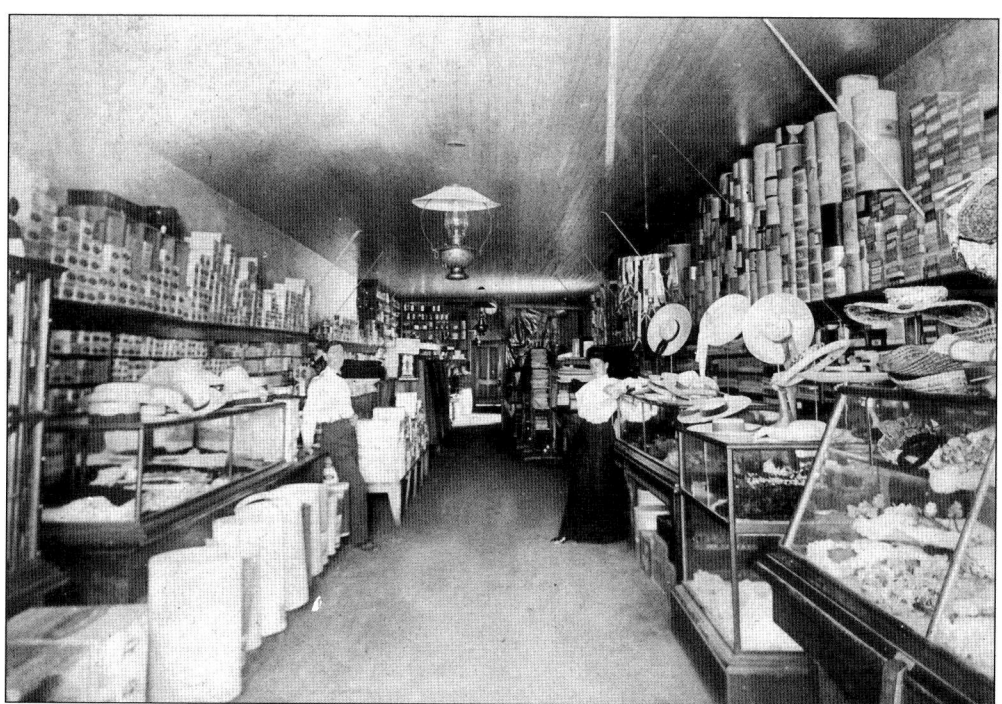

Ben Cagle and Frances Williamson stand inside the Hearin, Barnwell, and Cagle store in Gurdon, 1904. Cagle was also one of the founders of the Bank of Gurdon. Walter Scott Hearin and James B. Barnwell were the other owners of this dry goods establishment. (OBU.)

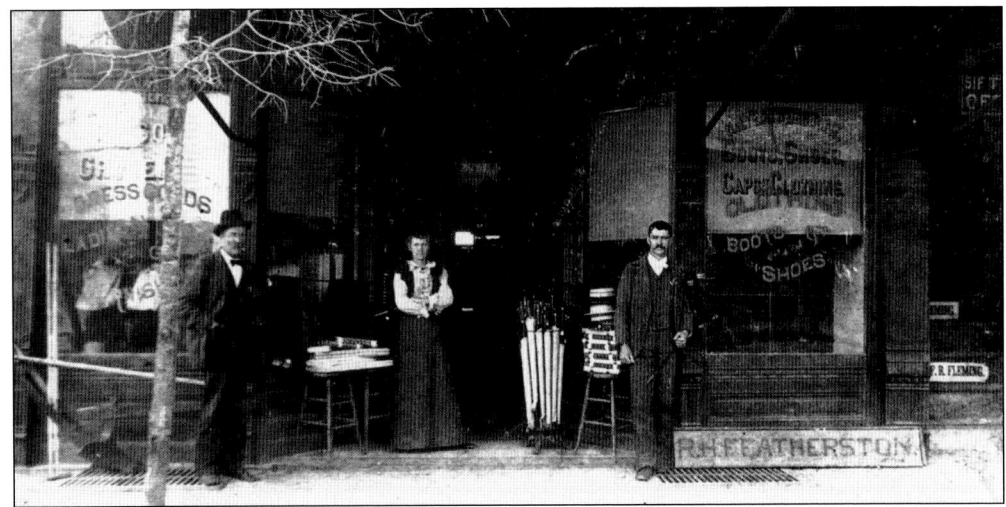

The R.H. Featherston store at Sixth and Clinton Streets, Arkadelphia, opened around 1890. Richard Henry Featherston came to Arkadelphia from Scott County, Arkansas, possibly following the Civil War. Featherston was in business as a merchant in Arkadelphia by the 1870s and, by 1890, had bought out the interest in R.W. Huie & Company. After 1910, Featherston and his wife, Virginia, possibly included in this photograph, moved to Oklahoma. (HSU.)

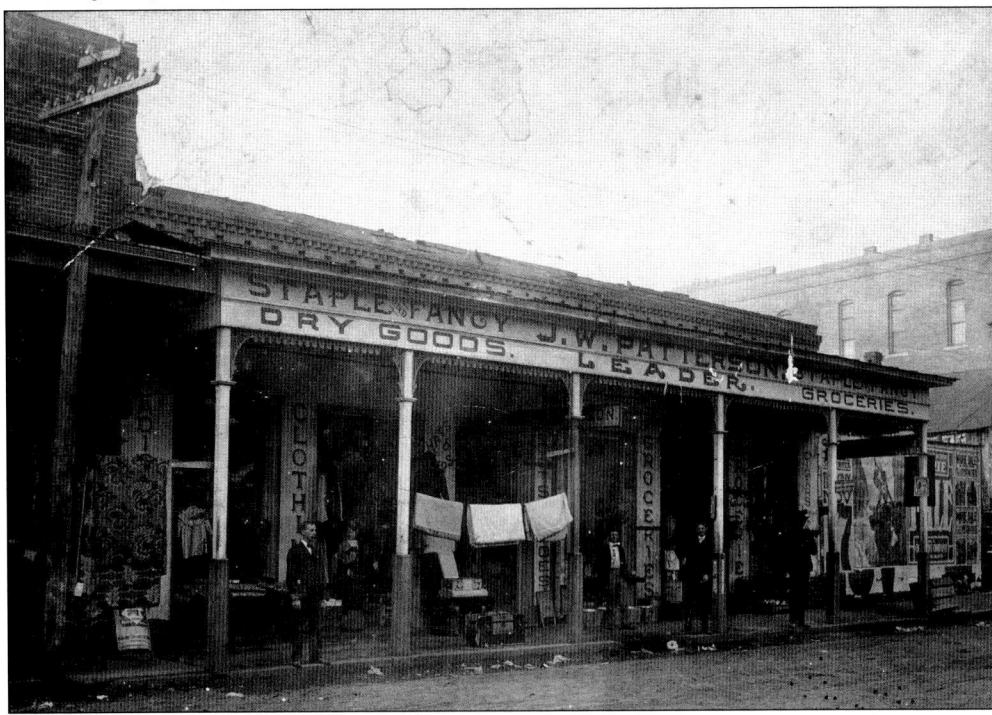

In 1875, John W. Patterson, originally from Georgia, opened a dry goods store on Main Street in Arkadelphia. His partner in the business was Luke Gibney, who also became Patterson's brother-in-law when the two men married sisters. In 1895, Patterson bought out Gibney's interests and expanded the business to include a grocery store. In 1905, he also opened a furniture store called Model. Identified in this photograph are Charlie and Nora Rudolph, Dick Petty, Jay Hardage, and George Abraham in Ouachita Baptist College military uniform. (HSU.)

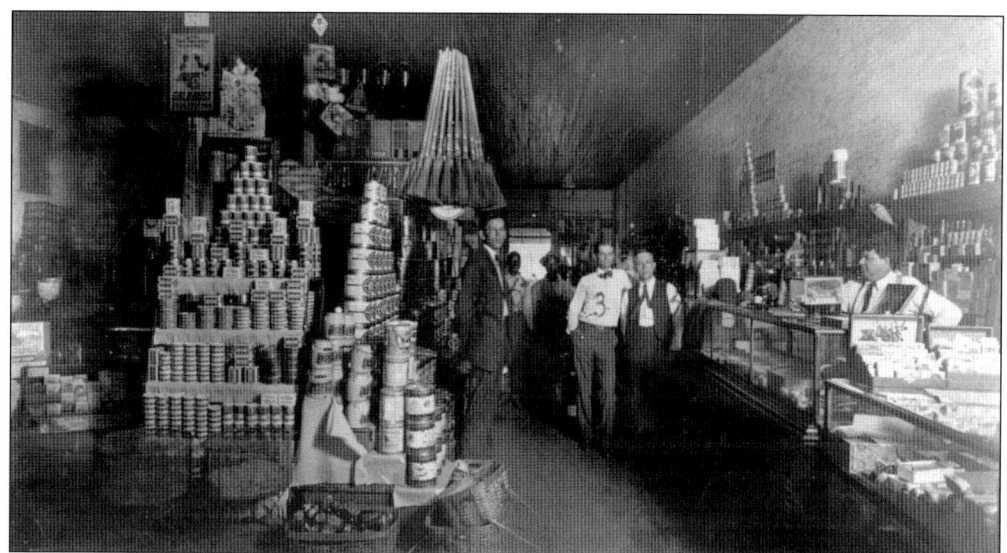

T. Abraham, George Abraham, Jay Hardage, A.P. Thompson, Columbus Trigg, and one unidentified man stand inside of the McNutt Supply Company in Arkadelphia, date unknown. Samuel Ralston McNutt, a native Mississippian, started what would become a very successful mercantile business in Arkadelphia in 1874. The store occupied most of the north side of Main Street between Seventh and Eighth Streets. McNutt died of tuberculosis at the age of 52 in 1905, but several prominent Arkadelphia men formed a corporation and continued to operate the McNutt Supply Company. (HSU.)

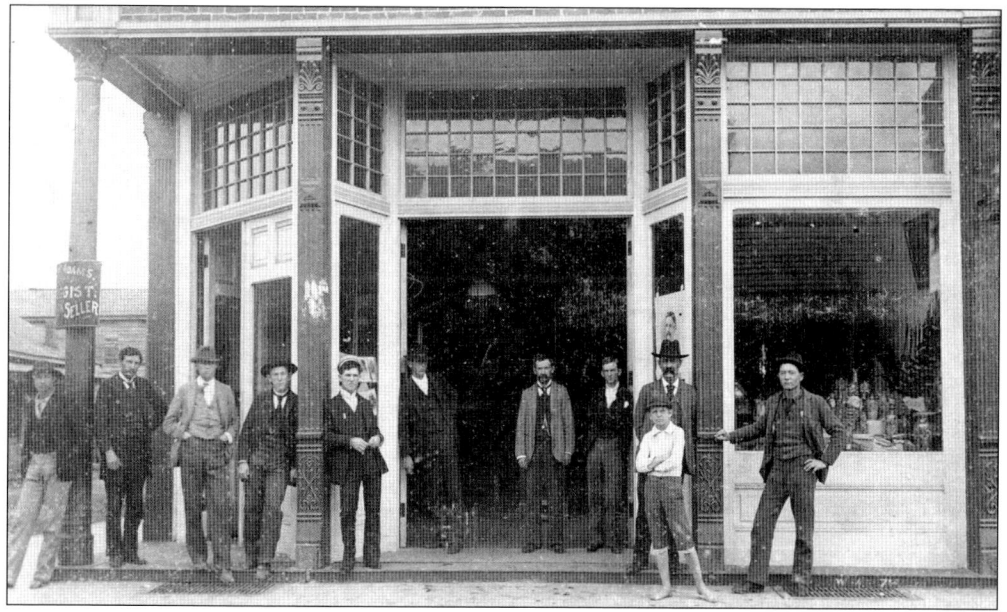

A group of men and one barefoot boy pose for the camera in front of McAdams Drug Store located on the corner of Johnston and Maddox Streets (now Main and Sixth) in Arkadelphia. Albert Clifford McAdams (center, doorway), a native of Cincinnati, Ohio, came to Arkadelphia in 1883 and opened the drugstore around 1888. In addition to filling prescriptions, the store stocked a wide range of patent medicines, was the town's exclusive seller of school textbooks, and offered a cold drinks and ice-cream counter. (HSU.)

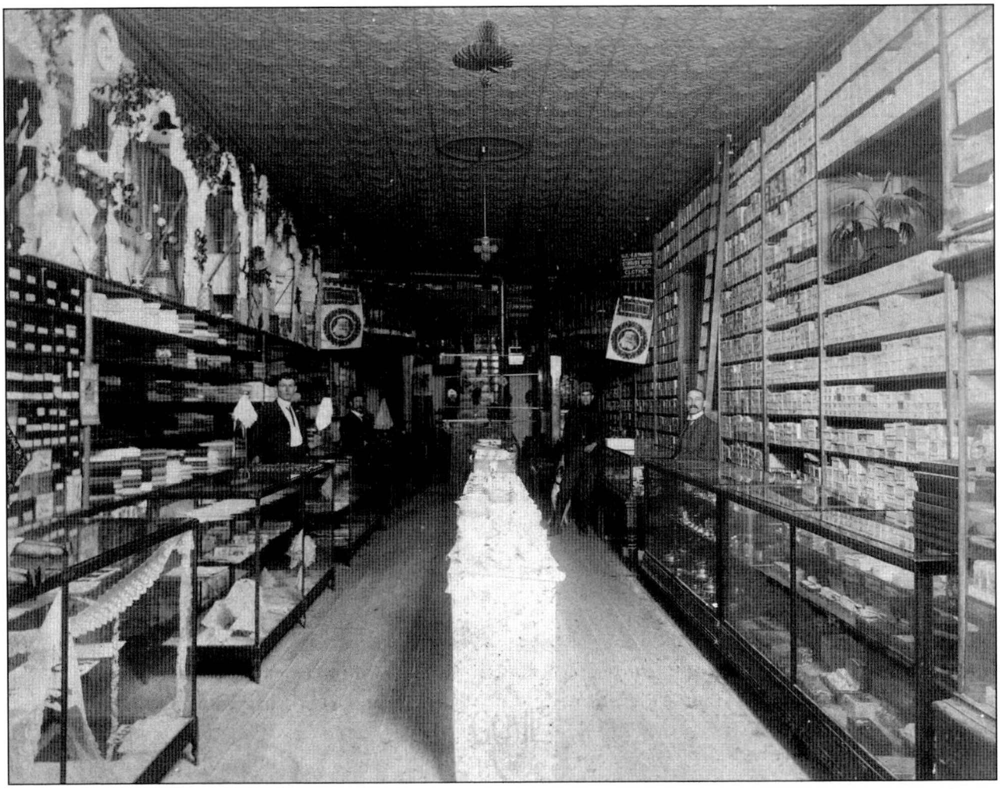

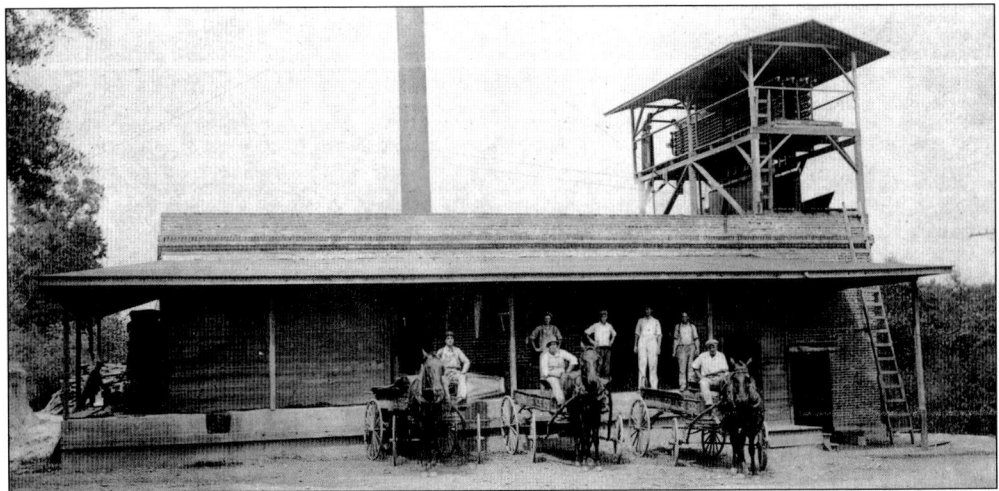

The Racket Store in Arkadelphia operated at the corner of Maddox and Johnston Streets (now Sixth and Main) in Arkadelphia for over 20 years. Owners Charlie and Bobe Thomas opened the store in 1893 in the location of a previous dry goods store. The stairway at the back of the store led to a small balcony where clothing for men and boys was displayed. The store operated until 1914. (OBU.)

The Arkadelphia Ice Plant, once located on Caddo Street near the train depot, opened around 1901. Before the plant opened, townspeople could purchase shipped-in ice from various enterprises around the city, including a drugstore, grocery, and a dairy, all of which kept icehouses. The Caddo Street plant, managed by Albert Moore, shut down operations around 1905. (HSU.)

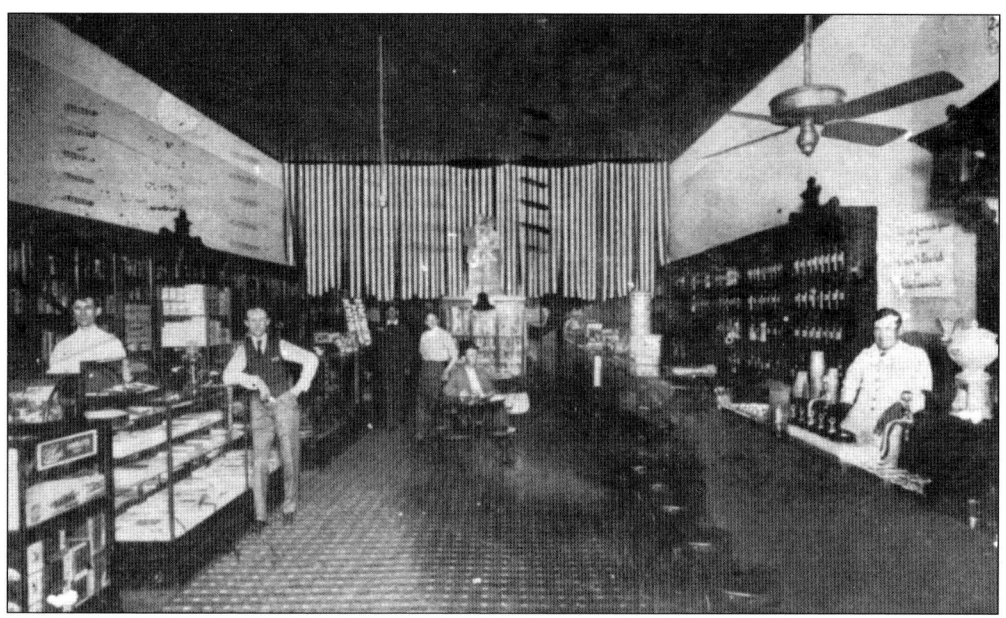

Clark, Sloan & Company (above) was established in November 1906 when Paul Sloan purchased Clark, Stewart and Company Drug & Book Store near the corner of Sixth and Main Streets in Arkadelphia. The company became Sloan Brothers in 1917, under the management of brothers Paul and Harold Sloan. The occasion for this parade float (below) sponsored by Clark, Sloan & Company was likely the Clark County Woodmen of the World picnic held on July 28, 1910. An estimated 5,000 people attended the event at Henderson Park. Arkadelphia High School is visible at the right of the float. (Both, OBU.)

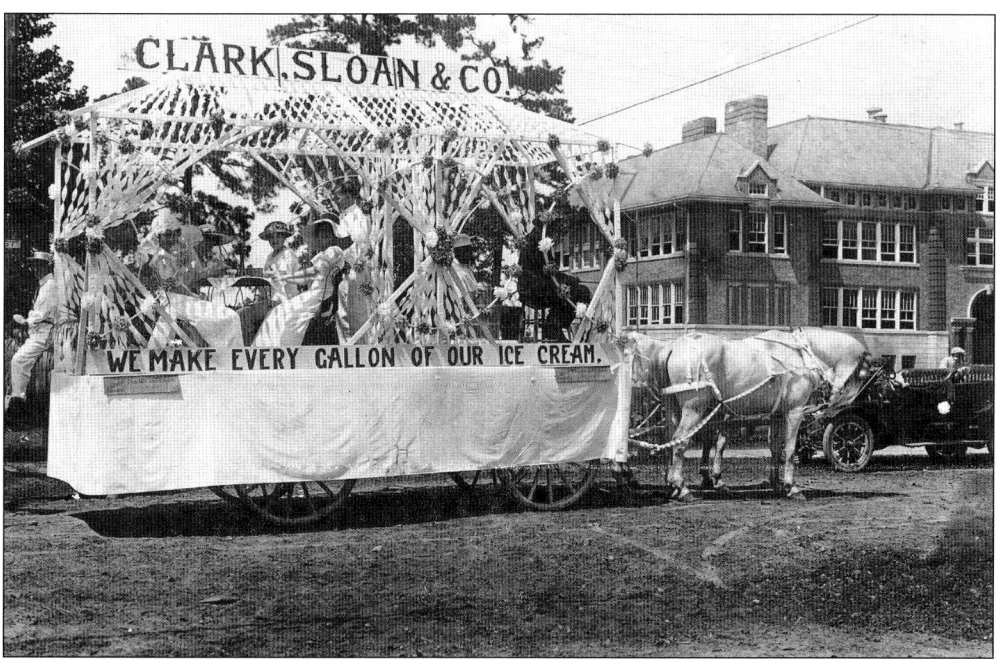

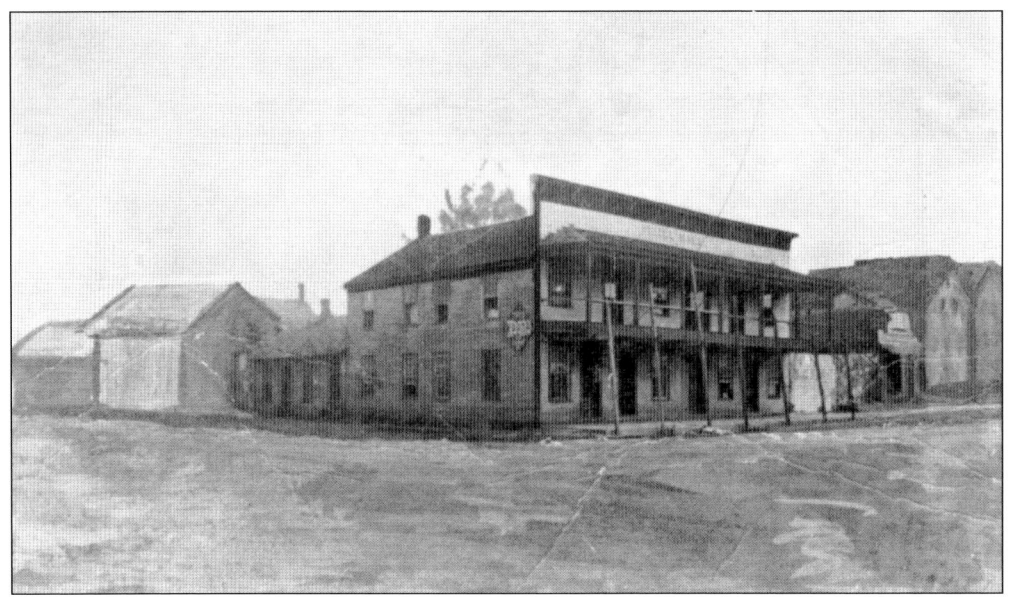

Hotel Hall in Gurdon was the site of the 1892 founding of the Concatenated Order of Hoo-Hoo, a fraternal organization of lumbermen and related trades. Hoo-Hoo is the oldest industrial fraternal organization in the United States. In 1981, Hoo-Hoo relocated its international headquarters back to Gurdon from Boston and opened the fraternity's museum in a renovated Works Progress Administration (WPA) log cabin on Main Street. A Hoo-Hoo monument located on West Main Street in Gurdon was added to the National Register of Historic Places in 1999. (OBU.)

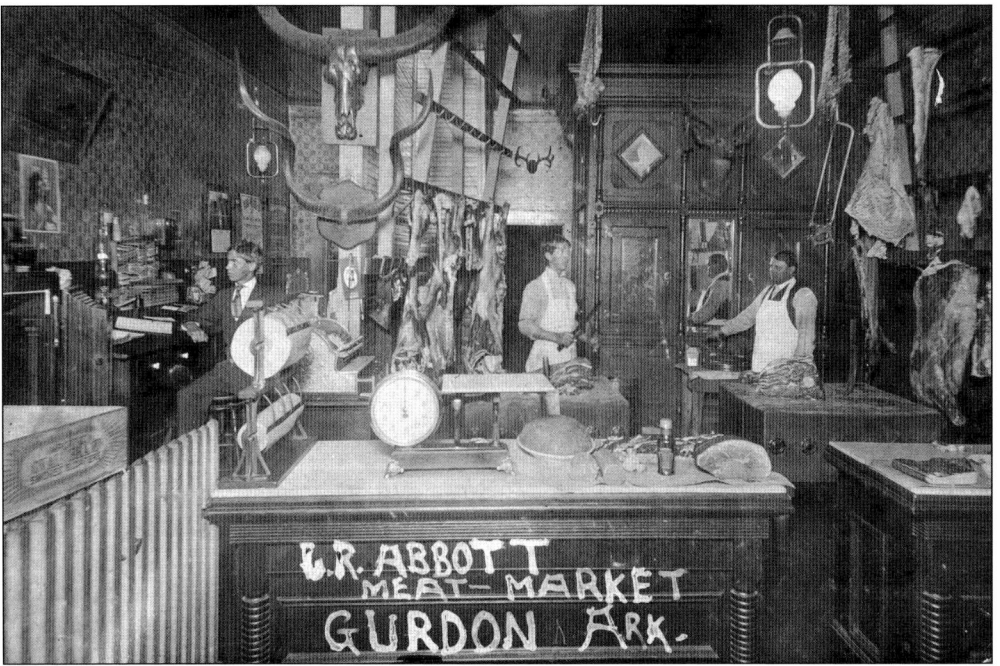

James Robert Abbott was a farmer and proprietor of a meat market in Gurdon in the early decades of the 20th century. Abbott also was one of the founding members and stockholders of the Merchants and Farmers Bank at Gurdon and served as the bank's first president. (OBU.)

Opened in 1912 on a half-block bounded by Caddo and Clinton Streets in Arkadelphia, the Caddo Hotel was the preeminent establishment serving travelers for decades. Built by R.W. Huie, founder of the Arkadelphia Progressive League, the building housed retail enterprises on the first floor, while the second floor served lodgers. The coming of Interstate 30, which bypassed Arkadelphia's downtown, caused the hotel to close. On November 19, 1989, a fire destroyed this city landmark. (OBU.)

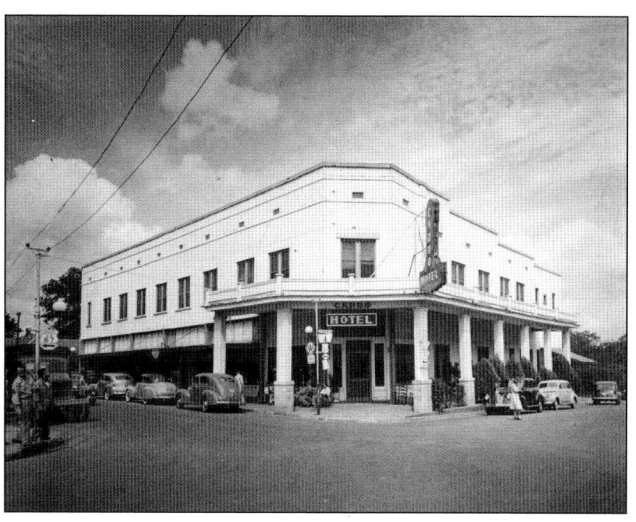

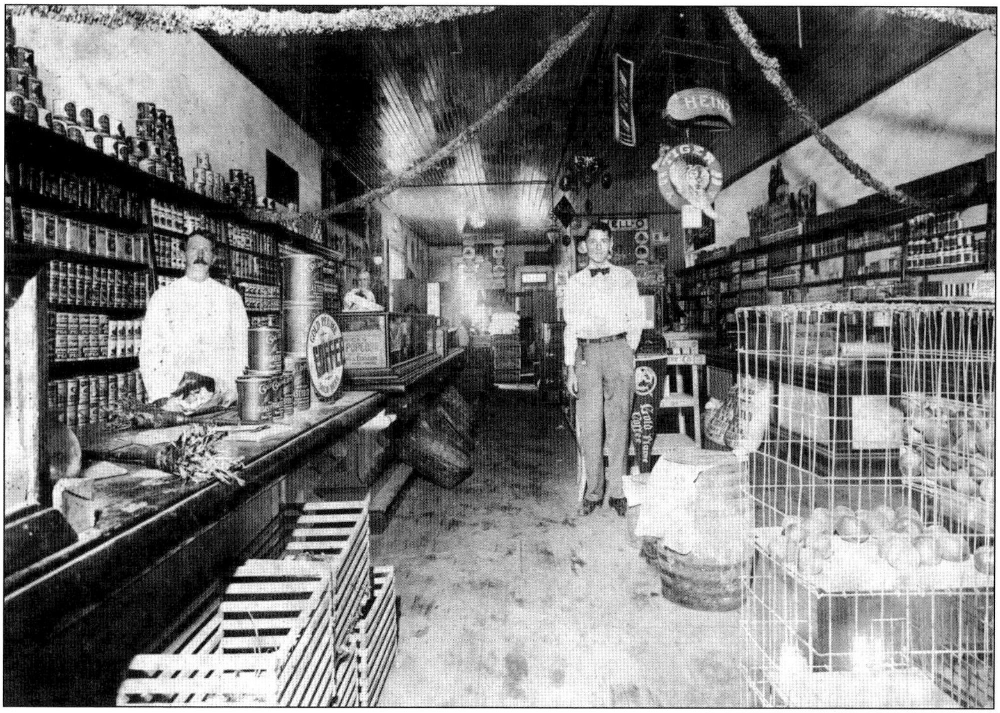

W.W. Banks (left) and Herbert Stanford (right) stand inside the W.W. Banks & Son grocery store at Sixth and Clay Streets in Arkadelphia around 1915. Banks came to Arkadelphia in 1913 from Bristow, Oklahoma, to start a grocery concern and, in 1915, hired Stanford as a clerk. In 1916, Banks sold the store to Stanford and Monroe Francis and moved back to Oklahoma. Some of the wares displayed in this photograph include Gold Plume Coffee, Rick's Popcorn, and Jell-O Ice Cream Powder. Anheuser-Busch crates are stacked at the rear of the store. The binned items at the front right are possibly onions. (OBU.)

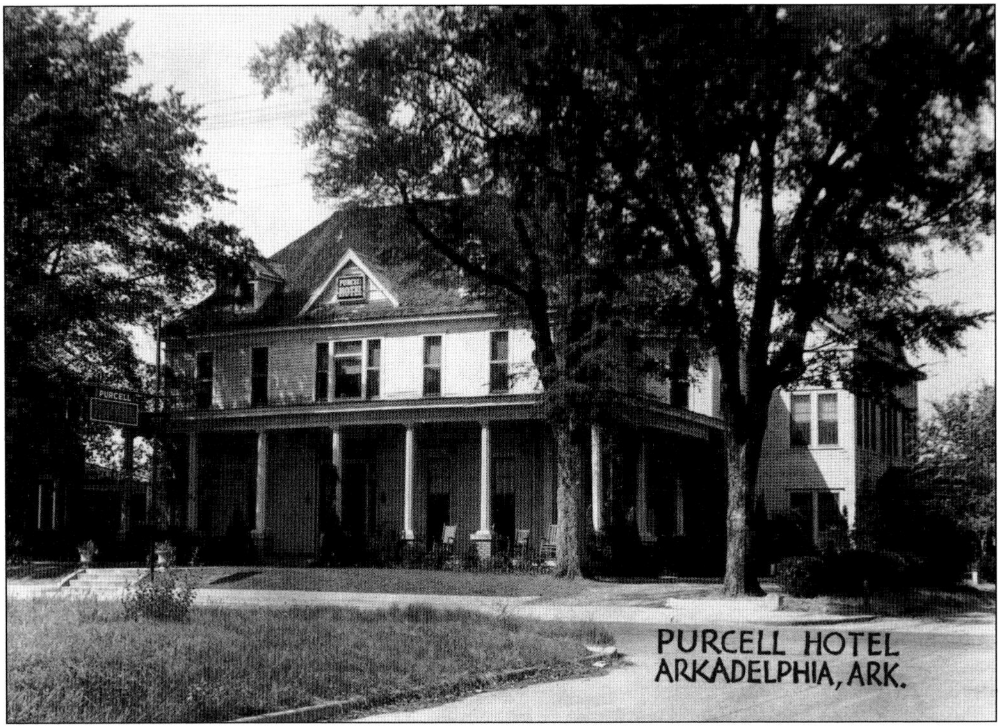

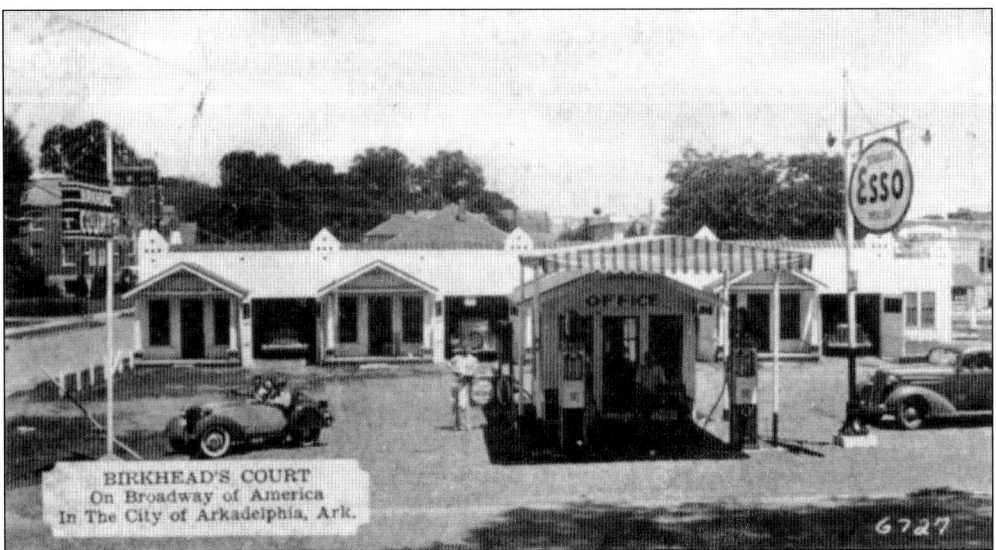

The Purcell Hotel operated at this Arkadelphia residence in the late 19th and early 20th centuries. The home was originally built by steamboat captain and merchant Capt. Thomas R. Tennyson around 1872. The hotel was owned and operated by Thomas H. and Elizabeth Purcell. Elizabeth continued to operate the hotel following her husband's death in 1923. In 1929, the house passed to the Purcells' daughter Fannie, wife of Dr. Samuel N. Doane. Doane operated his medical clinic from the house. The home was substantially damaged by fire in January 1952. (HSU.)

Birkhead's Court and Esso station at 900-902 Clinton Street in Arkadelphia was owned by Bonnell C. Birkhead Sr. and his wife, Corinne (Bevill). The Birkheads opened the tourist court around 1931 along US Highway 67. (OBU.)

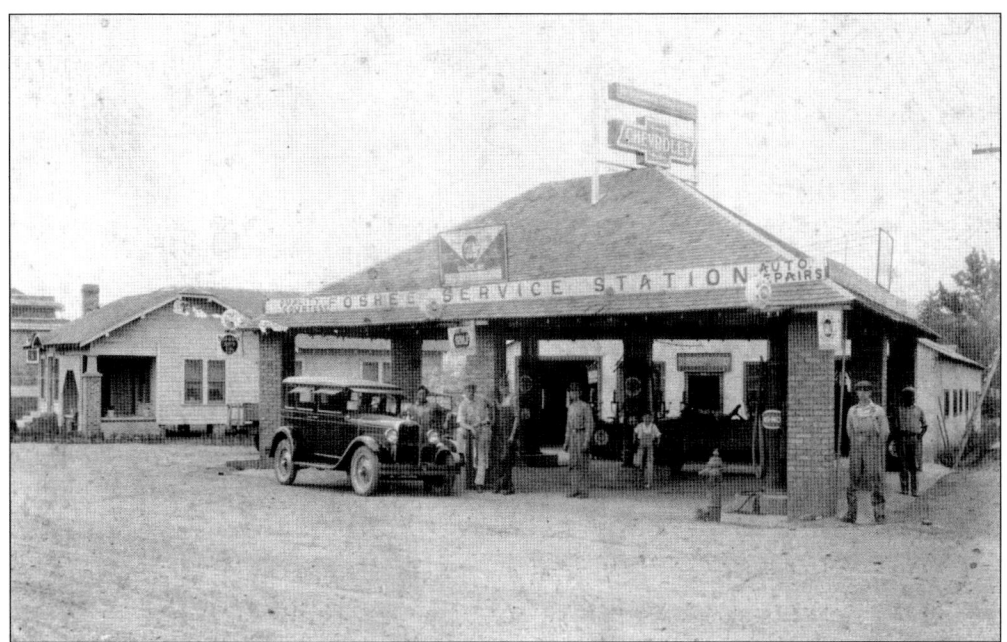

Foshee's Service Station and auto repair shop operated in Gurdon in the early part of the 20th century. Likely operated by Clarence Brice Foshee (1899–1971) on East Main Street in Gurdon, the shop sold Gulf gasoline and Dunlop tires. (OBU.)

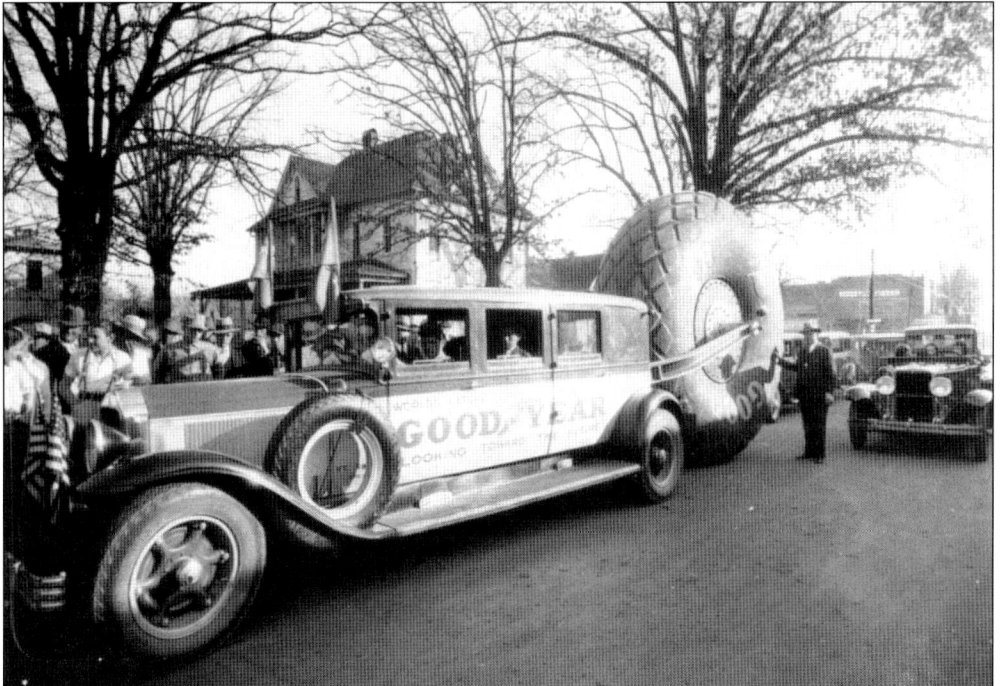

In 1929, the Goodyear Tire and Rubber Company introduced the Airwheel, its first low-pressure balloon tire for airplanes. Towed by a specially built 1929 Buick with a lengthened chassis, the giant tire, measuring twelve feet high and four feet wide, toured the United States, visiting almost half of the 48 states over a two-year period. (HSU.)

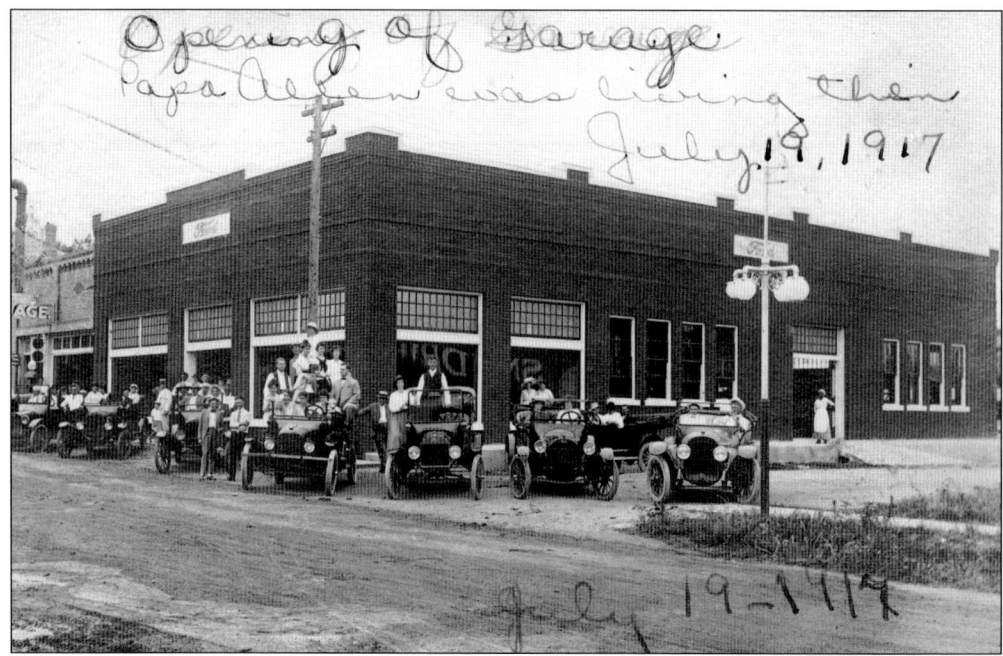

On July 19, 1917, the Allen & Allen Ford garage opened to over 500 excited spectators in Arkadelphia. While proprietor John Allen had been selling Ford automobiles in Arkadelphia for over a decade, the new garage had space to keep a large supply of replacement parts on hand and to display the newest models of Ford cars. Local newspapers reporting on the new business seemed most impressed that the automotive store had a restroom for women. (OBU.)

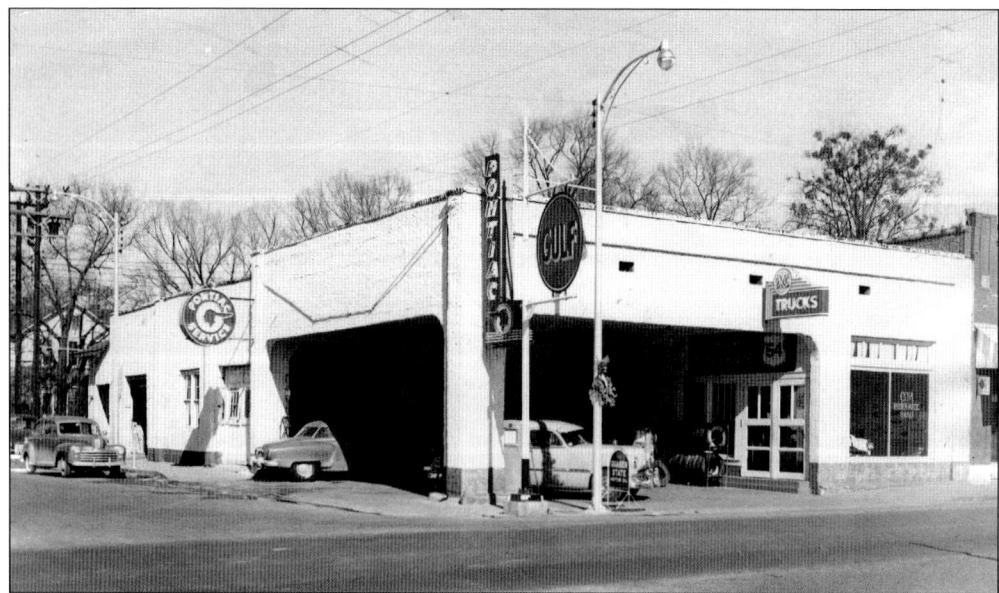

Johnson's Service Station opened on the corner of Eighth and Clinton Streets in Arkadelphia on July 19, 1920. Located on the Bankhead Highway, the station was a prime location for serving cross-country drivers. Dr. W.S. Johnson, a former college professor of psychology, started the station after retiring from teaching. Johnson, incidentally, was the first Arkansan to earn a doctorate, graduating from Yale in 1890. (OBU.)

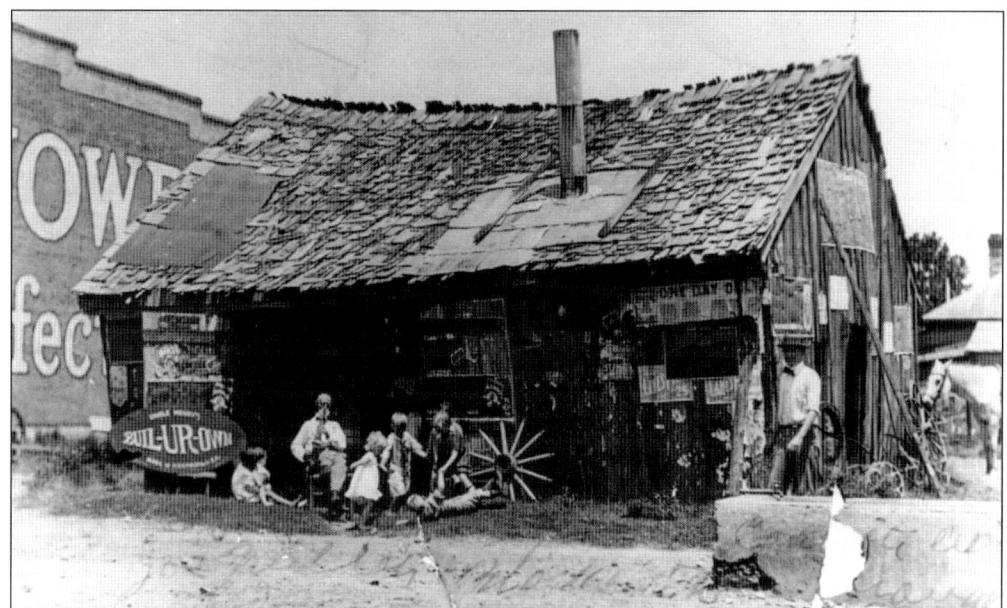

Joe C. Miller's blacksmith shop faced east on Fifth Street between Main and Crittenden Streets in Arkadelphia. Miller was a Confederate veteran who came to Arkadelphia sometime in the 1870s, first residing in adjacent Hot Spring County, where he also operated as a blacksmith. During the Civil War, he served as a member of the 9th Mississippi and later in a cavalry regiment commanded by Wirt Adams. The man seated is John Butler; the others are unidentified. (OBU.)

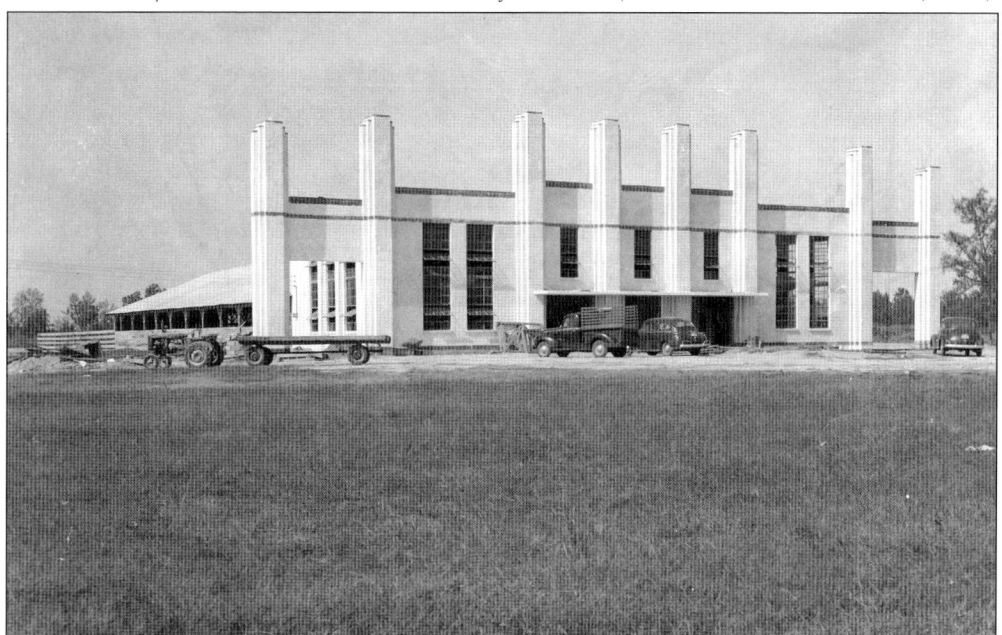

The Clark County Livestock Auction opened on US Highway 67 north of Arkadelphia in 1948. The T-shaped structure was built by Tom G. Clark and leased to Jack Brewer, Harold Arnold, and Elgy Taylor, who previously operated a livestock auction in downtown Arkadelphia. The auction contained stadium seating for 1,000 people and stalls for 1,500 heads of stock. While the building still stands, livestock auctions ceased in 2002. (OBU.)

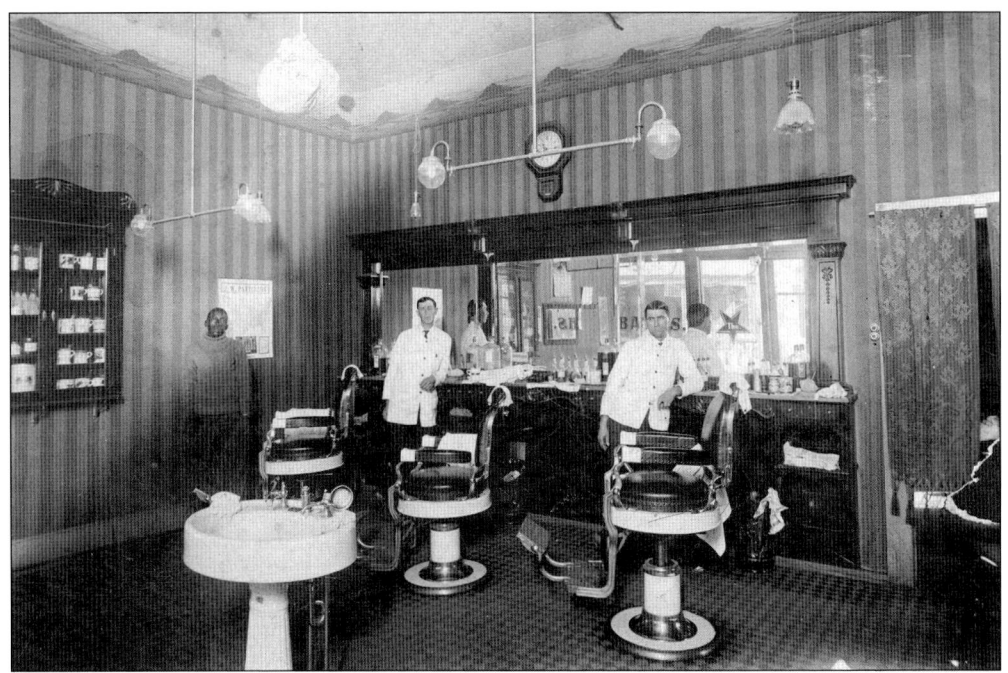

Sanborn Fire Insurance maps show a barbershop operating on Main Street in Arkadelphia (formerly Johnston Street) by 1896. The Star Barber shop moved into a new building on Main Street in February 1913, but how long the business had been in operation is not known. Over the years, Star Barber's ownership changed hands a number of times, being owned and operated at various times by William P. Whittle, H.T. Carmack, Louis Stroope, J.T. Allen, Newt McDaniel, and Gilbert Jones. (OBU.)

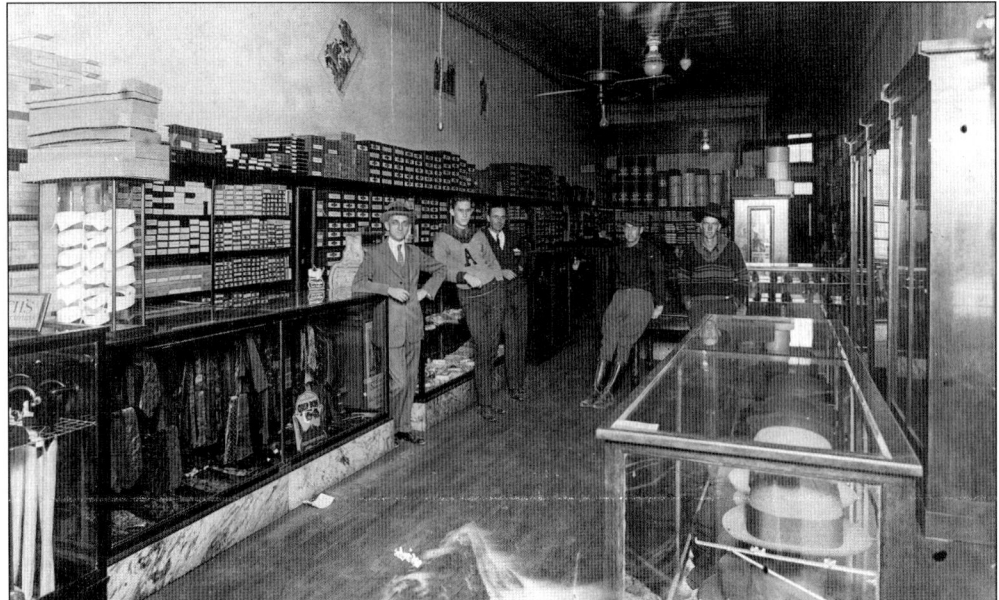

Originally called Whitten & Hall and named for proprietors Floyd Whitten and Charles Hall, the Whitten's men's clothing store opened in Arkadelphia in early 1907. This photograph was taken on November 3, 1921. The men in the photograph are unidentified. (HSU.)

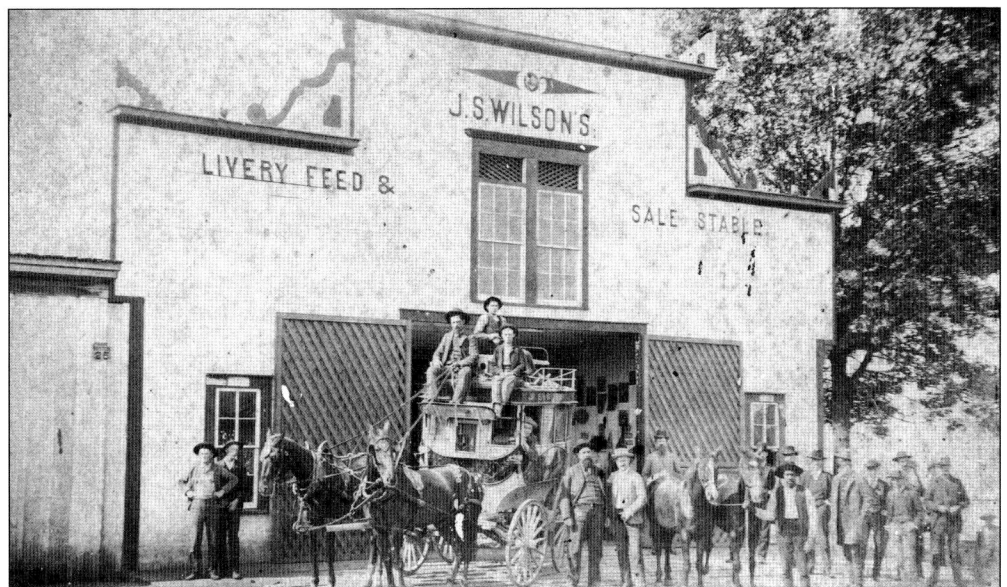

J.S. Wilson's Livery, Feed & Sale Stable was located at Fifth and Main Streets in Arkadelphia. Taken around 1895, this image shows the old stagecoach that met all the trains. Wilson's livery was established in 1887 near Hall House, Arkadelphia's leading hostelry of the period. The livery served traveling salesmen and rented surreys and horses to carry groups on outings to Davidson's Methodist Campground and Brown Springs. The bearded man standing right of the wagon is Nash Flanagin, who may have been the proprietor at this time. (HSU.)

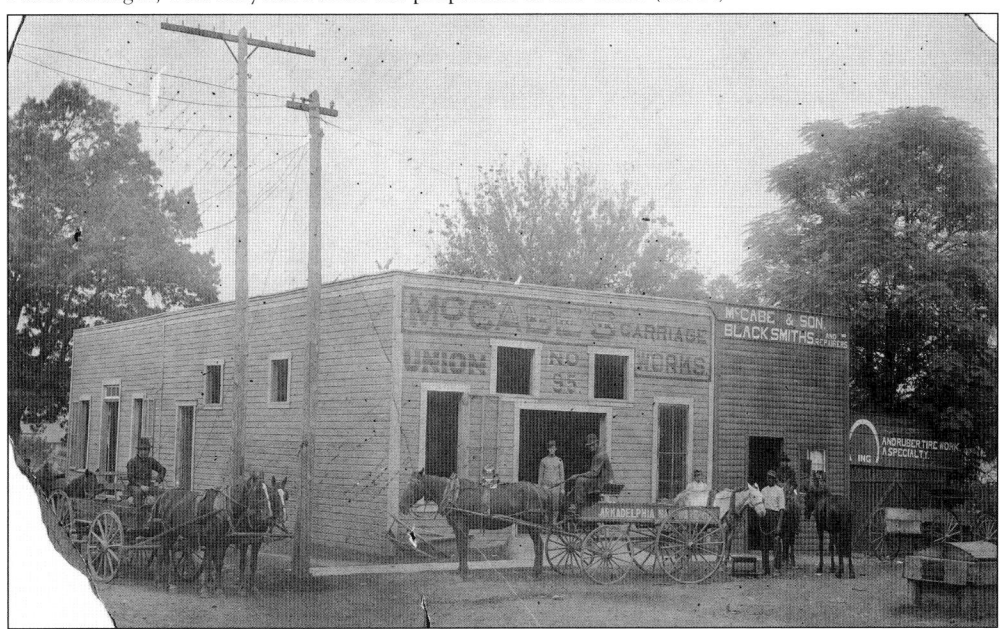

In 1904, A.L. McCabe opened this Arkadelphia carriage and blacksmith shop, which he ran with his son Harry. In 1906, the East Main Street business expanded operations to include a carriage painting shop. A local newspaper, the *Southern Standard*, noted that between this new service and their rubber-tire-making operation, McCabe's was "an enterprising concern." McCabe's went out of business sometime around 1908. (HSU.)

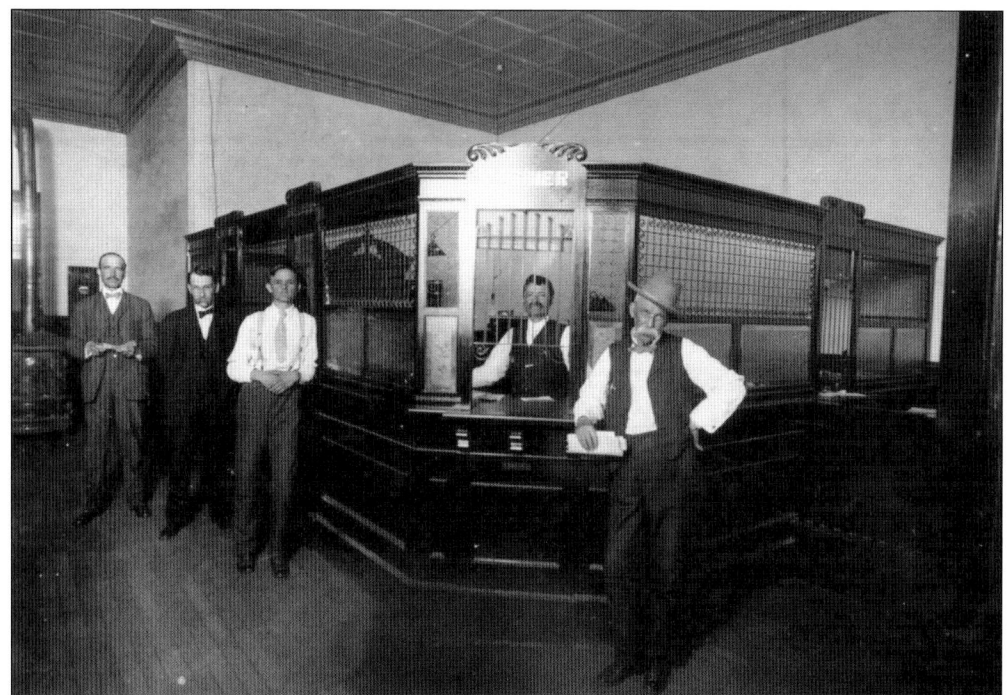

Elk Horn Bank was organized in Arkadelphia in 1884 by businessmen S.R. McNutt and John N. Stuart. Allegedly, the bank was named Elk Horn for a mounted elk's head on the wall of McNutt's store after naming deliberations stalled. The bank originally was located in McNutt's general store but later moved into the building shown here at Sixth and Main Streets in 1903. Three of the men in this photograph are identified as C.C. Scott, Willis Brand, and W.E. Barkman, cashier and bank officer. (HSU.)

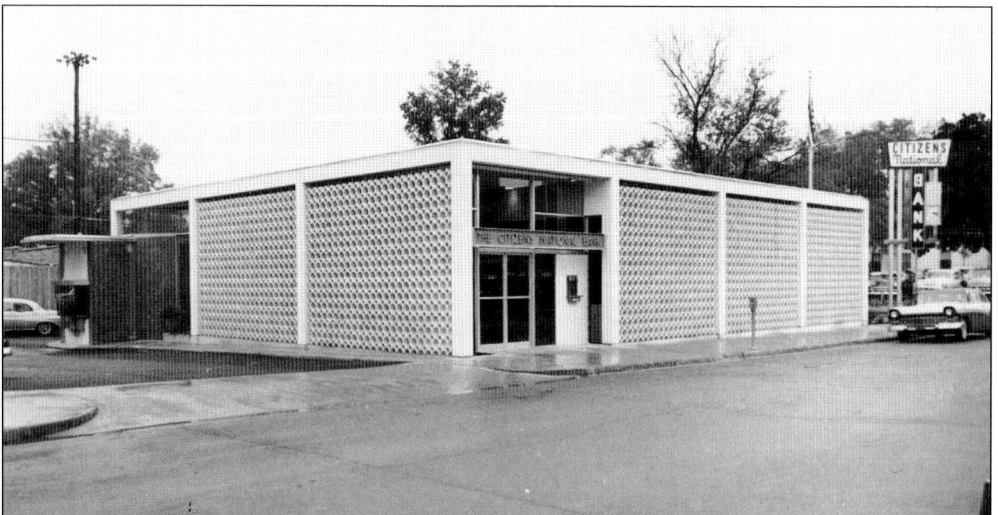

Founded in 1888 as Citizens Bank and Trust Company by C.E. Neely and R.W. Huie, who served as the first president, Citizens Bank has operated in Clark County for over 130 years. The bank has operated under several names during its history, including Citizens National Bank and later as Citizens First State Bank. For much of its history, the bank was located on Sixth Street but later moved to the building shown here at Fifth and Main Streets in 1957. (OBU.)

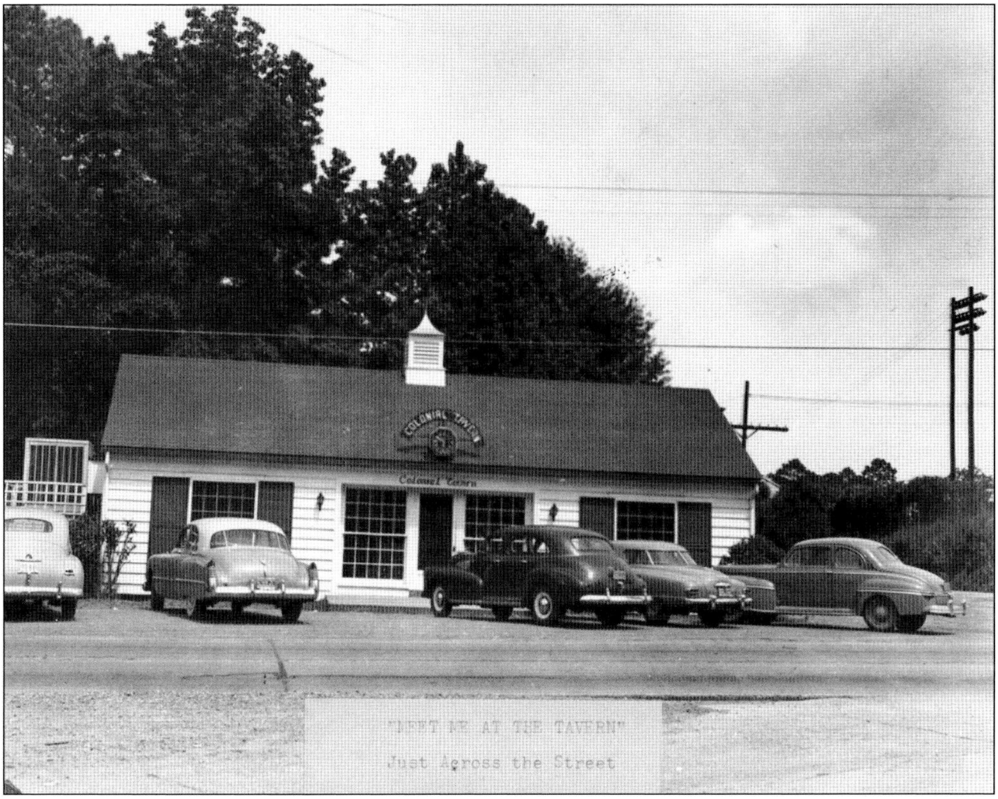

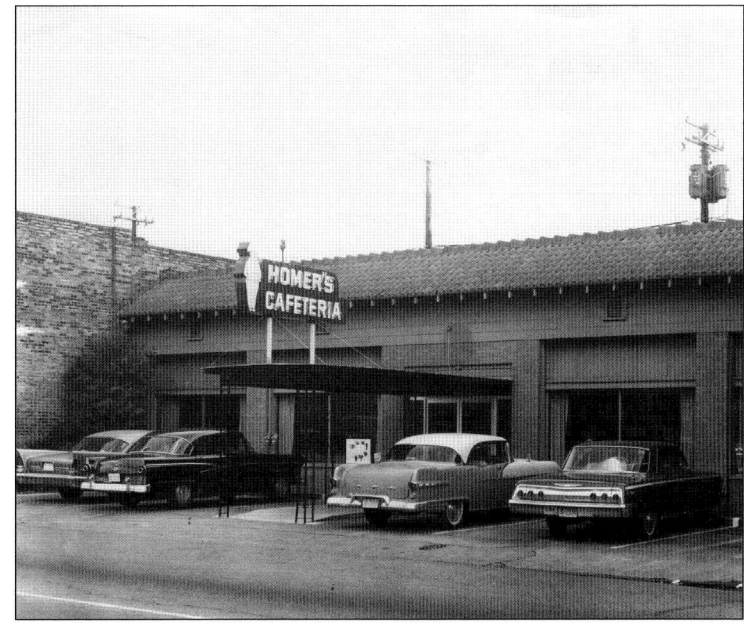

The Colonial Tavern on Tenth Street, just across the road from Henderson State Teachers College, was a popular dining spot in Arkadelphia. The tavern was owned by Cecil Cupp, a businessman involved in banking, communications, and movie theaters. Cupp also owned Arkadelphia's Royal Theatre and the Sky Vue drive-in. (OBU.)

Homer's Cafeteria, named for owner Homer Moore, served diners at 617 Clinton Street in Arkadelphia, the current site of Slim & Shorty's Restaurant. Prior to becoming Homer's, Neel's Grocery occupied the site. (OBU.)

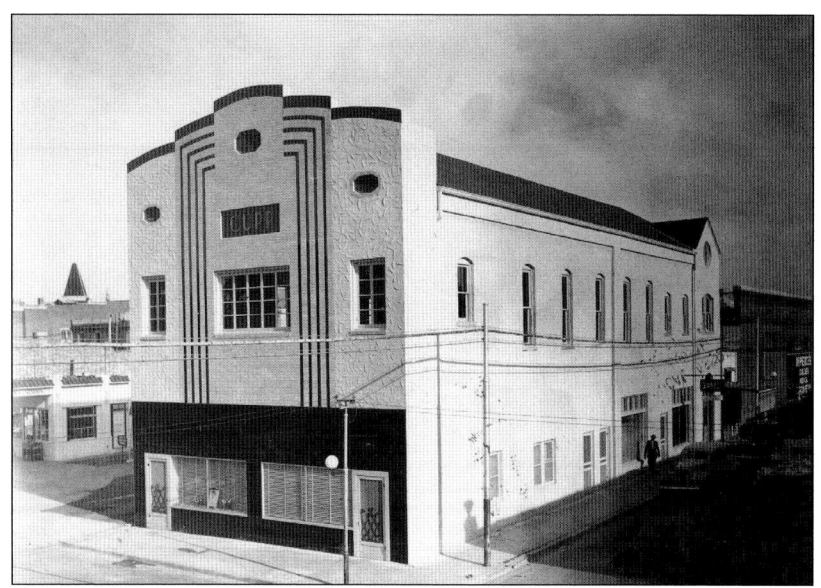

The striking Art Deco Cupp Building at Clinton and Seventh Streets in Arkadelphia was the home of the KVRC AM radio station, which went on the air in September 1947. KVRC was established by Cecil Cupp. (OBU.)

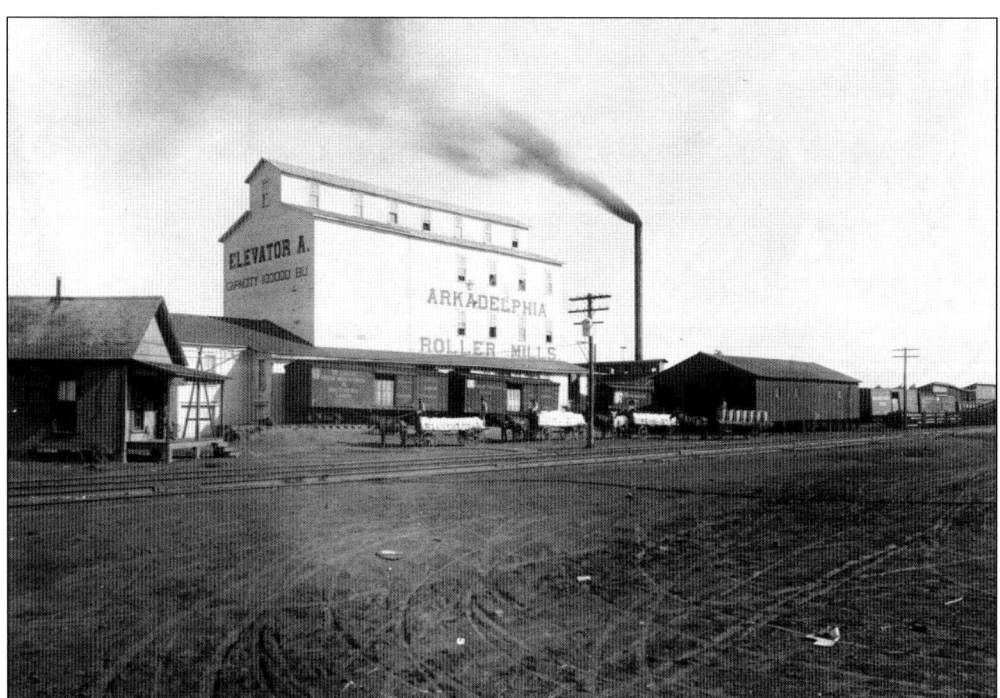

One of the first successful large industries in Arkansas was the Arkadelphia Roller Mill, later known as the Arkadelphia Milling Company. Established in 1898 by brothers W.E. and Joe H. Adams, the mill was a major manufacturer of flour, cornmeal, stock feed, and staves. Located just southeast across the tracks from the train depot, the mill was one of the railroad's largest customers, providing materials across the United States and to seven foreign countries. The mill buildings were twice destroyed by fire, in 1909 and again in 1926, but were rebuilt each time. The mill shuttered operations permanently during the Great Depression. (HSU.)

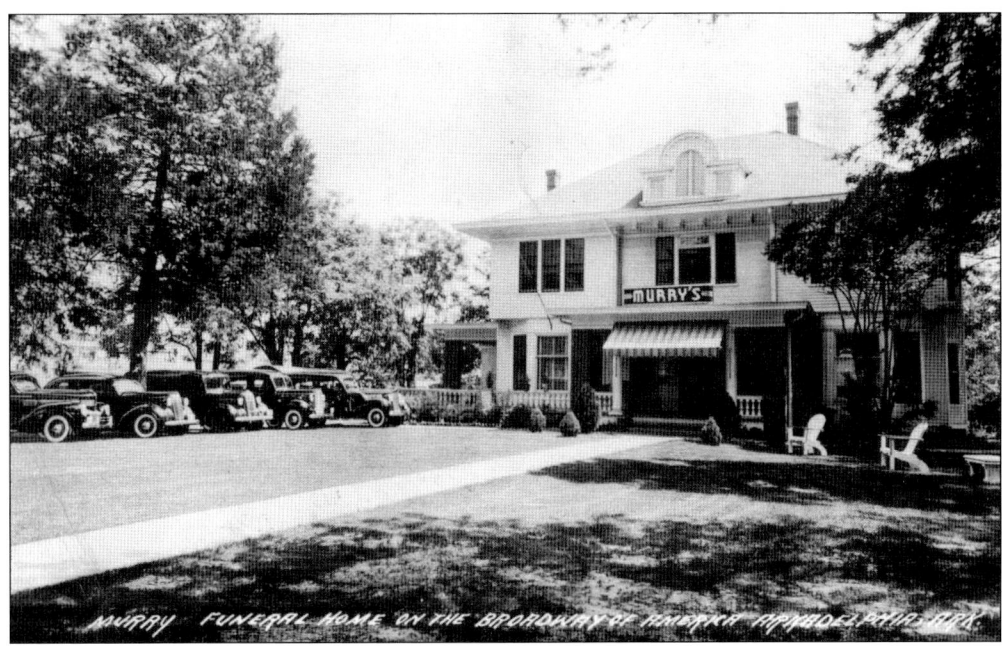

The Murry Funeral Home was established in Arkadelphia in 1905 by C.B. and Fairy Lee Murry. The funeral home business previously existed as part of McDaniel, Murry & Lee, a business that also sold furniture and hardware. The company's motto was "We serve you from the cradle to the grave." The Murry Funeral Home moved into a former two-story residential home (above) on the corner of Seventh and Main Streets, which it occupied until 1942. The company's horse-drawn hearse is pictured below. (Both, OBU.)

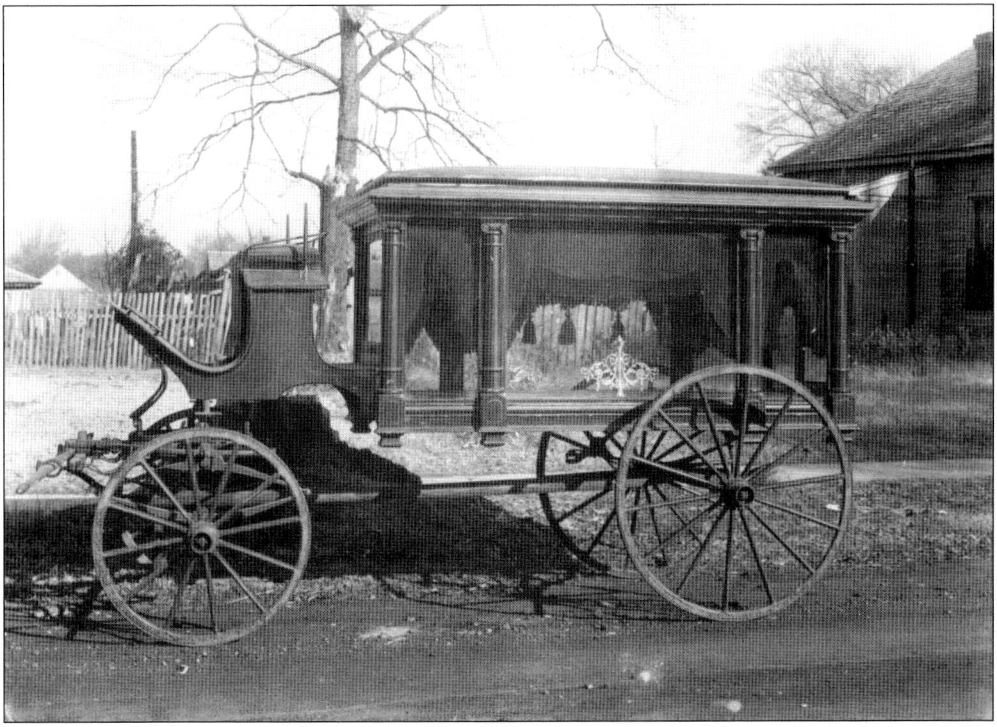

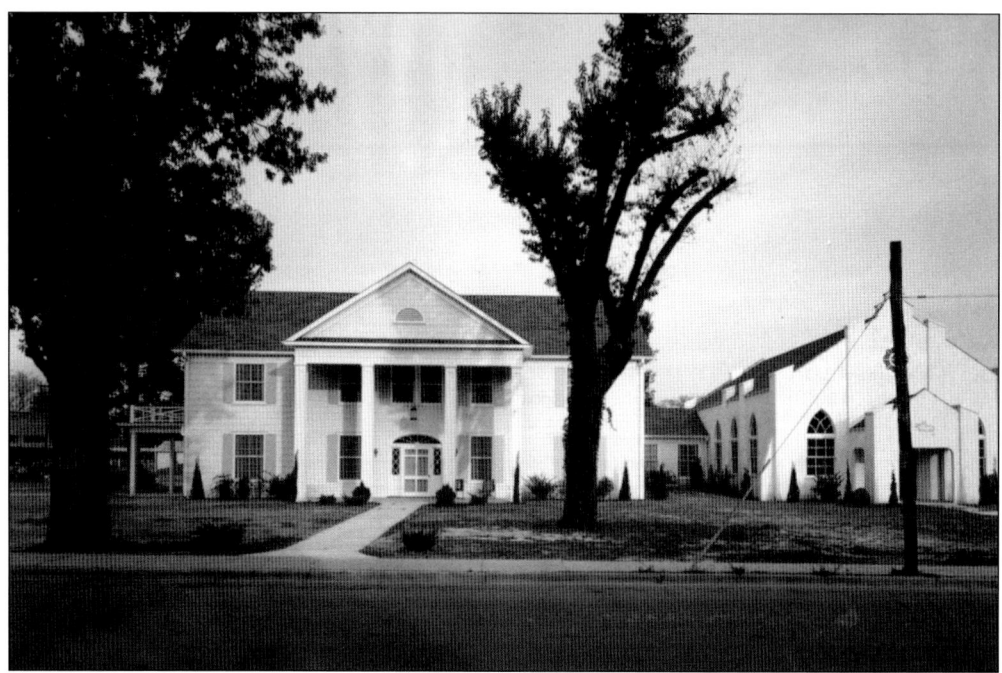

In 1942, the Murry Funeral Home moved into this new two-story Colonial structure between Clay and Crittenden Streets. This building and its adjacent chapel served the community until 1997, when they were heavily damaged by an F-4 tornado along with much of Arkadelphia's downtown. Today, Smith Family Funeral Homes occupies this site. (OBU.)

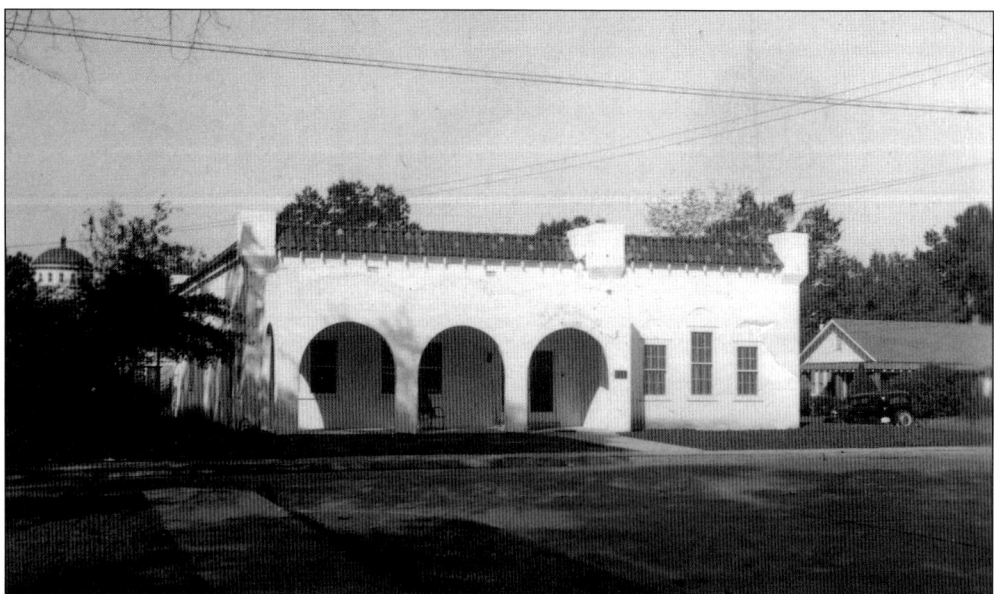

The Harris Funeral Home, located at the corner of Sixth and Pine Streets in Arkadelphia, was originally established as Newberry and Harris in 1905. The business was a partnership between Alva Harris and L.C. Newberry. In 1934, the partnership dissolved, and the name of the business became Harris Funeral Parlors. Alva Harris built this Spanish-style structure in 1940, only to see it destroyed by fire in April 1942. (OBU.)

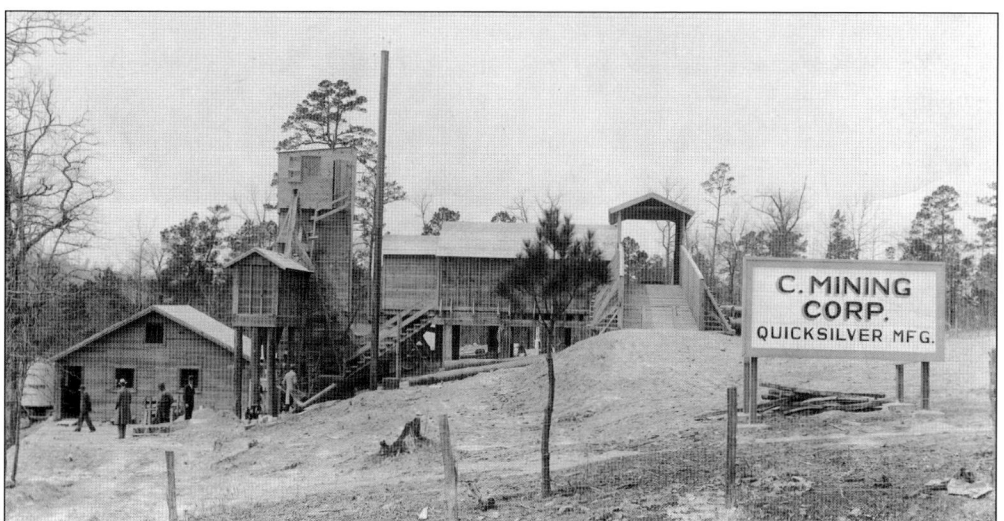

In 1931, cinnabar, used in the production of mercury, began to be mined in an area of southwest Arkansas running from Howard County into western Clark County. This mine operated at Kirby in adjacent Pike County. The production of mercury was important during World War II in the manufacture of tracer bullets and chemical warfare compounds. The southwest Arkansas mining district produced mercury yearly until around 1946, when activity petered out. (OBU.)

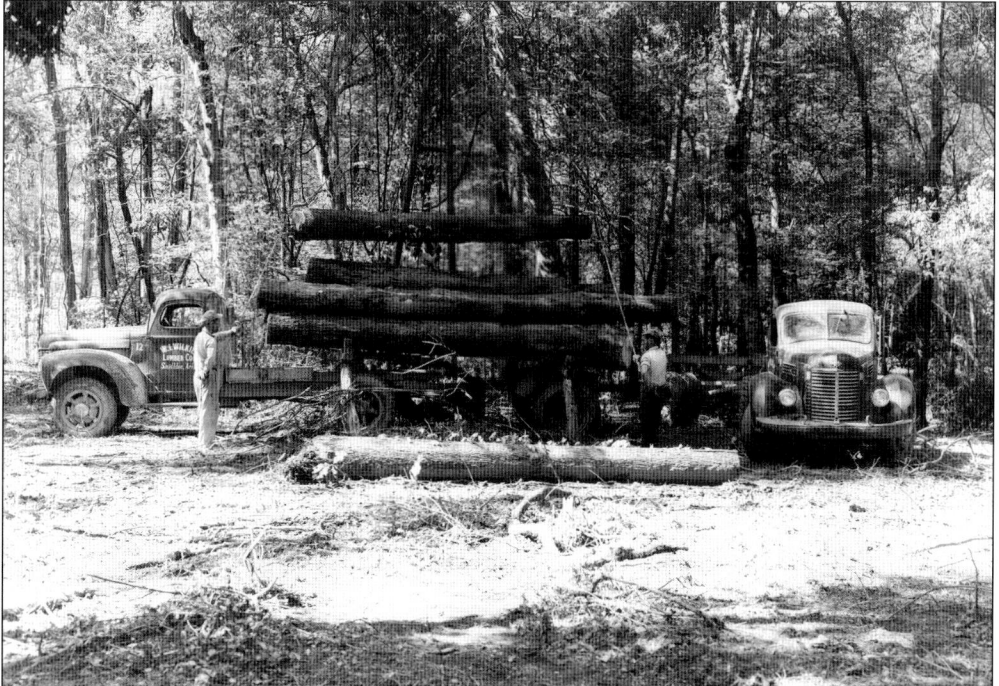

Men from the W.I. Wilkie Lumber Company at Smithton load cut logs onto the back of an International Harvester truck. Smithton, located about two miles northeast of Gurdon, was founded as a lumber town when James A. Smith organized the Smithton Lumber Company there in 1888. An Irish immigrant, Smith came to Clark County in 1873 as a railroad worker. At one time, the Smithton lumber mill boasted the "world's largest sawdust pile," according to *Ripley's Believe it Or Not!* (OBU.)

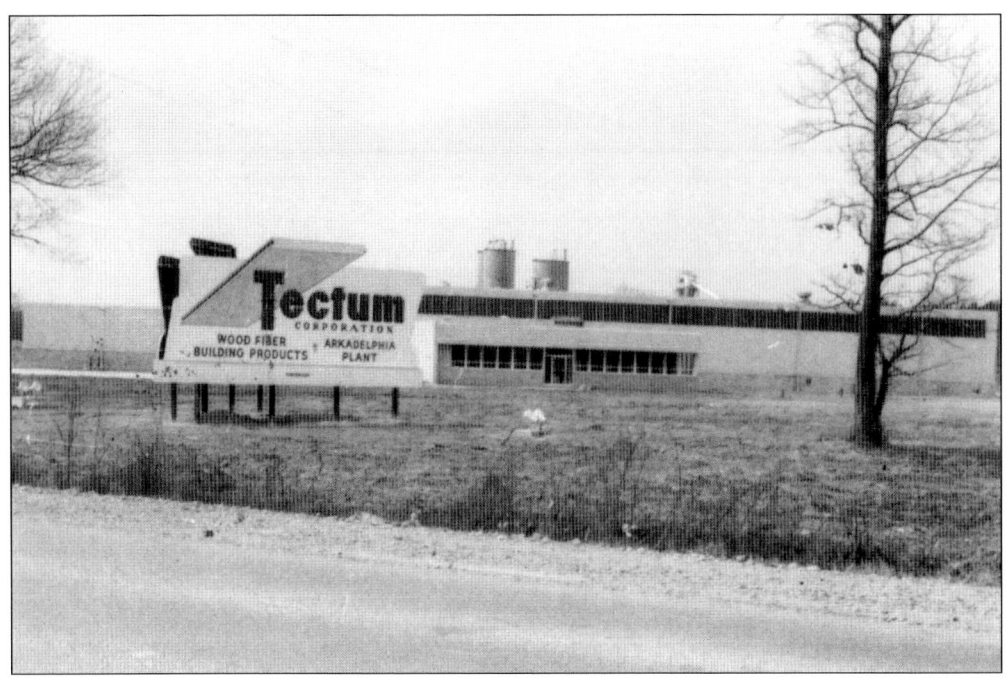

In 1957, the Tectum Corporation of Newark, Ohio, contracted with the Arkadelphia Chamber of Commerce to construct a new facility (above) for the manufacture of building materials made from pine excelsior or wood slivers. The City of Arkadelphia loaned Tectum $240,000 for the construction of the plant, which cost $3 million to build. The Tectum Corporation agreed to lease the plant site for sufficient time for the city to retire the indebtedness. Winthrop Rockefeller (below, standing at left), director of the Arkansas Industrial Development Commission (AIDC), welcomes officials from the Tectum Corporation at an event at the Arkadelphia Country Club around 1956. Seated to the left of Rockefeller is Arkansas governor Orval Faubus. Siplast now occupies the facility built for Tectum. (Both, OBU.)

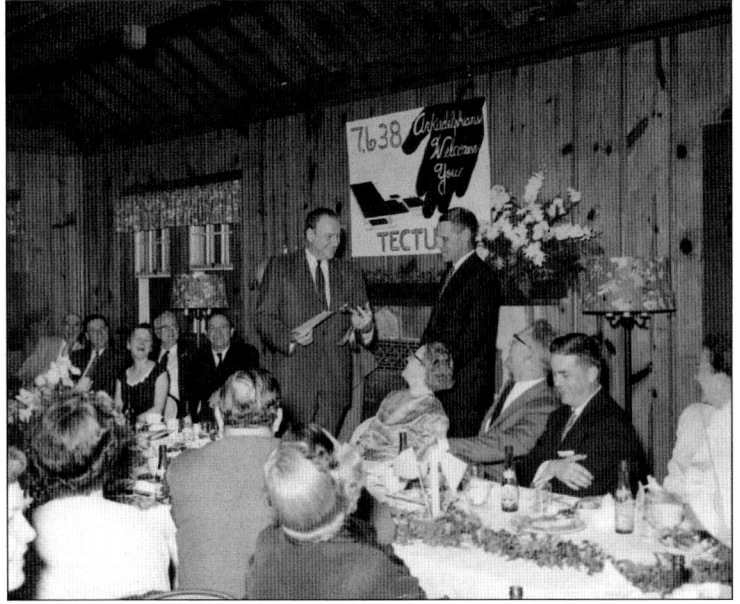

Arkansas Power and Light Company shareholders from Clark County pose near the Arkadelphia Public Library in 1926. Stockholders pictured here are, from left to right, (first row, seated on ground) Bill Allen, Clyde Key, Joseph E. Callaway, and John Ernest Couch; (second row, seated) W.S. Johnson, L.C. Newberry, Mayme Callaway, Almedia Couch, Frances Crawford, Mary Zenas Clark, and Flave Carpenter; (third row, standing) Will Lee, Frank Delamar, Claude Phillips, J.D. Holder, C.C. Tobey, J.D. Brock, Doc Greene, and Roy Golden. (OBU.)

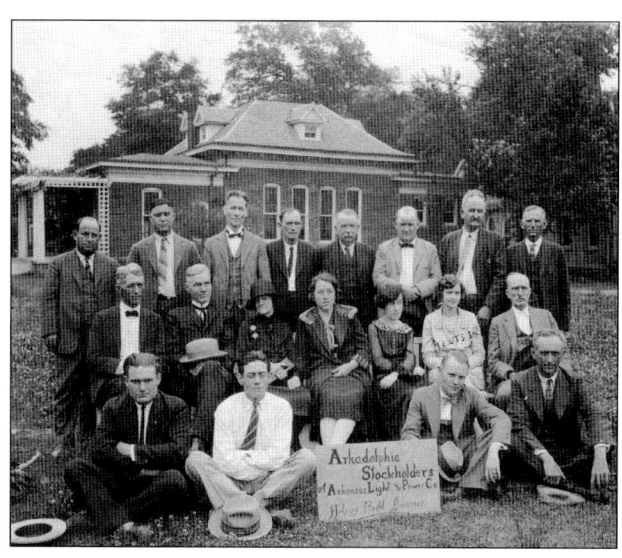

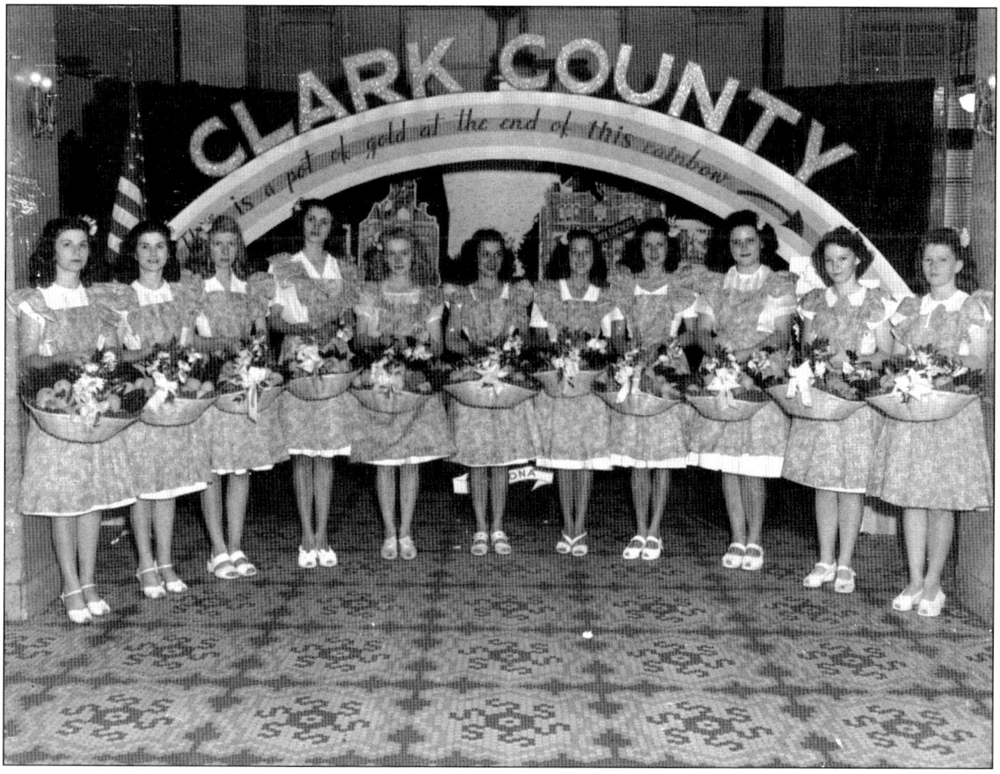

June 14, 1946, was "Clark County Day" at the Little Rock Chamber of Commerce luncheon. In celebration of the "Pot of Gold" theme, 10 young ladies from the area displayed an assortment of goods representing materials produced and grown in Clark County. The young ladies representing Clark County are, from left to right, Ruth McLain and Esther McLain (twins from Gurdon), Jackie Hill and Jean Ann Hardin (Okolona), Ann Culley Yates, Sarah Savage, Anne Dews, and Martha Frances Harris (Arkadelphia), and Irene Callaway, Jackie Garner, and Joyce Beene (Amity). (OBU.)

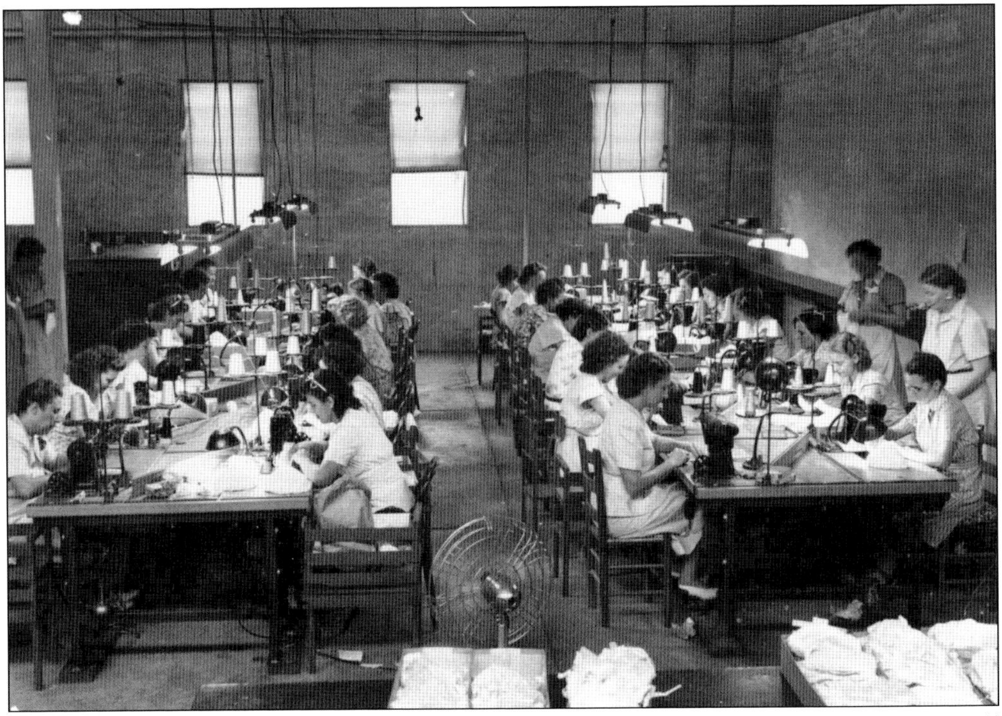

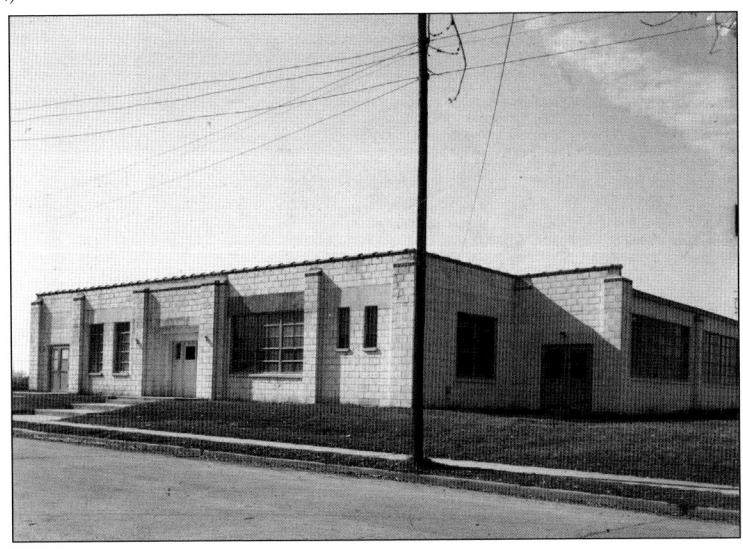

Two garment manufacturing plants opened in Arkadelphia in the 1940s, the Hollywood-Maxwell Company and Oberman & Company Manufacturing. The Hollywood-Maxwell Company (above), a brassiere manufacturing plant, began production in November 1941 at Main and Fourth Streets. The company provided numerous jobs for women entering the workforce during and after World War II. The plant and successor corporations—Vassarette and Munsingwear—manufactured women's apparel until 1981. In 1947, Oberman Manufacturing Company (below) opened at Main and Twelfth Streets and initially employed 300 men and women in the production of men's work clothes. Oberman later became the Levi Strauss & Co. The Arkadelphia Foundation raised $75,000 to construct the building for Oberman in order to secure the enterprise for the town. (Both, OBU.)

Three

THE ATHENS OF ARKANSAS

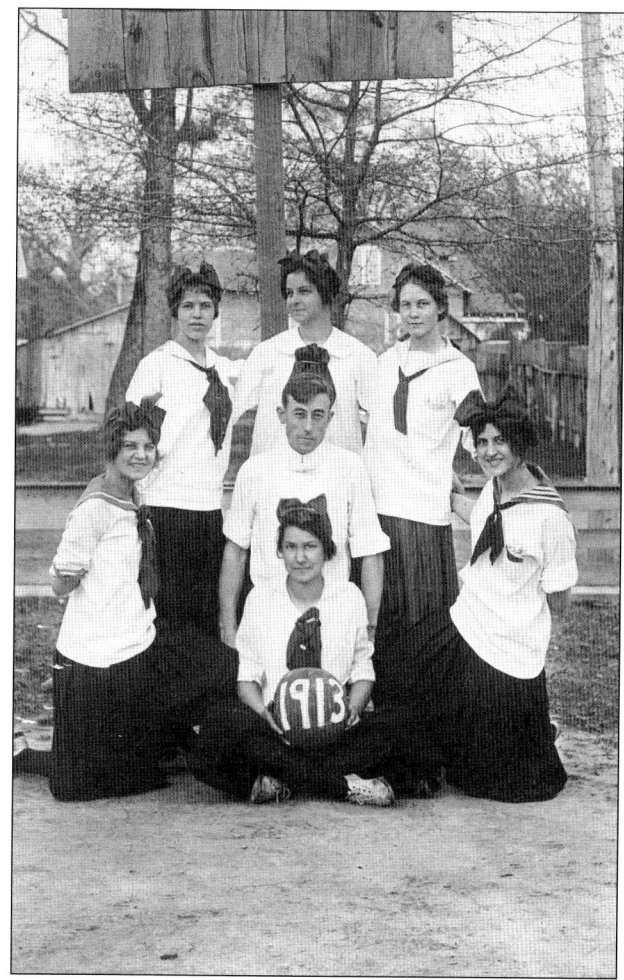

The game of basketball was introduced to Arkadelphia in December 1901 when the "girls of the Methodist College" hosted an exhibition game. According to the *Southern Standard* newspaper, "much interest was manifested [and] an immense crowd assembled on the campus." By 1908, female students at Arkadelphia High School (AHS) were playing local teams, including Hope, Camden, Hot Springs, and Ouachita College. In 1913, the AHS coach was Brice Martin Mace, and some of the players included Rose Dews, Pauline Deene, Helen Beck, Louise Finger, Anna Grace Adams, Alma Brown, Roberta Carpenter, and Cosie Patterson. (OBU.)

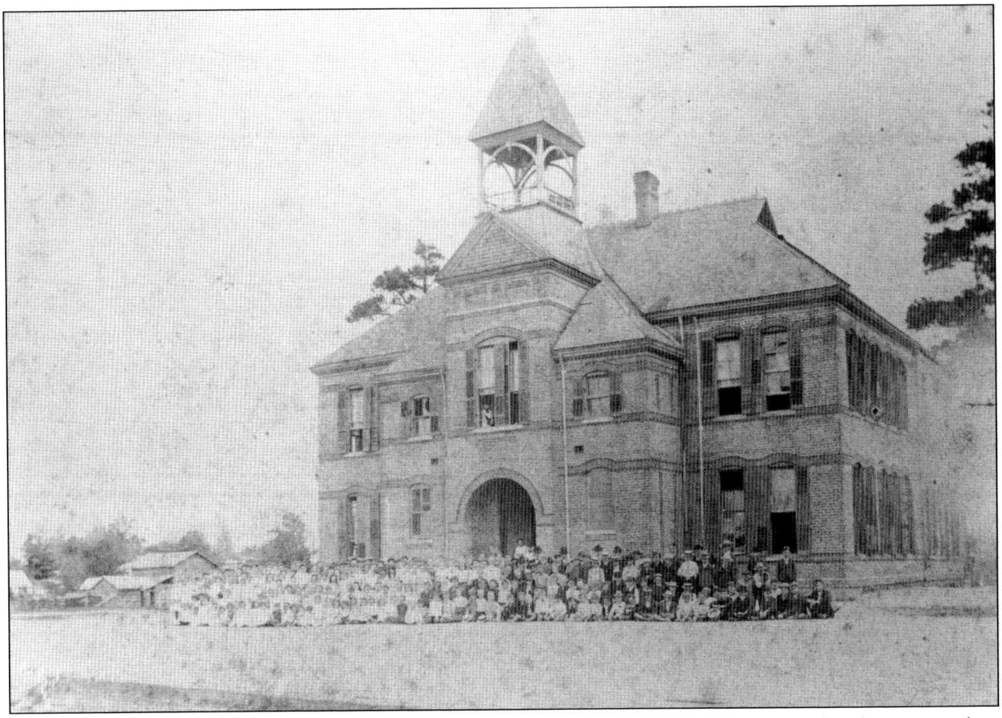

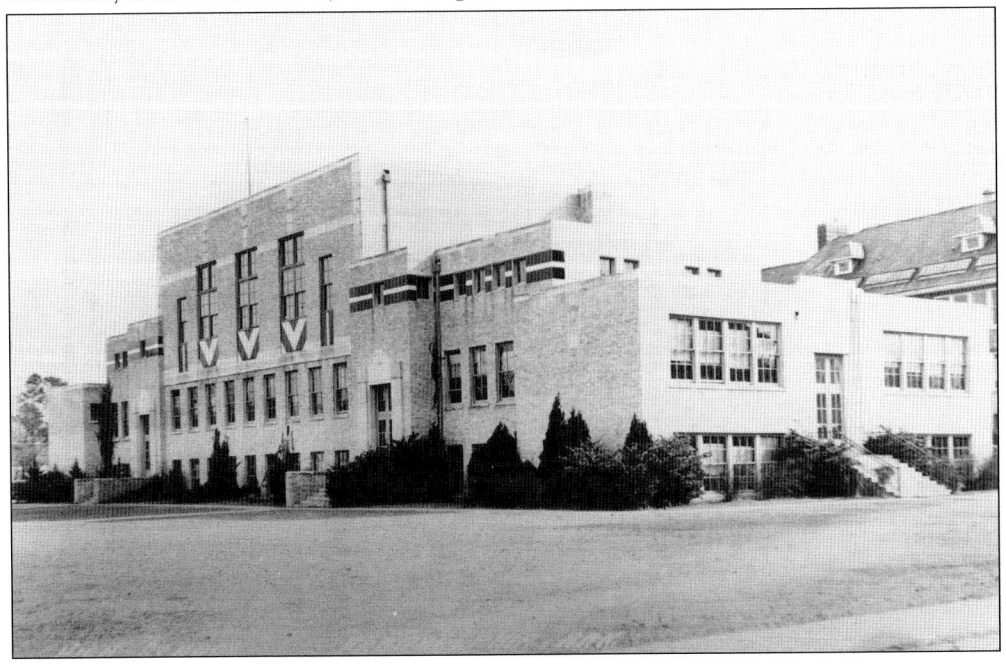

Public education came to Arkansas after the Civil War. Prior to this time, schools were either private, funded by subscription, or operated by religious organizations. The Arkadelphia High School on Pine Street (above) opened in 1899 as a free public school for White students. A new building opened in 1906 but later burned and was rebuilt in the 1940s. The Art Deco school building (below) was constructed in 1931. It served as the high school and later as Central Elementary until 2020. In 2024, the building was sold and torn down. (Both, OBU.)

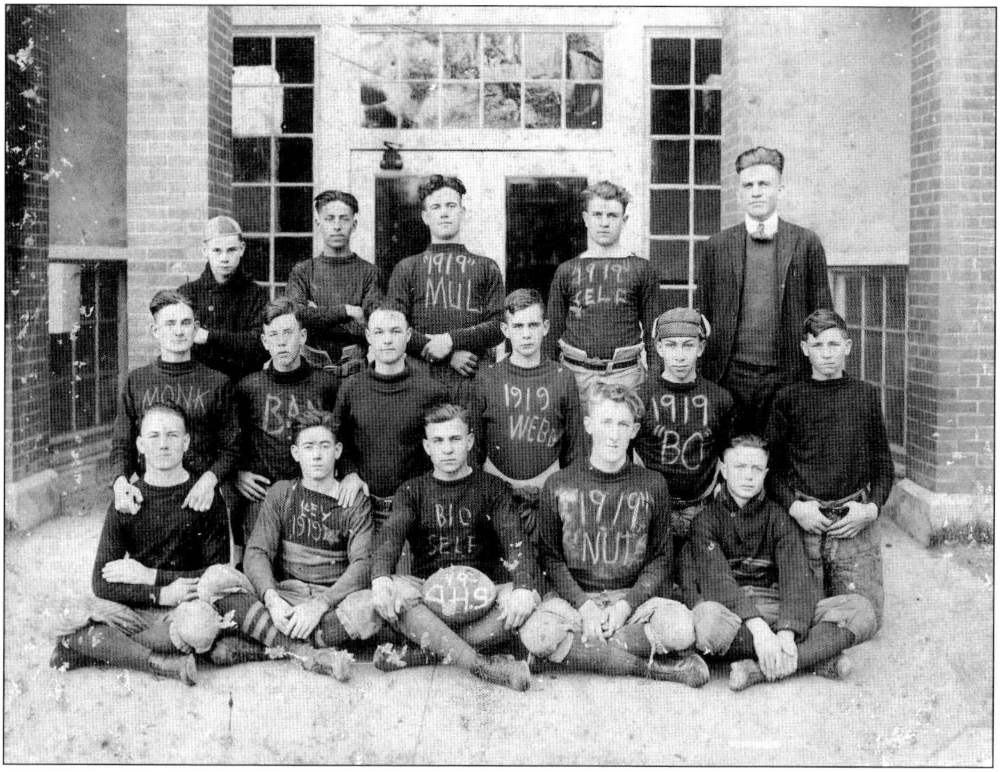

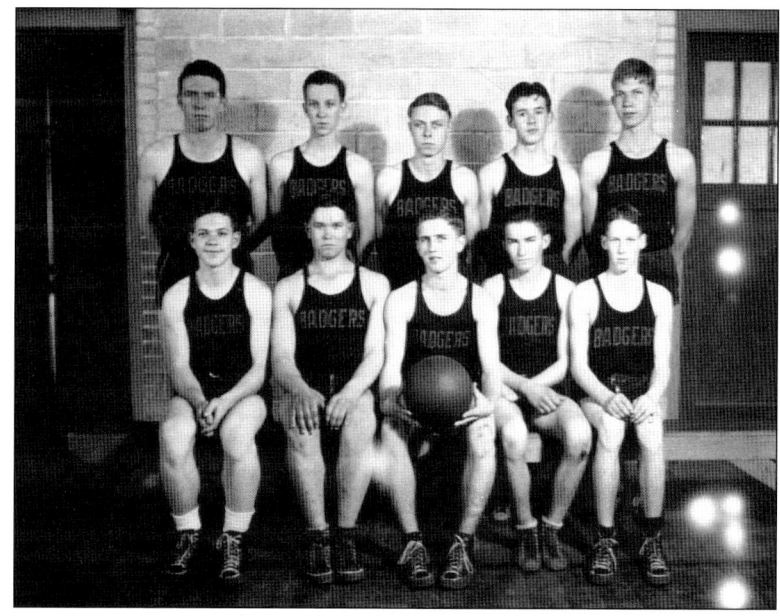

Arkadelphia High School first fielded a football team around 1908. In 1919, the team shown above played six games between October 20 and November 27. Their opponents were Hope, Little Rock, Texarkana, Hot Springs, and Benton, with an open date on Thanksgiving. (OBU.)

The members of the 1938 Arkadelphia High School Junior basketball team included, from left to right, (seated) Thomas Halsell, Sidney Thomas, Buster Jordan, Gale Dunlop, and Delton Rice; (standing) Robert Strickland, Jay Ray, Arnold Helms, Bill Millsapps, and George Hendricks. (OBU.)

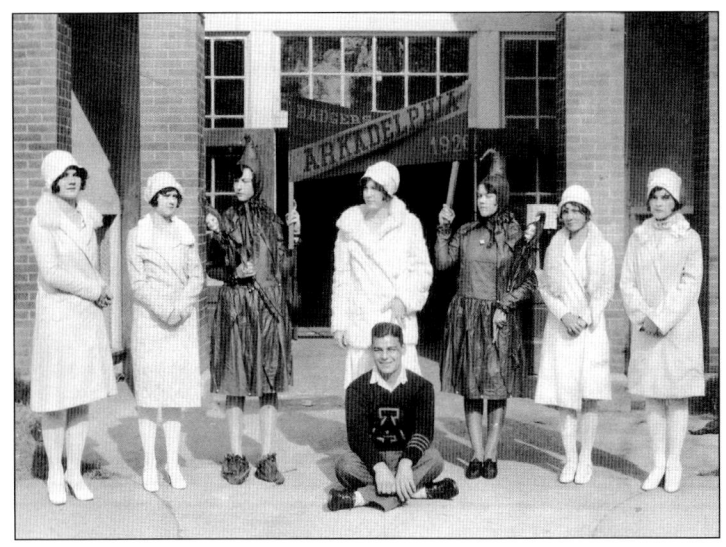

The occasion for this amusing photograph of Arkadelphia High School students in 1926 is not identified. However, it is possible that the photograph was taken in conjunction with the annual "Skule Karnival," held during Mardi Gras. The carnival involved the election of class candidates who vied for carnival queen. Martha Virginia Stuart was crowned the 1926 carnival queen. (OBU.)

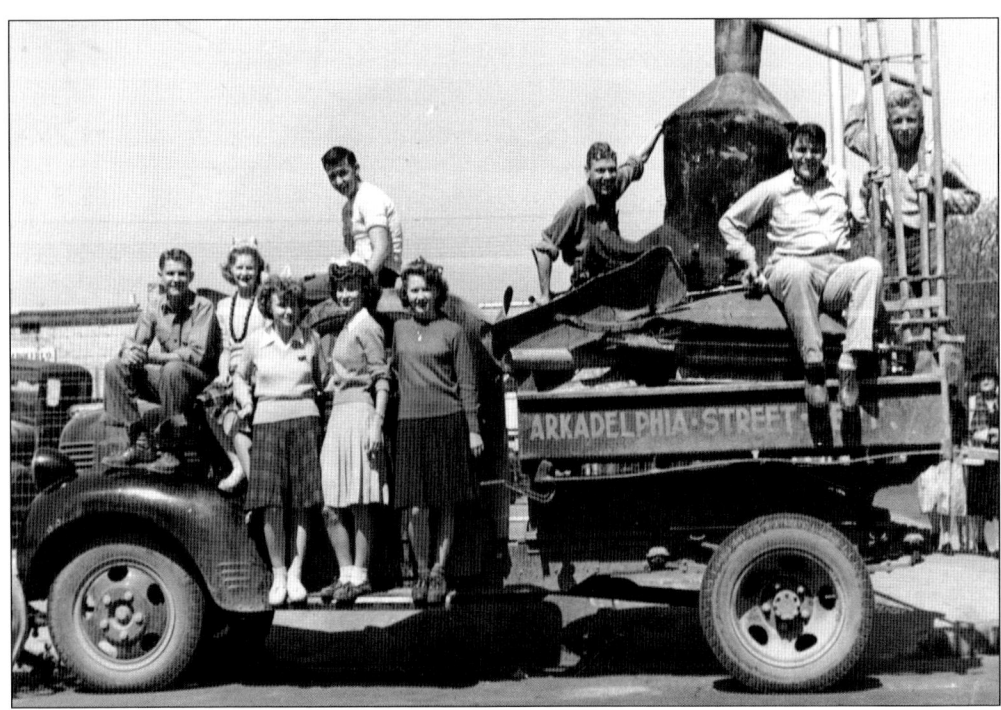

During World War II, local students assisted with the county's scrap and rubber drive. During the 1943 scrap drive, coordinated by the Clark County Defense Council, Clark County collected an estimated 125,000 pounds of scrap from Arkadelphia, Gurdon, Amity, and Okolona. Boys and girls, including the Arkadelphia High School students pictured here, were asked to help with the drive as part of a National Junior Army. (OBU.)

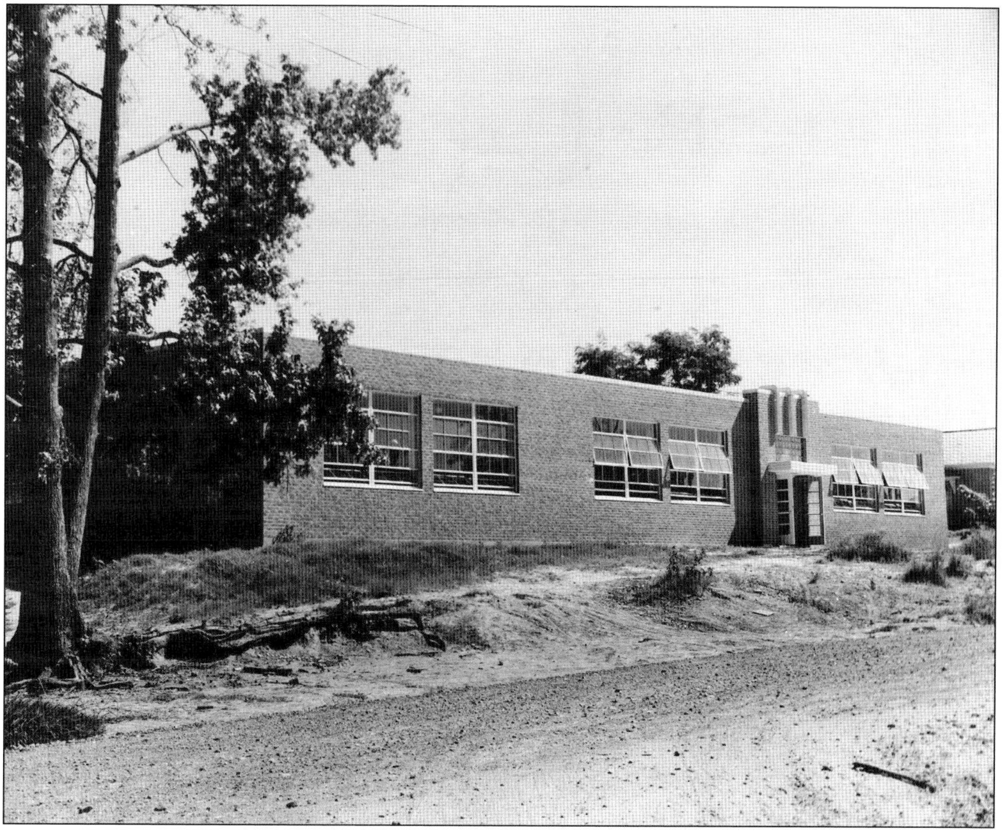

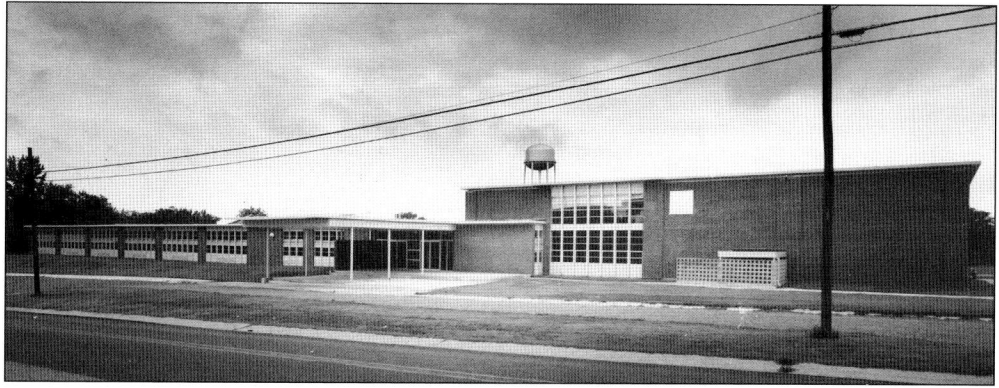

The building shown above is the original Peake school in Arkadelphia, constructed in 1928 and partially funded by the Julius Rosenwald Fund. The land on which the building still sits was donated by the family of John Ed Peake (1851–1906), a well-known African American educator in Arkansas. The original school served as the town's only public school for African American students until the new Peake High School, pictured below, opened in 1960. While the Peake-Rosenwald School continues to be owned and used by the Arkadelphia School District, the 1960 Peake High School was demolished in 2024, and a new and larger facility for elementary school students was built in its place. The Peake-Rosenwald School was added to the National Register of Historic Places in 2005. (Both, OBU.)

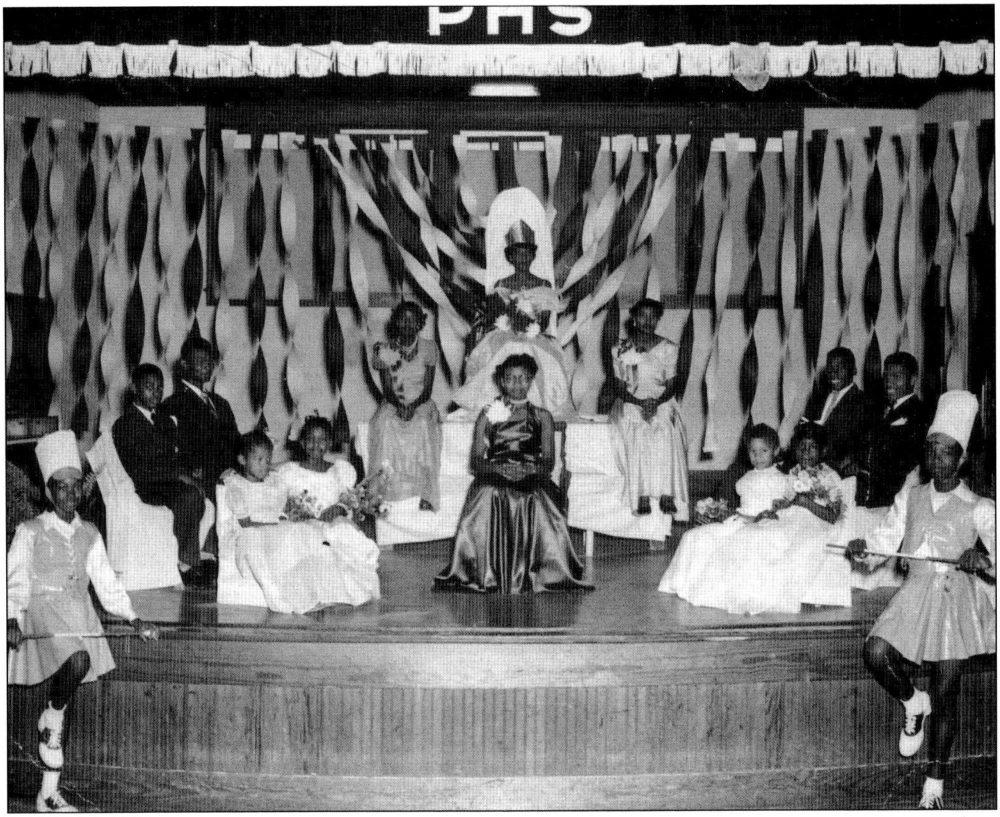

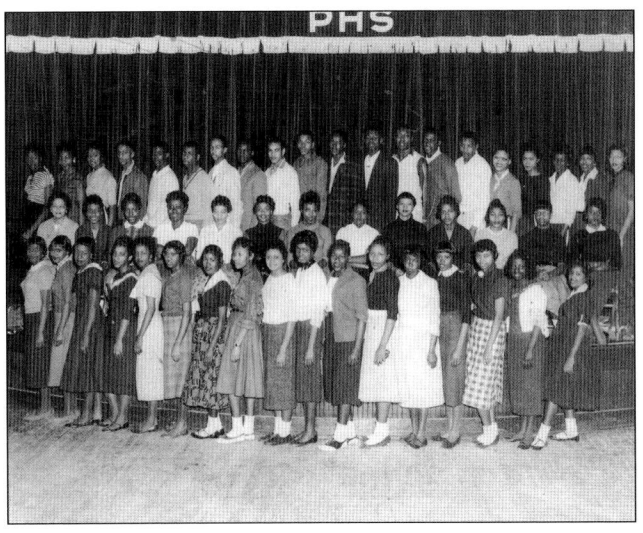

Willor R. Somerville (center) was elected queen at Peake High School's homecoming in 1953. Maids were Charlene Beard (left of Somerville) and Mary Joyce Hill, seated below Somerville. The maid standing at the right is unidentified. Escorts at right were Willie T. Somerville (left), twin brother of Willor, and Maurice Horton (right), who later became the first African American student to receive a degree from Henderson in 1957. The majorettes were Edith McCloud (far left) and Bobbie Hinkle (far right). Escorts on the left and the junior maids are unidentified. (OBU.)

The class motto of the 1958 Peake High School senior class was "Finish What You Attempt." In 1993, alumni established the Buffaloes Foundation Inc., a nonprofit named after the Peake mascot, the buffalo. Dedicated to the preservation and celebration of Clark County and Arkadelphia African American historical achievements, the organization annually awards the Brownlee, Deloach & Ware Memorial Scholarship to a local high school student of African American descent. (OBU.)

The 1952 Peake High School football team, pictured here, was coached by Jerome Muldrew, at far left. Identified players include Maurice Horton (22), Arthur Lee Williams (23), U.S. Cummings (14), Willie "Snap" Jackson (26), Perry Bragg Jr. (11), Robert Charles Jones (17), Willie T. Sommerville (10), Raymond Crite (27), Charles Newborn (19), Henry Todd (24), Will McFadden (29), Vernon Preston (21), and Henderson Nevels (15). Kneeling with the ball are, from left to right, Carrol Dean Forte, Ruben Edmondson, and John Andrew Taylor. (OBU.)

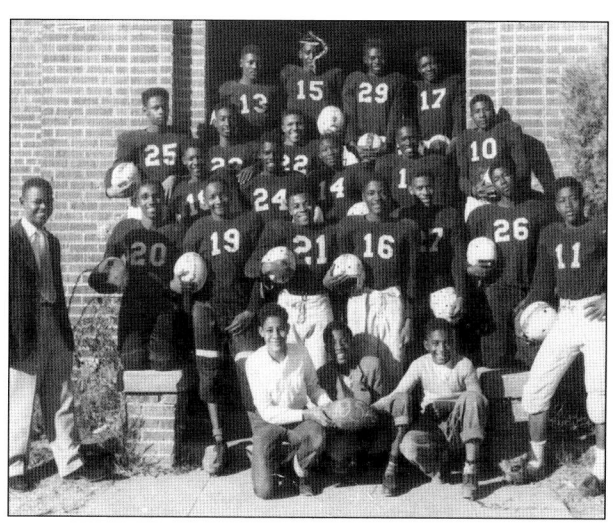

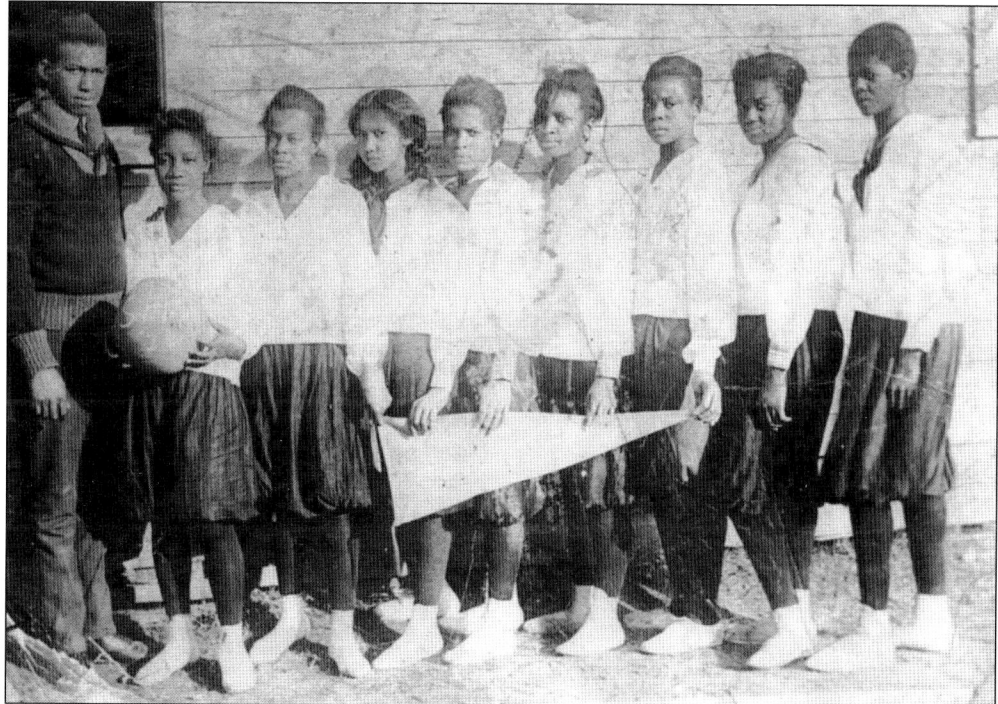

The Sloan School girls' basketball team poses with a ball and pennant around the 1920s. The school was the original public school for African American students in Arkadelphia, operating between 1872 and 1926. Located at Main and South Fourteenth Streets, the Rose Hill Cemetery addition now occupies this spot. The school was a small wood-frame building in which seven faculty members educated students in grades first through eighth. The property was destroyed by fire in 1926. A historical marker at the corner of Main and South Fourteenth Streets commemorates the Sloan School. (OBU.)

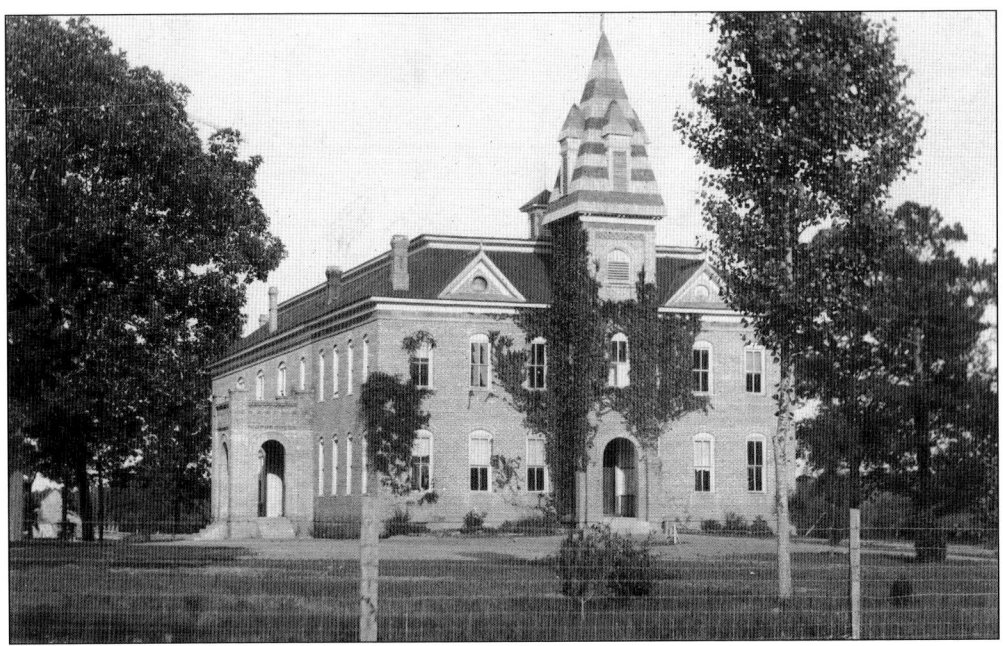

The public school at Amity was the life's work of Prof. Samuel M. Samson. While a school had operated in the community since 1845, the arrival of Samson in 1888 heralded a turning point. Under his leadership, enrollment grew, and enough funds were raised to construct this two-story, four-room brick building. This building served as the high school until it was torn down in 1954. (OBU.)

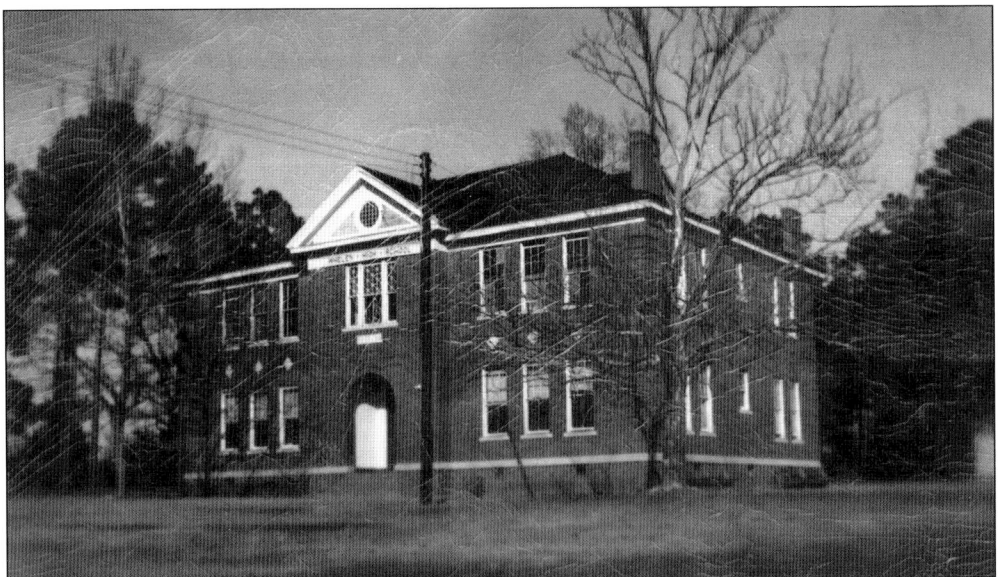

The Whelen Springs High School opened in 1915 following the consolidation of several rural schools in southern Clark County. The two-story building was constructed of locally manufactured brick from J.A. Barringer's brickyard and trimmed in white stone. Two large classrooms sat on either side of the downstairs hallway, while the second floor housed an auditorium and lodge hall that also served as a community center. The Whelen Springs High School closed in 1958 when the district consolidated with Gurdon. (OBU.)

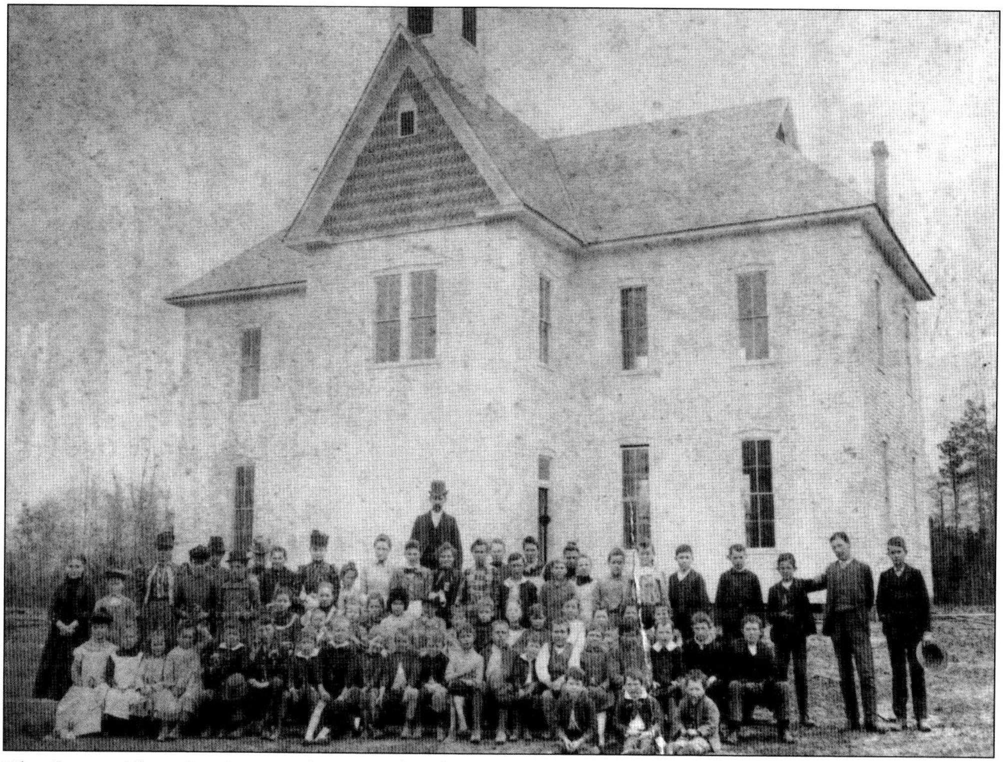

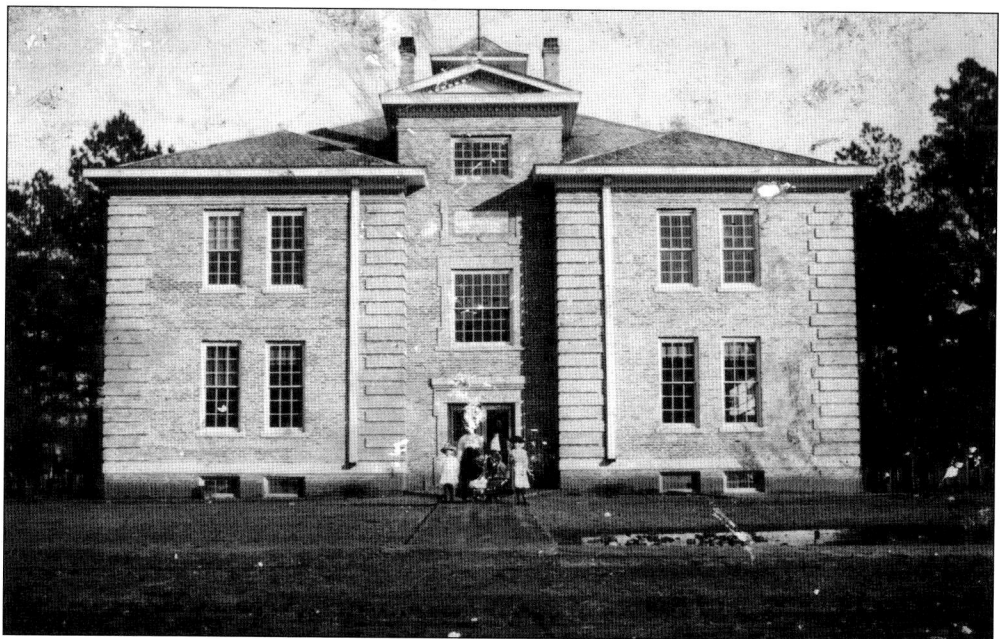

The first public school opened in Gurdon between 1878 and 1881. This one-room structure was built on what is now North Elm Street on US Highway 67. The building was used as a school and a place of worship. By 1892, the two-story frame structure, shown above, had been built on South Third Street. This building burned on January 1, 1907, and was replaced in 1909 by the structure shown below. (Above, OBU; below, HSU.)

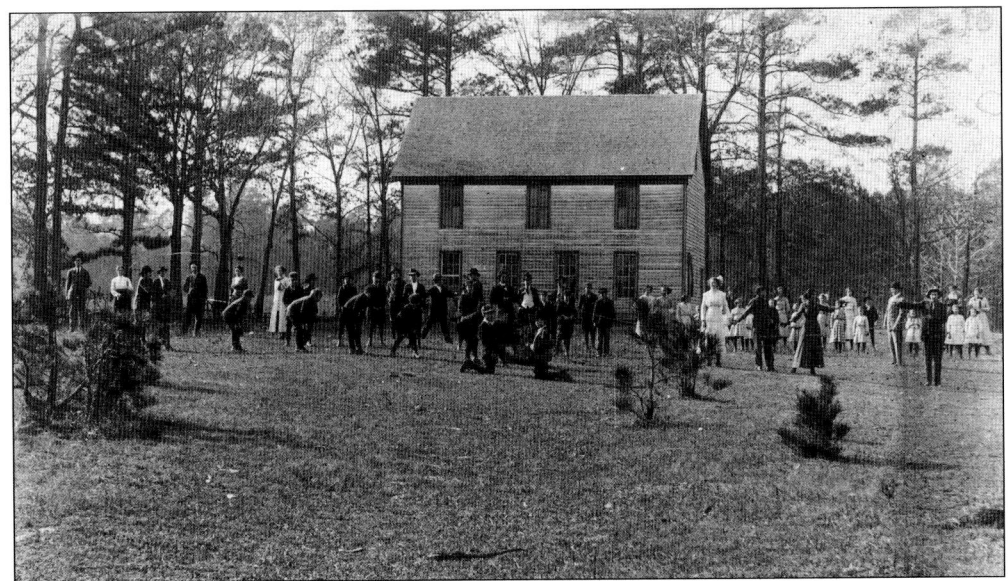

The Hollywood School was likely one of the first nonresidential structures built in that community around 1861. The school served the community for over 70 years. The second floor of the school also served as the community gathering place for the local Masonic chapter. In 1931, the process of consolidation with the Arkadelphia School District began, and by 1950, the Hollywood School closed. (OBU.)

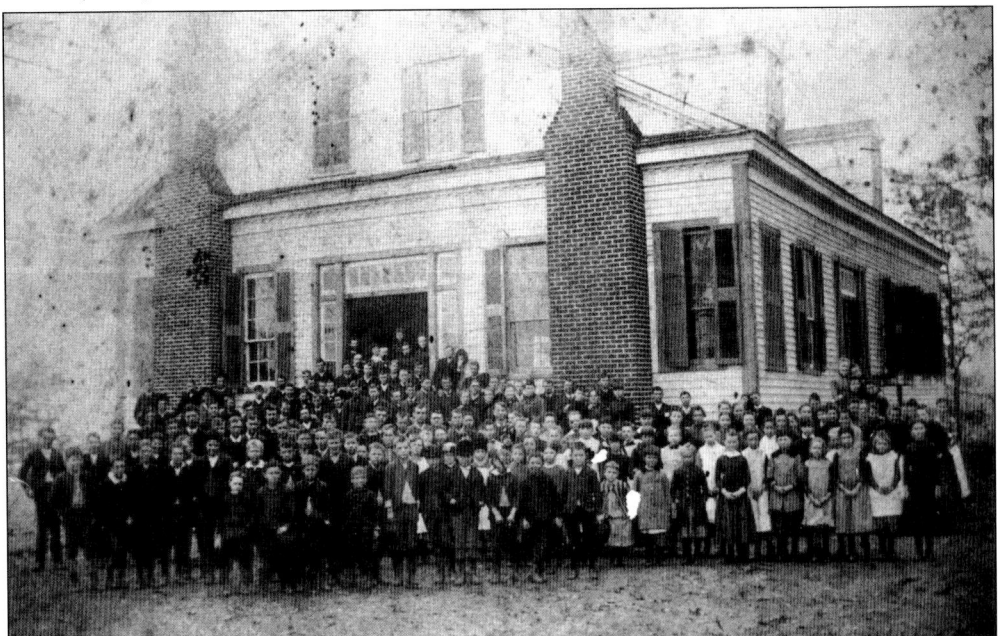

Between 1858 and 1868, this building housed Arkansas's first Institute for the Blind. After the state legislature relocated the institute to Little Rock, the Red River Baptist Association ran an academy there between 1876 and 1886. This photograph was likely made during those years. In 1886, the association donated the building and land to the newly established Ouachita Baptist College. Today, a historical marker designates the site formerly occupied by Arkansas's first state school for blind students. (OBU.)

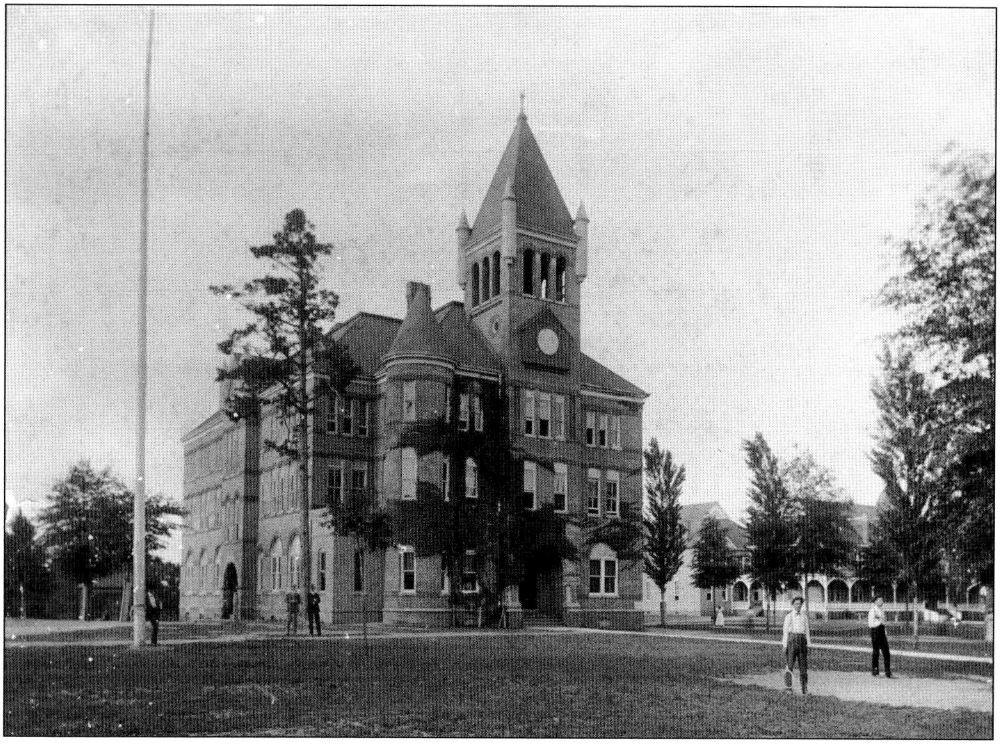

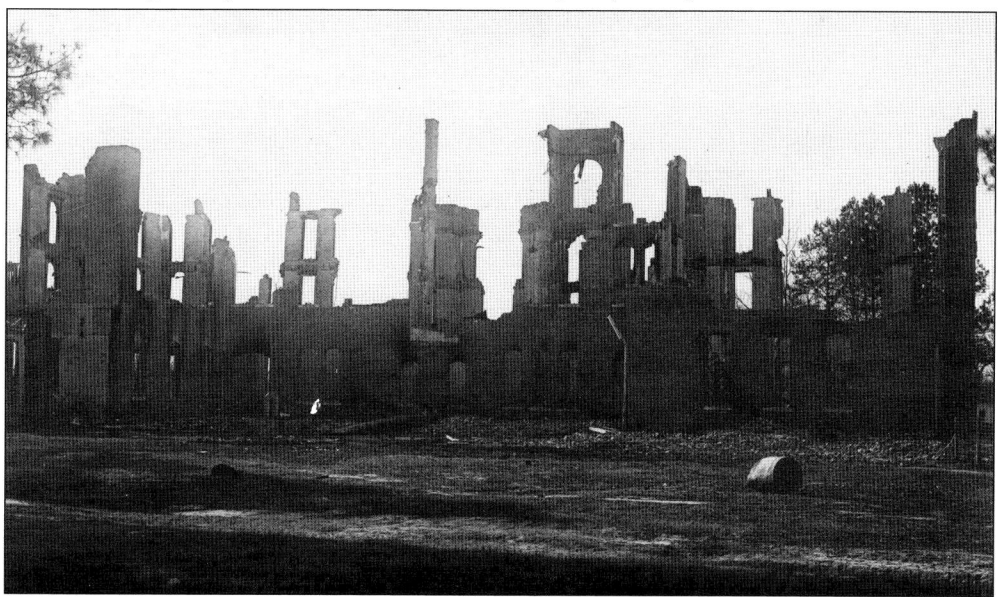

Ouachita Baptist College constructed the building that would become known as "Old Main" (above) in 1889, three years after the school opened. The picturesque three-story brick building housed the college president's office, business office, library, literary society rooms, and science department. Old Main was destroyed by fire caused by lightning on the night of commencement in May 1949. Reportedly, hundreds of townspeople and students responded to help salvage valuables from the building, including a safe from the registrar's office containing college records. The ruins of the building shortly after the fire are shown below. (Both, OBU.)

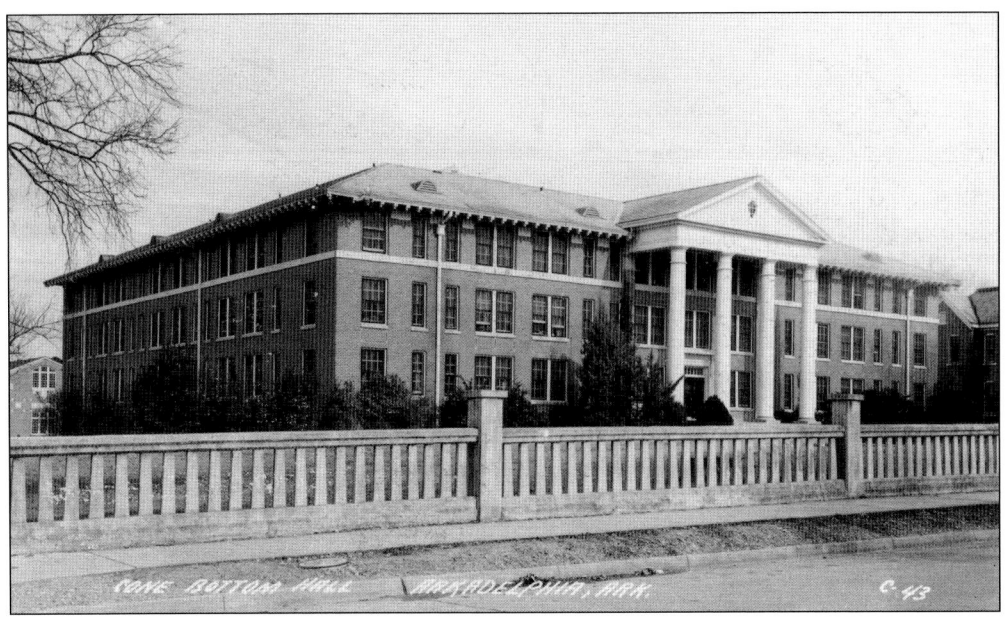

Cone-Bottoms Hall is the oldest surviving building on the campus of Ouachita Baptist College, which was renamed Ouachita Baptist University in 1965. Completed in 1923 and named for donors W.T. Cone and George W. Bottoms, the building served as a dormitory for women until the mid-1980s. This photograph shows the "Nowlin Wall," an ornamental concrete fence constructed with funds donated in 1923 by brothers Everett and Edger Nowlin in honor of their father, Andrew. The building now houses administrative offices. (OBU.)

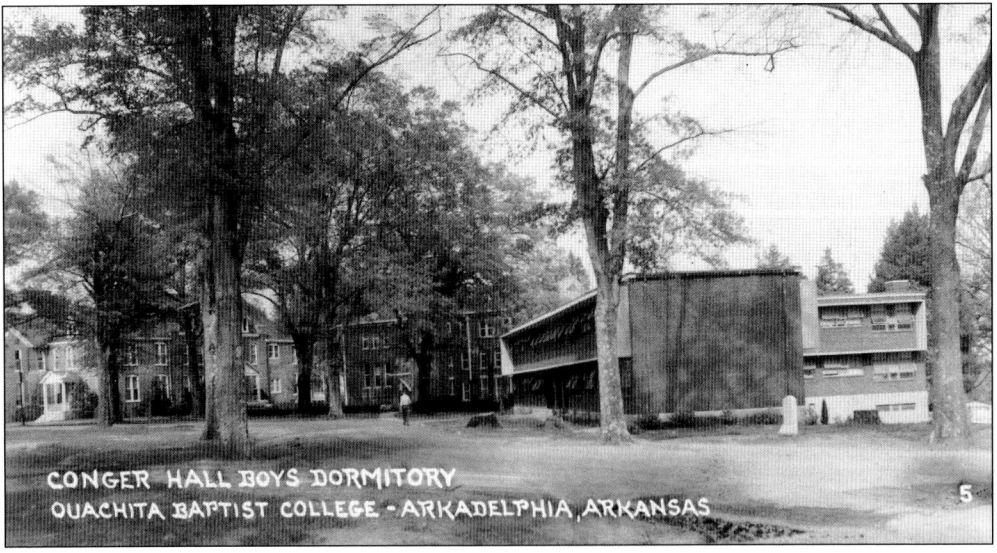

Conger Hall, shown at right, served Ouachita's campus for many years as a men's dormitory. Built in 1952 and named in memory of Dr. John W. Conger, the college's first president, the dormitory was located near the current site of Anthony Hall. A gravestone marking the burial place of Conger and his wife, Tennie, is visible at the side of Conger Hall. The Conger grave has twice been disinterred and relocated. It now occupies a spot next to the Ouachita River bluff near Evans Student Center. The Conger grave is the only legal burial in Arkadelphia outside a designated cemetery. (OBU.)

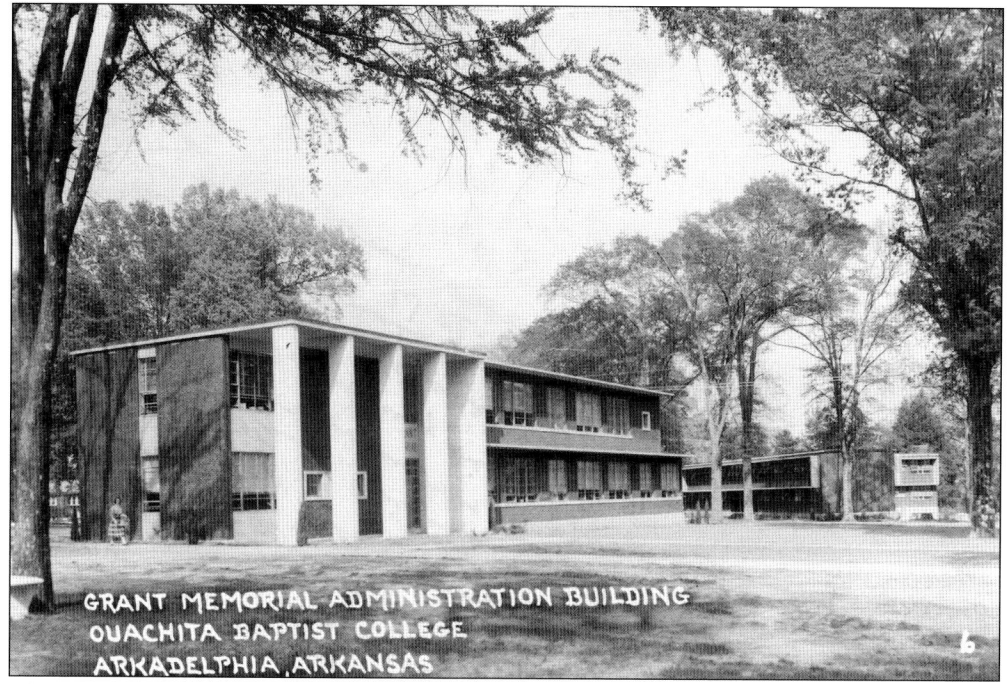

GRANT MEMORIAL ADMINISTRATION BUILDING
OUACHITA BAPTIST COLLEGE
ARKADELPHIA, ARKANSAS

The Grant Memorial Administration building served as Ouachita's main administration building for 42 years before being razed in 1995. The building was named for James Richard Grant, who served as the college's eighth president from 1934 to 1949. Grant Hall sat near the current location of the International Flag Plaza. Conger Hall is shown at the far right. (OBU.)

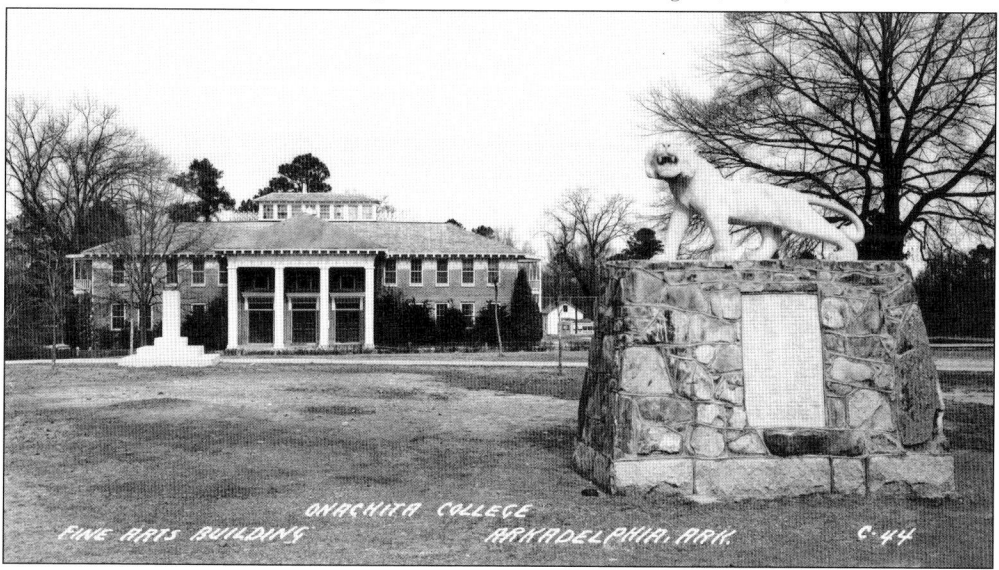

OUACHITA COLLEGE
FINE ARTS BUILDING   ARKADELPHIA, ARK.   C-44

The Fine Arts Building stood west of the Tiger statue on the Ouachita campus in this c. 1935 image. The iconic statue has been a school symbol since student B.F. Worley presented it to the college in 1935 in lieu of tuition. The tiger was a popular target for vandalism during Battle of the Ravine (BOTR) weeks through the years. Restored for its 75th birthday in 2010, the tiger is now protected by an iron fence. Ouachita students participate in a 24-hours-a-day, weeklong "guarding the tiger" event each year before the BOTR football game against Henderson. (OBU.)

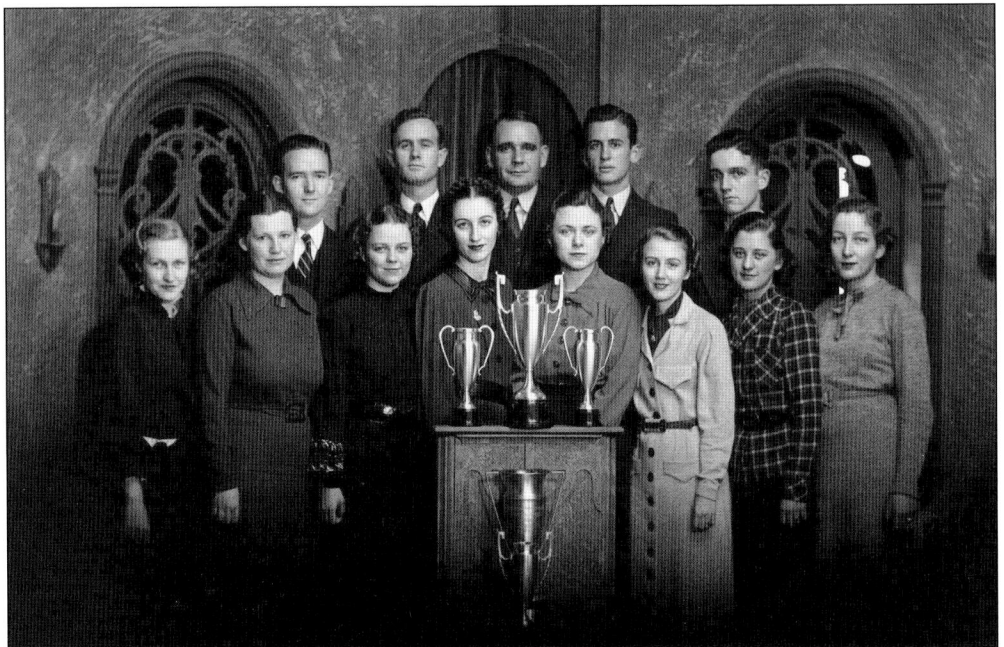

The Ouachita Baptist College chapter of Pi Kappa Delta, a national honorary society for speech and debate, won five trophies at the Arkansas Intercollegiate Forensic League tournament in December 1936. Team members pictured here are, left to right, (first row) Mildred Patishall, Bobbie Cooper, Pen Lile Compere, Juanita Pate, Doris Bradley, Janet Allen, Myrtle Bearden, and Maggie Flanagin; (second row) Monroe F. Swilley Jr., Paul Aiken, coach Dr. Ralph C. Daily, Charles Beasley, and Bill Parsons. (OBU.)

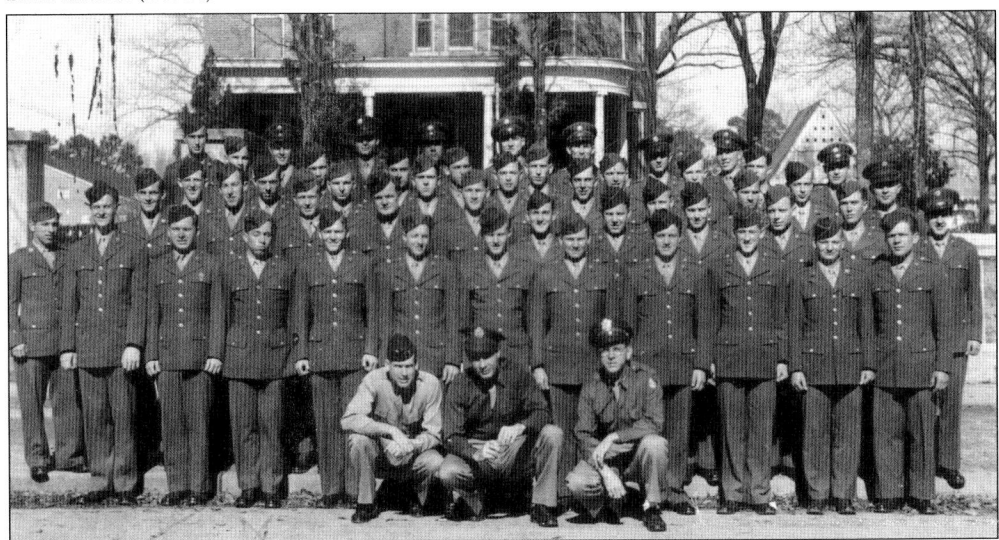

The 67th College Training Detachment (CTD) of the US Air Force poses in front of the Ouachita Baptist College President's Home around 1943-1944. The Air Force established the CTD in late 1942 to provide four months of accelerated education for cadets in the areas of mathematics, physics, chemistry, and astronomy. Both Ouachita and Henderson were assigned detachments, with the 66th training at Henderson. Approximately 1,300 students passed through the 67th Detachment, the most famous of whom was future Alabama governor George C. Wallace. (OBU.)

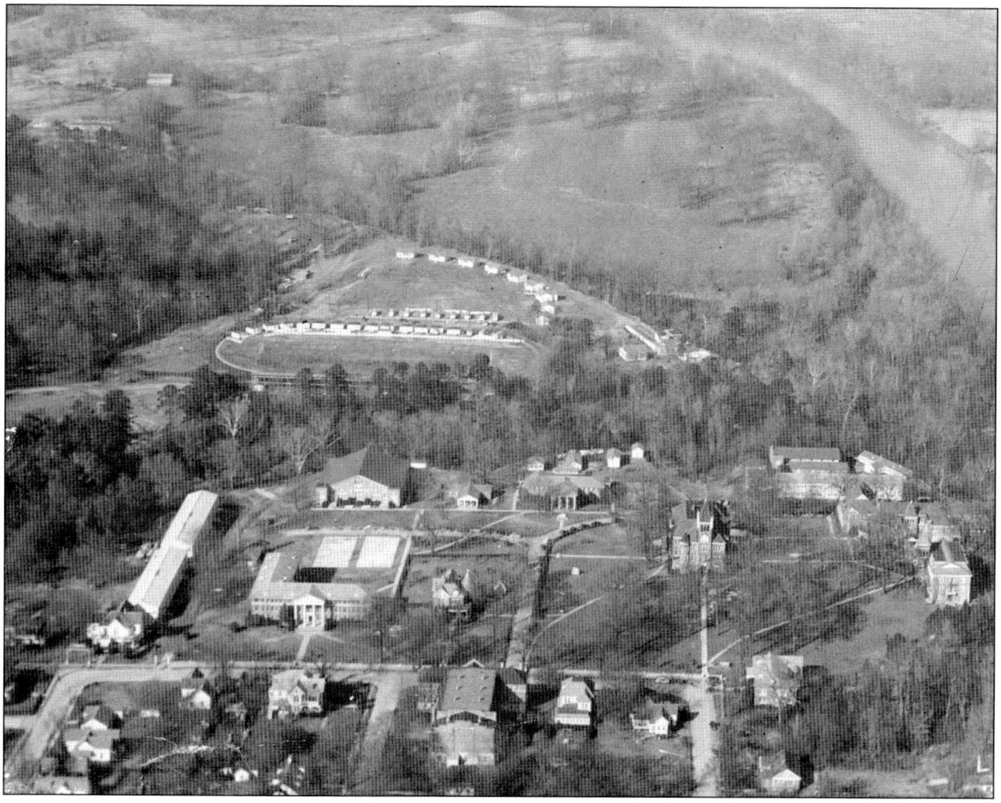

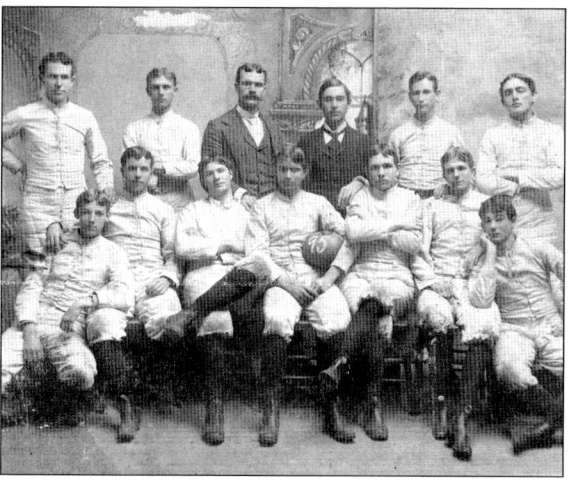

In 1948, thirteen brick and a few frame buildings made up the Ouachita campus. Old Main, a three-story brick building with a bell tower, housed administration, classrooms, the library, science labs, offices, and a museum. The year after this photograph was taken, a fire destroyed the building. The Fine Arts Building stood on the north side of campus. Cone-Bottoms Hall, an L-shaped brick structure with front columns, sat on the southwest side of campus. Behind Cone-Bottoms on the northwest corner of campus stood the recently completed gymnasium, which also housed the School of Military Science. The Ouachita President's Home sat to the right of Cone-Bottoms. (OBU.)

Ouachita's first football team was organized in 1895, the first year in which the Battle of the Ravine game was held between Ouachita and Arkadelphia Methodist College (now Henderson). Ouachita won the first game 8-0. Members of Ouachita's inaugural squad are identified as, from left to right, (first row, seated) Charles Weber, R.J. McCutcheon, L.V. Rogers, W.A. McGee, C.D. Guest, Curry Bowen, and Fred Pillsbury; (second row) Bynum Hinton, Raymond Smith, professor and coach Otto Schub, manager O.J. Wade, Albert Moore, and Lloyd Rowland. (OBU.)

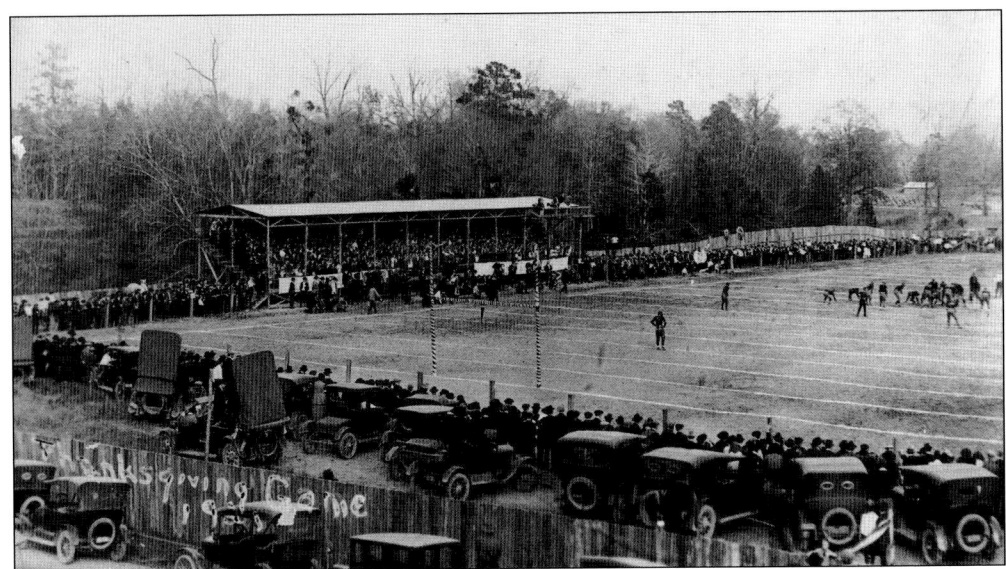

Over 3,000 people gathered to watch the 1921 Thanksgiving Day football competition between Henderson and Ouachita. The 1921 competition marked the first game played on Henderson's new athletic field. Ouachita emerged victorious with a score of 14-0. (OBU.)

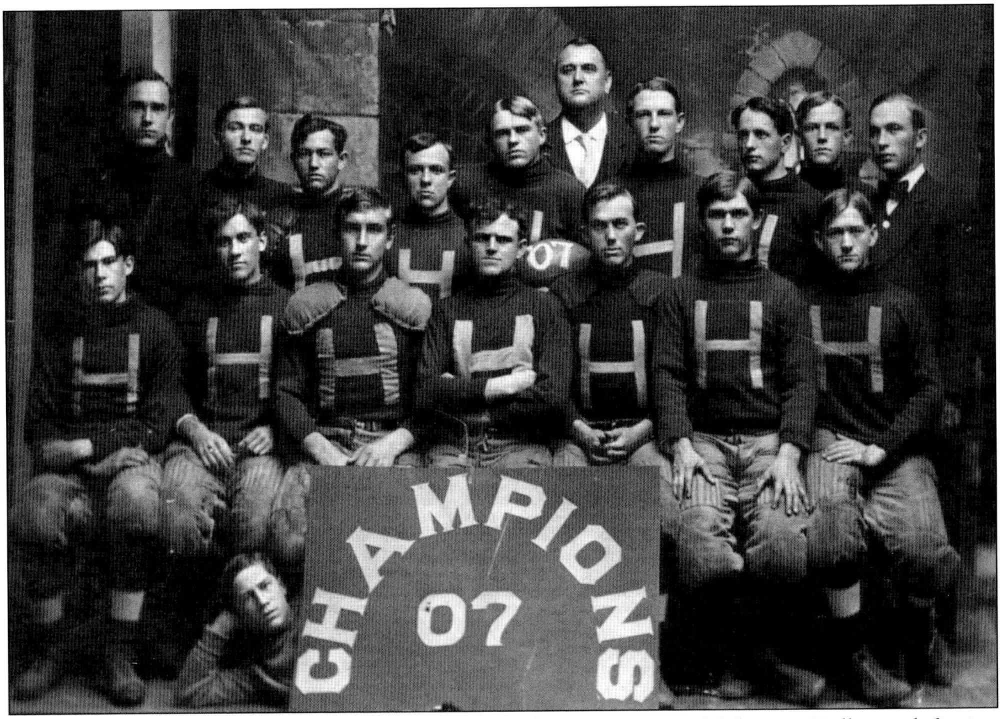

In 1907, Henderson captured the championship of the Association of Arkansas Colleges, defeating Arkansas Military Academy on Thanksgiving Day with a score of 6-5 under newly hired coach J.H. Lassiter. Members of the Henderson squad were Gus Brown, Wesley Rogers, Edgar Toombs, James Evans, McFerrin Gibbs, Hugh Wallace, Louis Agee, Ruford Turrentine, Gilbert Gillman, Dudley Tull, Charles McNeil, Welborne Berry, Whiteford Mauldin, and Elbert Edwards and substitutes Wood Hilliard and John H. Hinemon Jr. (OBU.)

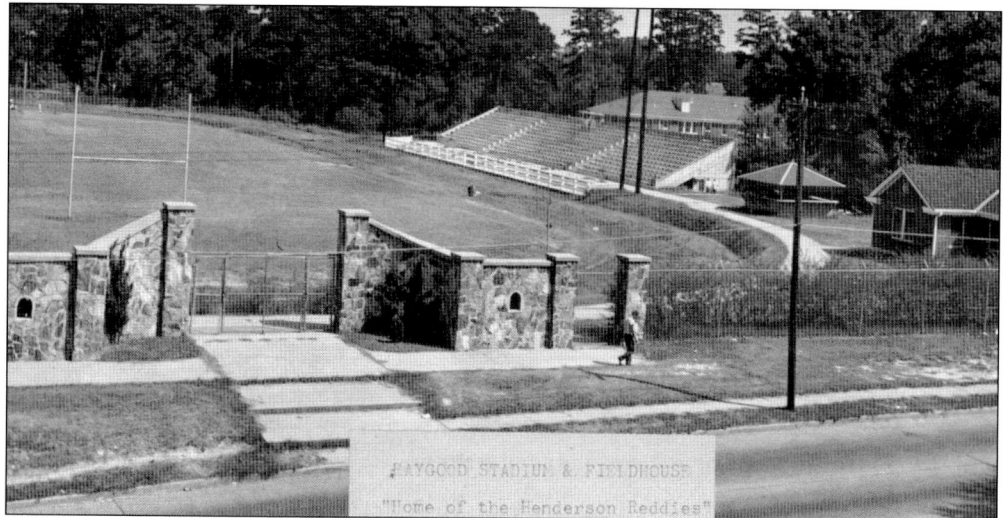

In 1935, Henderson filed an application with the Works Progress Administration (WPA) to improve Haygood Field, named for James Raymond "Jimmy" Haygood, who served the college as coach intermittently from 1907 to 1925. The New Deal public works program approved the college's application for the construction of a stadium, field house, lighting equipment, separate practice and game fields, and a track. The $55,000 project was completed in 1937, with the WPA furnishing all but about $10,000 of the funds. (OBU.)

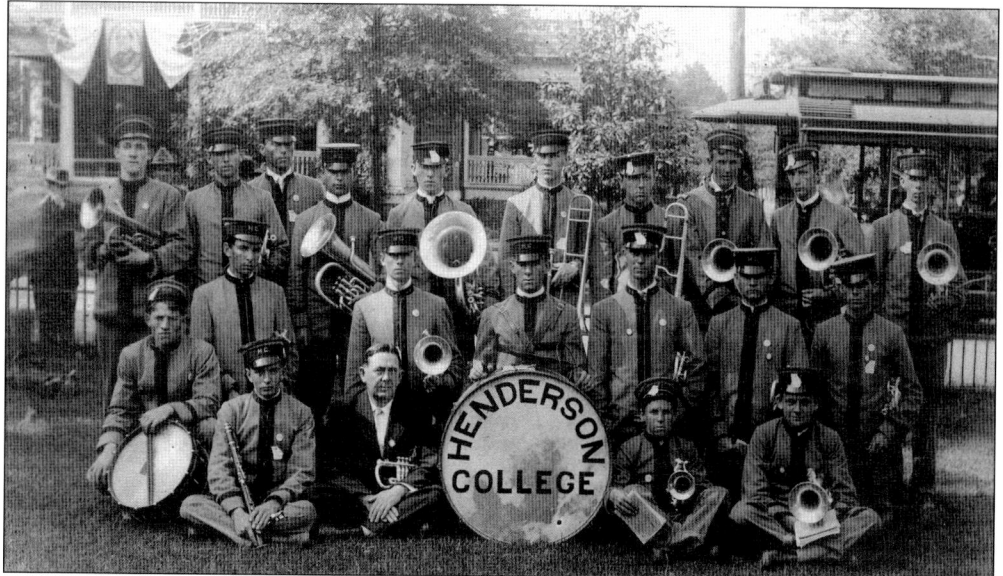

Members of the Henderson band pose with their instruments and director Dwight Blake (seated left of drum). Blake was the most well-known band director in Arkansas in the early 20th century. Blake had served as chief musician with the 2nd Arkansas Infantry during the Spanish-American War and was also a World War I veteran. Henderson band members are wearing the official college uniform for male students sometime around 1904–1911. Henderson was founded in 1890 as Arkadelphia Methodist College. The name was changed in 1904 to Henderson College and again in 1911 to Henderson-Brown College, both times to honor benefactors. In 1929, Methodist affiliation with Henderson ended, and the school became Henderson State Teachers College. (OBU.)

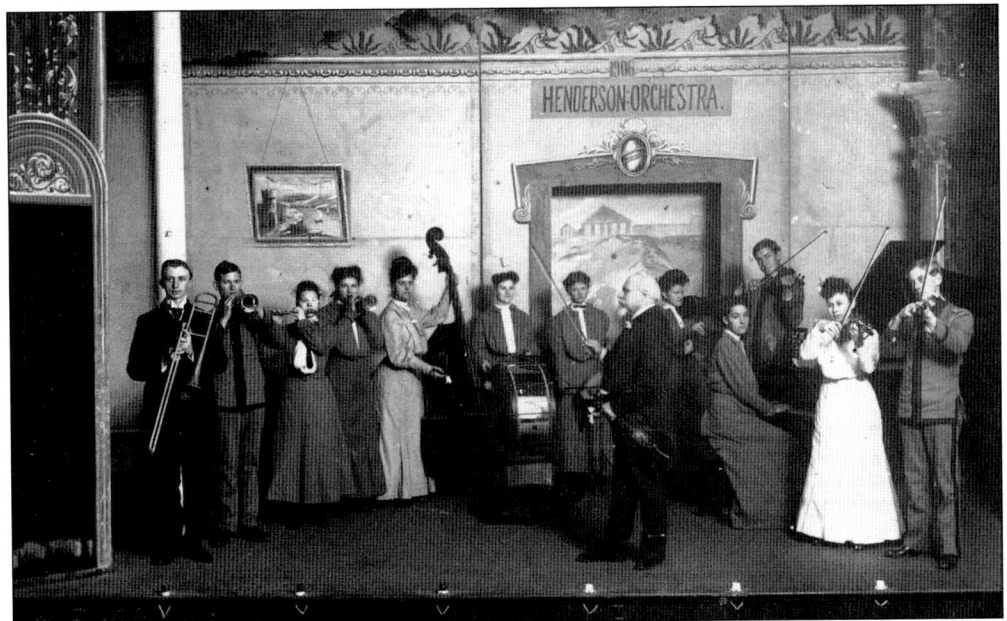

In 1906, the Henderson-Brown College Orchestra was under the direction of Prof. Carl Josef Schneider (center), who served as director of music for several years in the first decade of the 20th century. During his tenure, Professor Schneider was regarded as the "best-known director of music the college has ever had." He left Henderson in 1906. When he died in Rudesheim, Germany, in 1910, the Arkadelphia newspaper marked his passage with a front-page tribute. (OBU.)

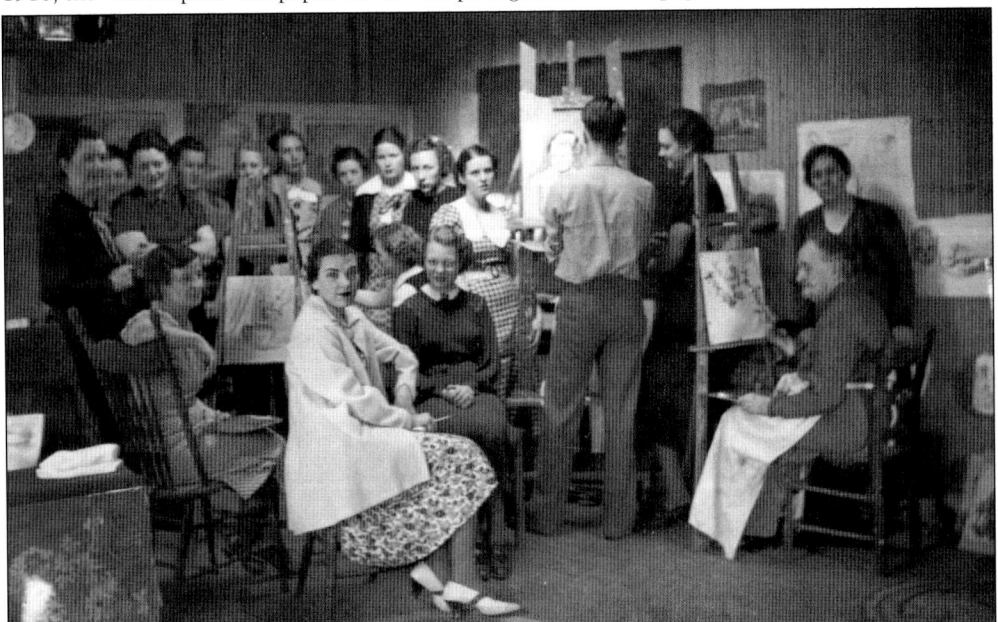

With back to the camera, artist Charles Dudley Richardson instructs an all-women class in his studio around 1936. Primarily a painter of landscapes, Richardson took on private pupils in Arkadelphia and, for a time, taught in the art departments of Henderson and Ouachita. Among this class of students is Estelle McMillan Blake, seated at right, the first female faculty member at Ouachita. Blake served the college in various capacities for 60 years. (OBU.)

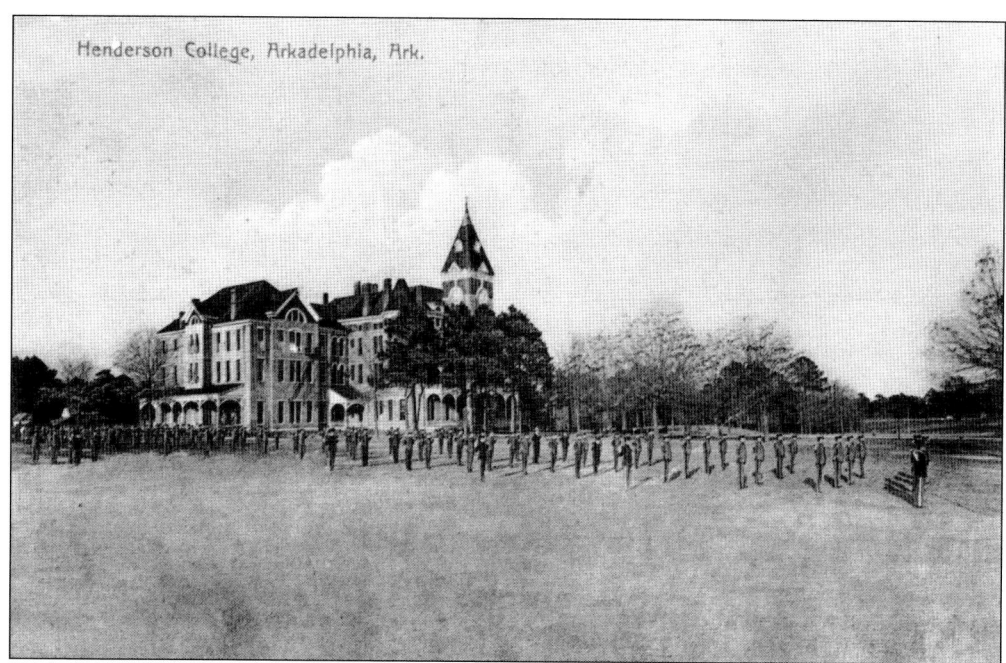

Henderson College, Arkadelphia, Ark.

In a strange coincidence, Henderson also had an "Old Main" building that was destroyed by fire in February 1914. The fire, which started in the college kitchen, quickly spread out of control. The college matron, a Mrs. Johns, speculated that the fire was caused by defective wiring or by "matches lighted by rats." Despite losing the college's primary building, Henderson officials carried on with the semester. Local residents took in female students, while male students relocated to the Caddo Hotel. Just one week after the fire, the local newspaper reported that temporary structures were already in place, including a dining hall and administration building, with "plans for a greater Henderson-Brown already well under way." The building's tower bell was preserved and sits on the university's lawn today. (Both, OBU.)

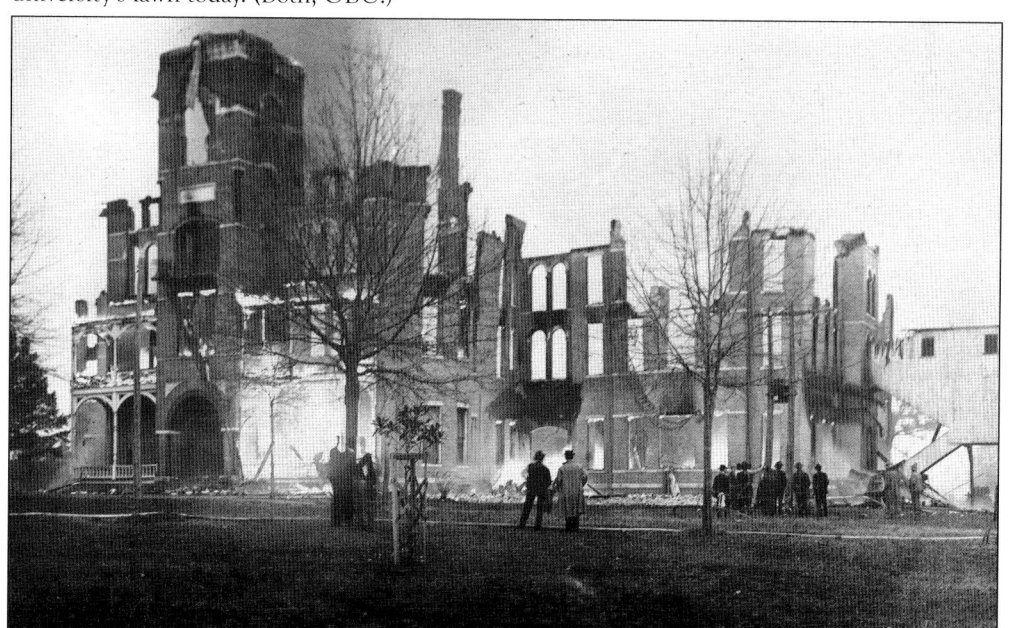

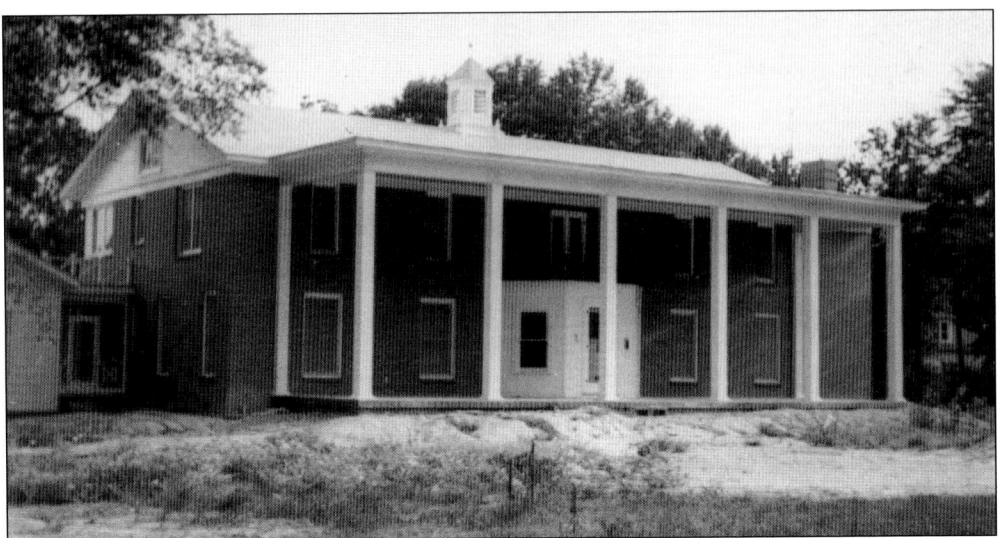

In January 1969, Henderson acquired a new home for its president. Farrar and Lila Newberry gifted their home at 1057 Henderson Street to the college for use as the President's Home. Newberry, a local historian and 1906 graduate of Henderson, specified in his will that the home should be used for the university presidents and their families. However, their gift allows the college to put the house to any use except as a dormitory. Henderson continues to use the Newberry house as the president's residence. (HSU.)

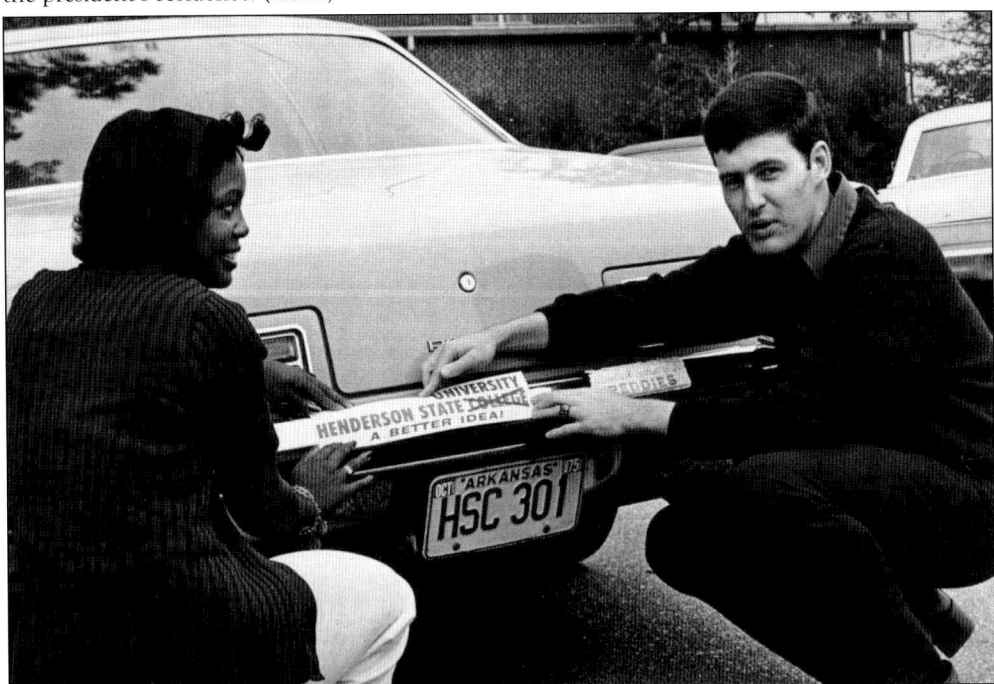

Henderson students Vera Jackson and John Berry apply a bumper sticker announcing the culmination of a successful campaign to have the college upgraded to a university. After becoming a public institution, Henderson greatly expanded. Enrollment more than doubled. Graduate classes were added in 1951. To reflect the growth, the school's name was changed to Henderson State College in 1967 and, in 1975, to Henderson State University. (OBU.)

Four

SACRED SPACES AND PRIVATE PLACES

The first Hollywood Methodist Church was a log structure built in 1812 on land near a creek. The structure served as a church and school for the growing community. In 1855, the Bridges family donated land closer to the Military Road for a new church, another log structure. In 1904, the church shown here was completed. The church and much of the village were destroyed by fire in June 1925. Within three months, the community had raised adequate funds to build a new sanctuary. Today, the church building is owned by the Clark County Historical Association. It serves as a meeting place and houses exhibits of the Hollywood community. (OBU.)

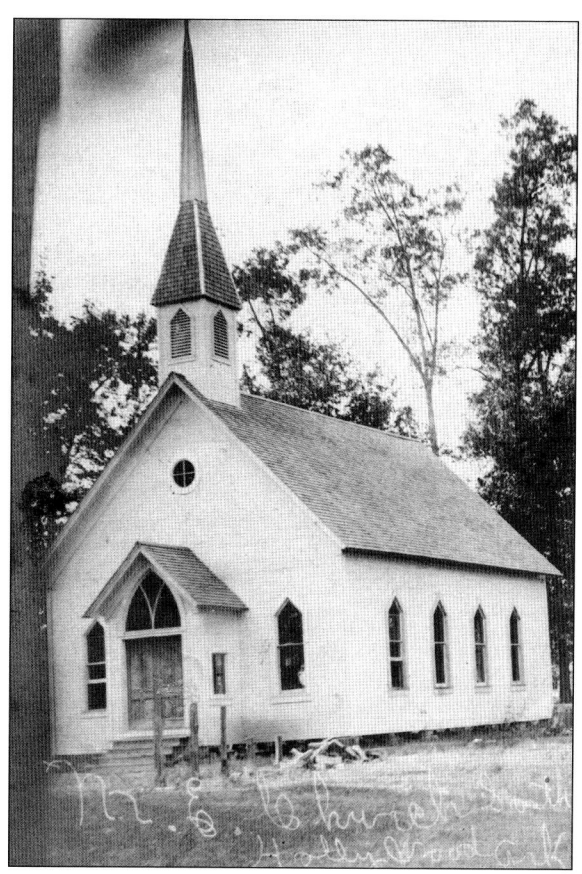

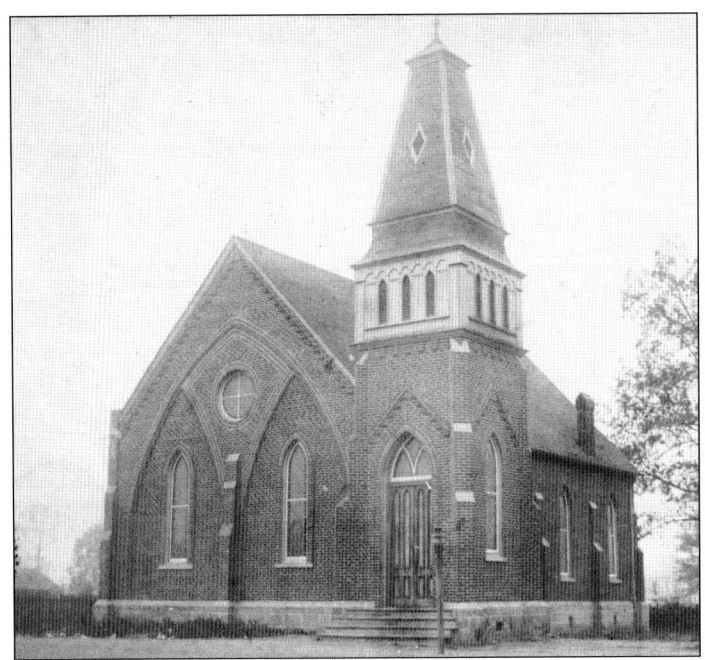

Arkadelphia's first Baptist congregation formed in July 1851, meeting at various locations around Arkadelphia until July 1884 when this 250-seat Gothic structure was completed on the southwest corner of Seventh and Caddo Streets. In 1909, the former Baptist church was sold to the First Christian congregation. In 1941, the building was sold again to the Deaton family, which operated a dry-cleaning business there until 1970. In 2007, the city of Arkadelphia condemned and later razed the building. (OBU.)

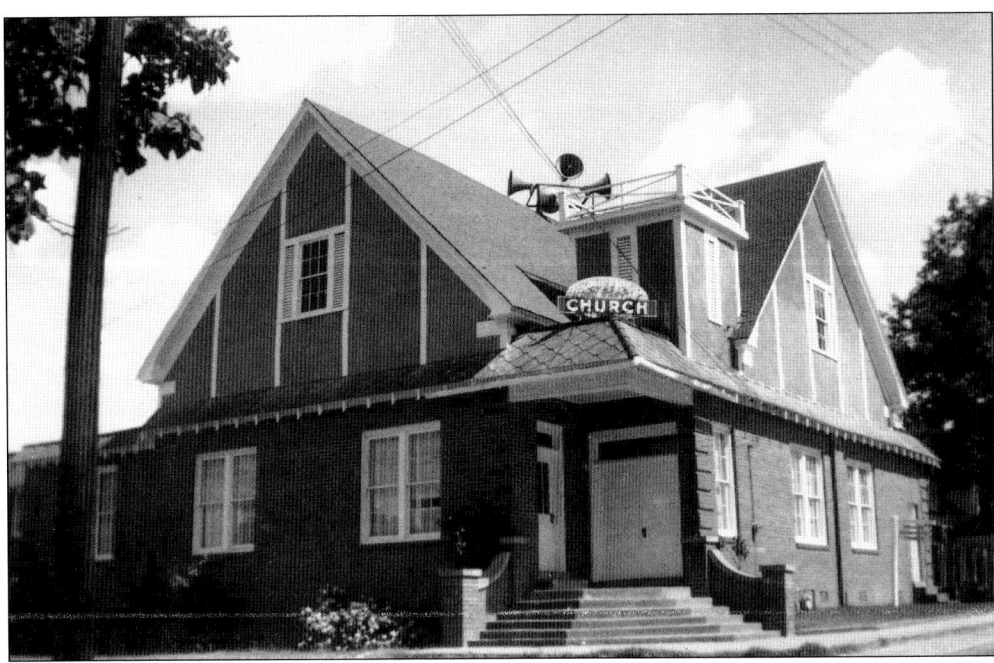

The Second Baptist Church of Arkadelphia was organized in 1904 as a mission of the First Baptist Church. In 1905, the church adopted the name Sweet Hill Baptist Church, which it retained until September 1928. The original church, shown here, was located just north of the current Second Baptist Church at Walnut and South Twelfth Streets. In 1938, the original frame structure was bricked. A new Second Baptist sanctuary was completed and dedicated in March 1968. (HSU.)

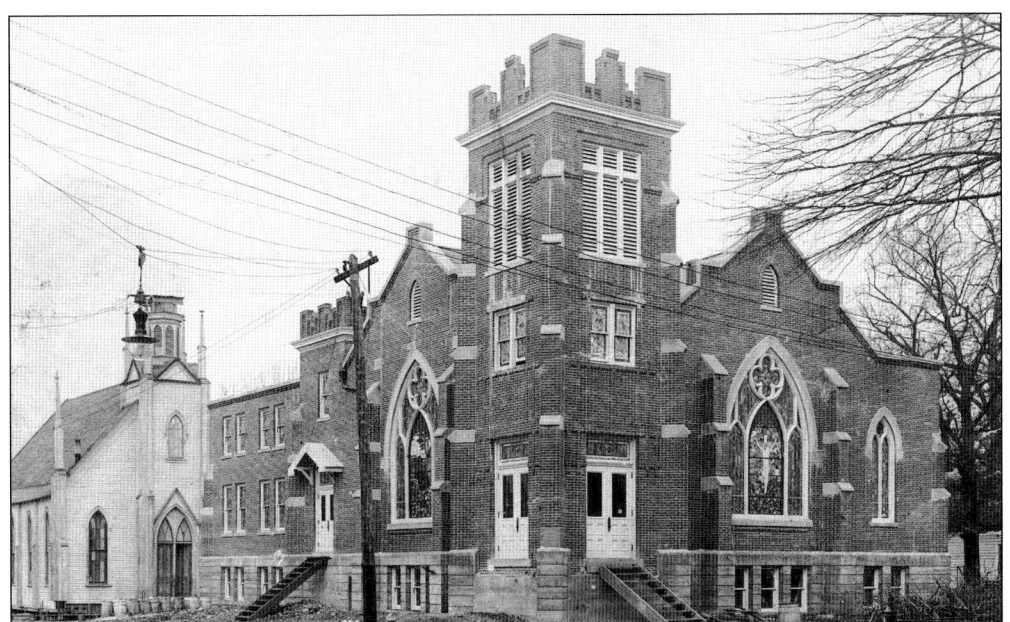

Methodism was formally established in Arkadelphia in 1851, although itinerant preachers had been delivering services in the area since the 1820s. Five structures have served Arkadelphia Methodists since 1851. In 1871, the frame church (above, far left) was constructed at Eighth and Center Streets. In 1907, a new brick sanctuary (above, right) was constructed next to the frame building. This structure served the First United Methodist Church congregation until 1973, when a new sanctuary was completed on Barkman Street. The Methodist Church boasted that it had the largest men's Sunday school class in Arkansas. The photograph below shows 205 members of the class who turned out to hear Dr. Matt Ellis, president of Hendrix College in Conway, Arkansas, and former Henderson president, talk about the resurrection of Christ on Easter Sunday in 1950. (Both, OBU.)

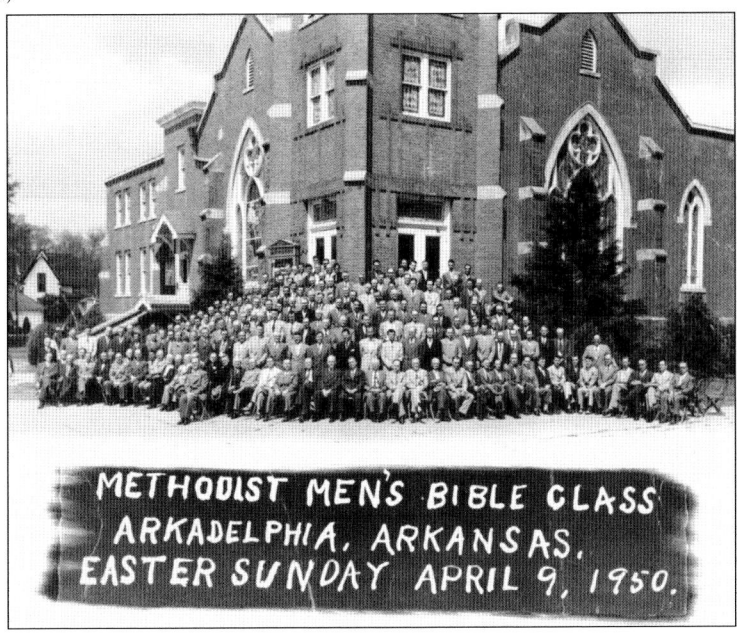

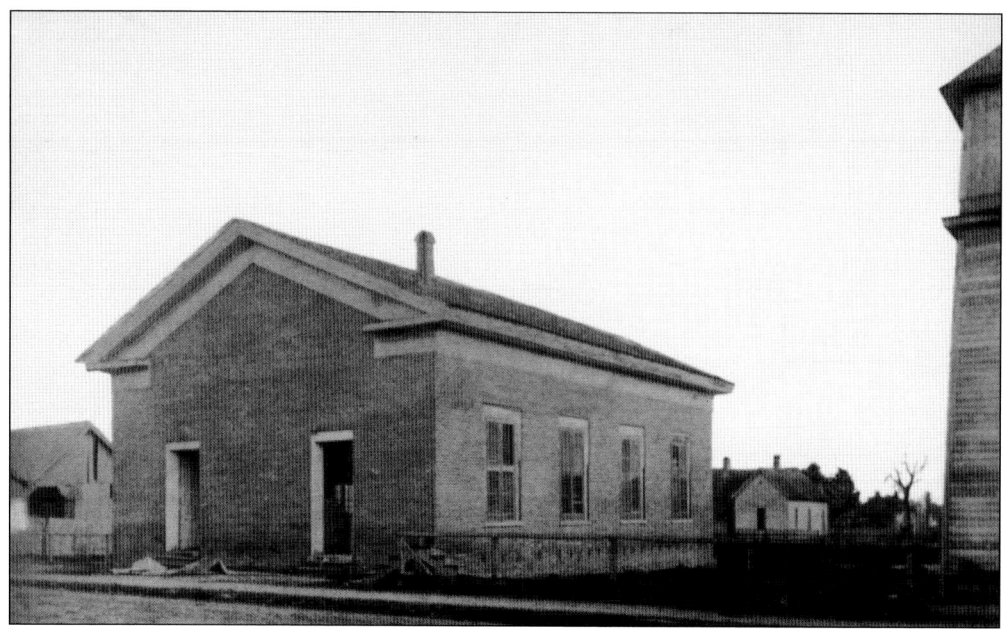

Arkadelphia's Presbyterian congregation was organized in 1858 with 14 members as part of the Ouachita Presbytery. The first church building (above), constructed on Clay Street, was a one-room brick structure with separate entrances for men and women and raised rows at the back of the church for enslaved African Americans. This building no longer stands. In 1902, the church began work on a new edifice at Caddo and Sixth Streets (below). This Gothic brown brick building was dedicated in 1903 and served the First Presbyterian Church of Arkadelphia congregation until the construction of the current church on Pine Street in 1954–1955. Also visible in this photograph is a corner of the first federal building and post office, at the left, and the columned entrance of the Arkadelphia Public Library, at the far right. (Both, OBU.)

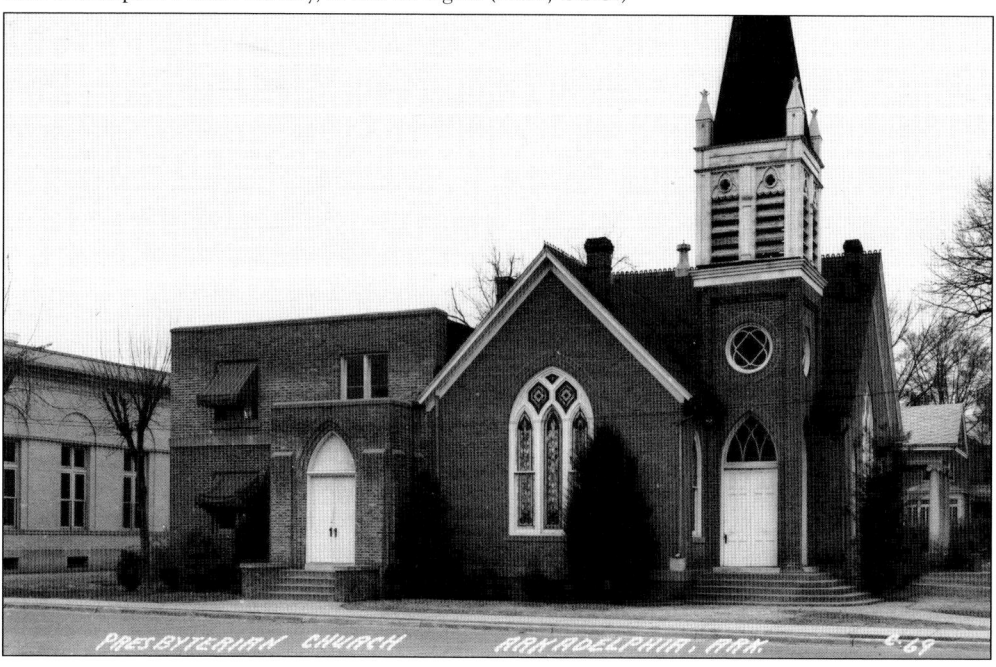

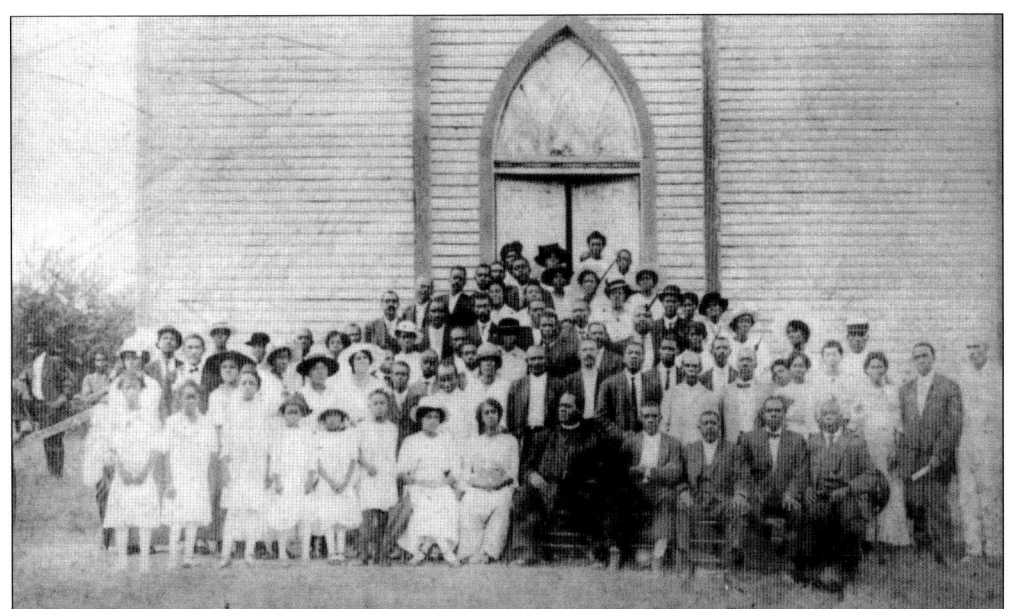

The congregation of St. Paul's African Methodist Episcopal (AME) Church poses outside their sanctuary at Main and Twelfth Streets, Arkadelphia, with Arkansas bishop J.M. Connor seated in the center in 1923. Organized in 1864, St. Paul's was the first church in the Arkadelphia district. Fire destroyed the white-frame church building in 1930, and members worshipped at Peake High School until a new sanctuary was completed at 1501 Caddo Street in 1940. (OBU.)

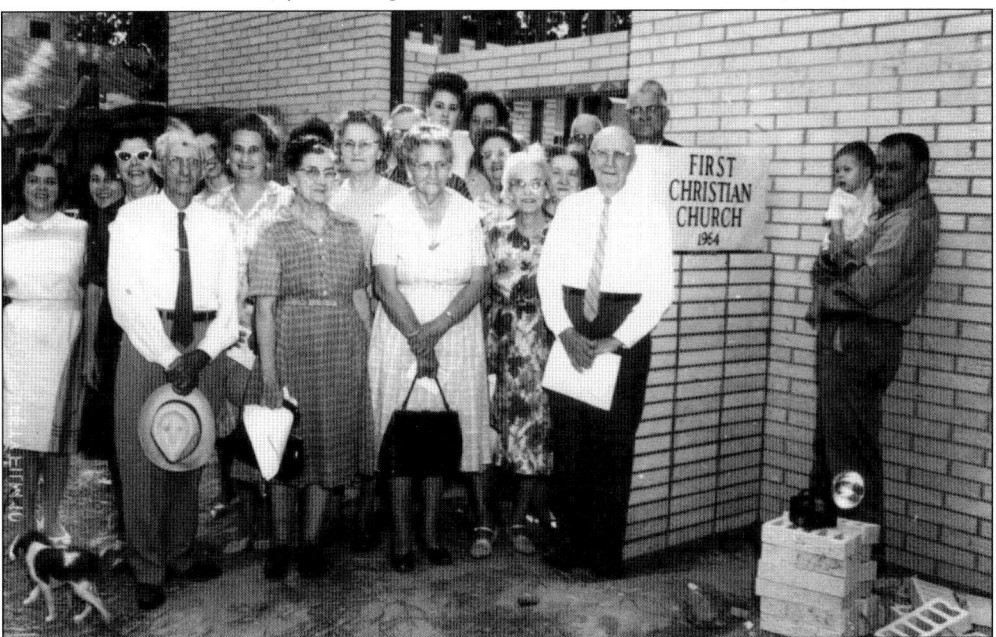

The First Christian Church of Arkadelphia was organized in December 1888. The first sanctuary was constructed in 1891 between Fourth and Fifth Streets. In 1908, the congregation moved into the old First Baptist Church at 107 South Seventh Street. The building shown here at the corner of Tenth and McNutt Streets was dedicated in 1964. The congregation disbanded in recent years, and Ouachita Baptist University now owns the property. (OBU.)

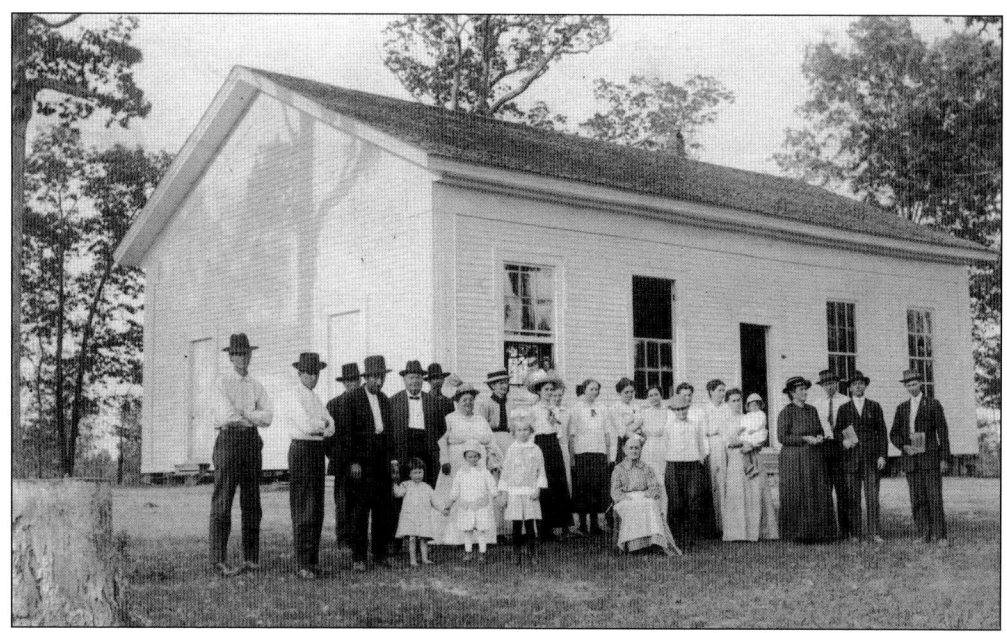

Mount Bethel Baptist Church, six miles west of Arkadelphia, was founded in 1836, making it one of the oldest Baptist churches in western Arkansas. In July 1851, fifteen members of Mount Bethel left to organize First Baptist Church in Arkadelphia. Fire destroyed the structure shown here in 1935. (OBU.)

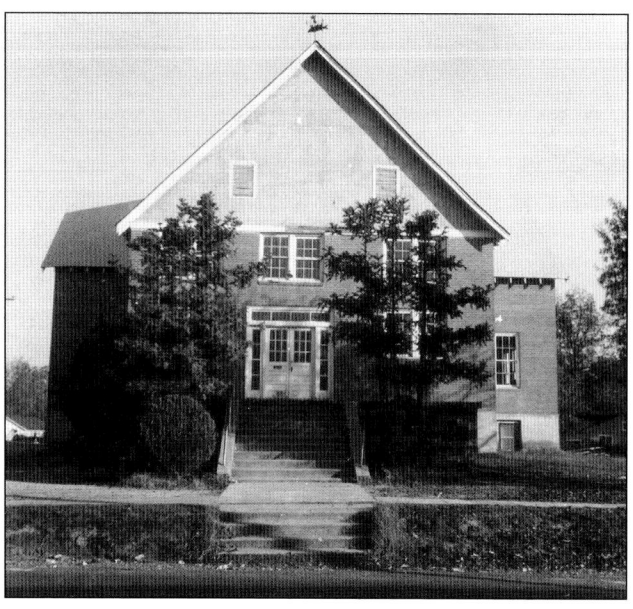

Pleasant Hill Baptist Church was organized in 1867 as a mission for African American residents. The first church building was erected in 1872. In 1887, the church organized the Arkansas Baptist Academy, which drew students from across Arkansas. The church's name was changed to Greater Pleasant Hill Missionary Baptist Church in the early 1930s, and a new sanctuary was constructed between 1935 and 1936. In August 1998, a new sanctuary was dedicated. The older building now serves as space for class and conference rooms, administrative offices, a library, and a smaller sanctuary. (OBU.)

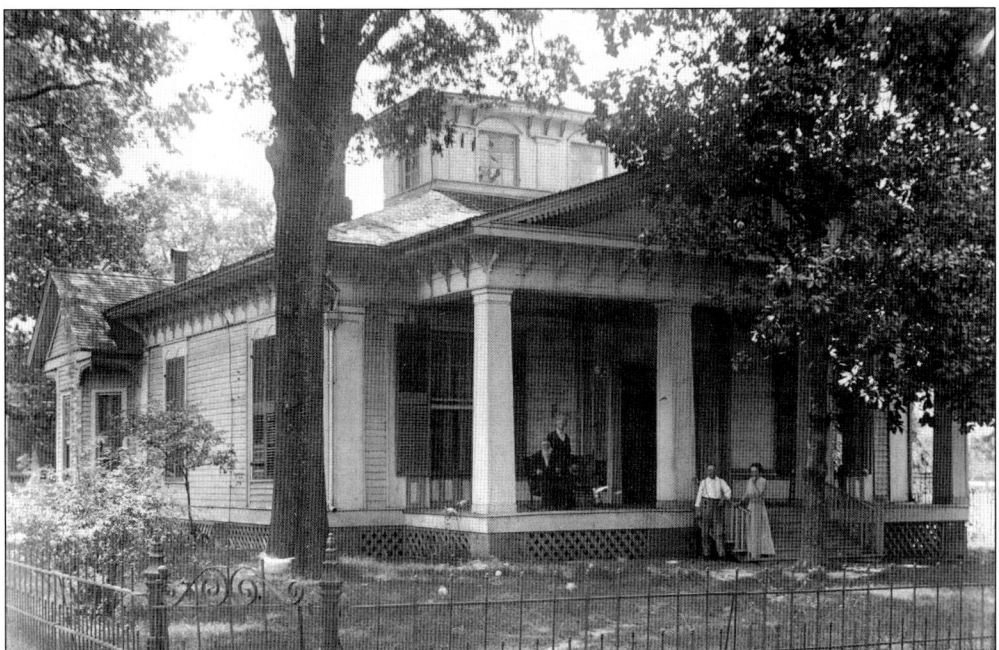

The Habicht-Cohn-Crow house at the corner of Eighth and Pine Streets in Arkadelphia was built in 1870 by Anthony E. Habicht, superintendent of the Clark County Freedmen's Bureau. In 1875, Habicht sold the home to Mark Matthias "M.M." Cohn, an Arkadelphia merchant who later established a department store in Little Rock. In 1880, Austin M. Crow purchased the residence. The home stayed within the extended Crow family until 1983 and today houses Apex Insurance Consultants. The home was added to the National Register of Historic Places in 1985. (HSU.)

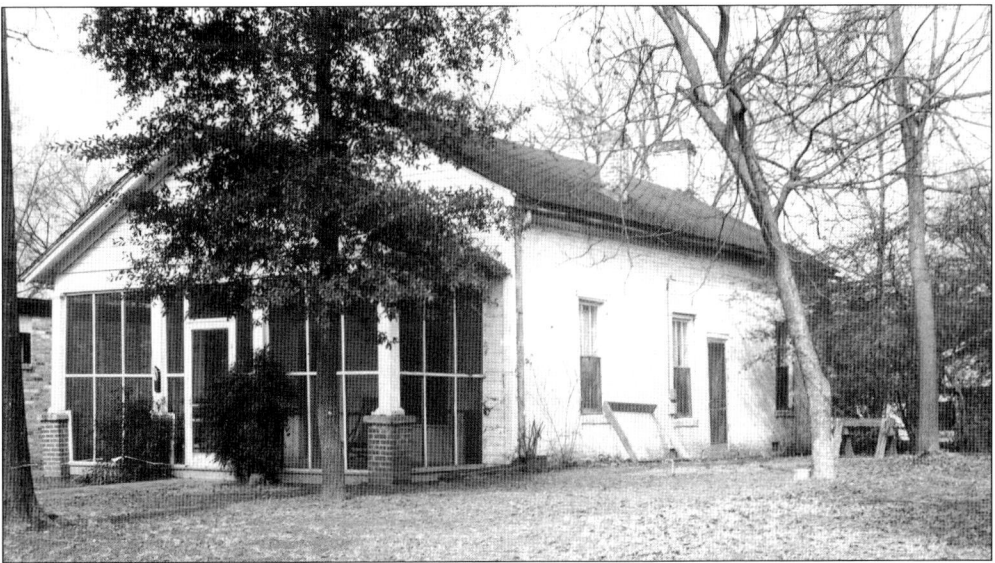

This modest single-story brick masonry building, known as the Benjamin Mercantile, may have been the oldest brick residence in Arkadelphia, constructed in the mid-1840s. James K. Benjamin acquired the land on Johnson (now Main) Street in 1845 and contracted with brickmason J.H. Obaugh to construct the combination store and residence. Later, the building served as a restaurant, carpenter shop, and dentist's office before being torn down in the mid-1990s. (HSU.)

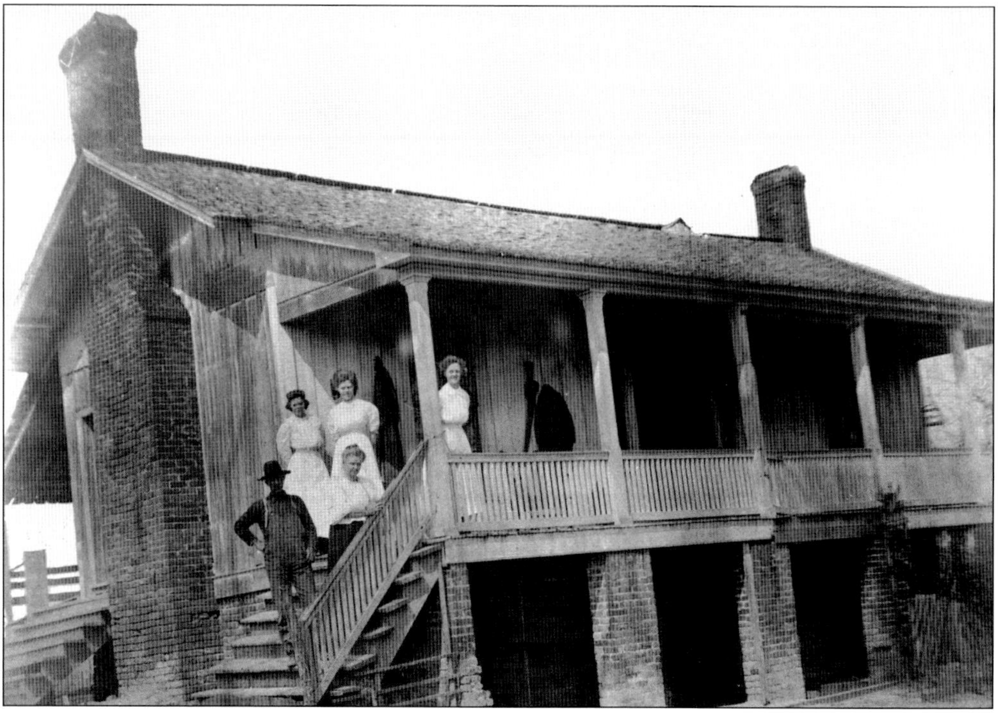

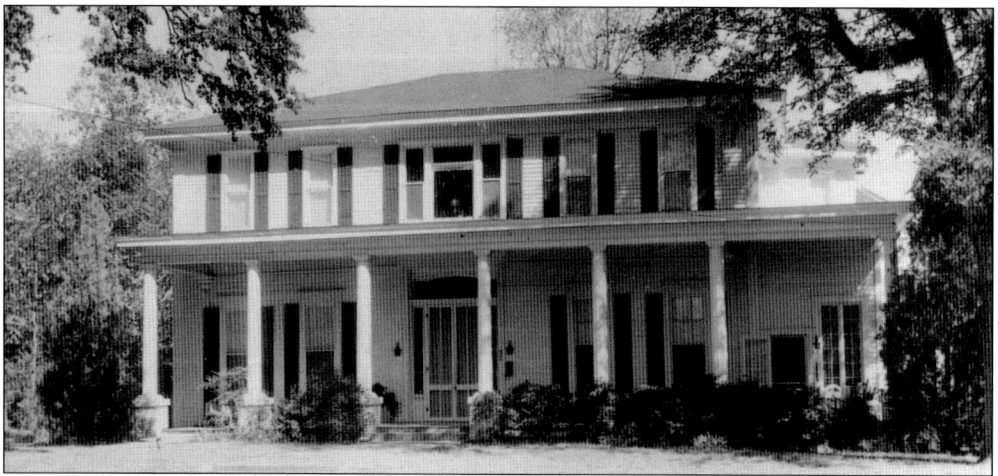

The McFadden home in Arkadelphia was originally built in 1869 by Ludlow Clark, who served as county clerk and supervisor from around 1869 to 1874. After Clark left the state, the house was sold at auction to Cynthia Smith. Smith deeded the house to her daughter and son-in-law, Tom and Mary Clara McFadden, shown here with their three daughters around 1895. The house was distinguished by its unusual construction, with the lower story built of brick and the only access to the second story via the outside staircase. (HSU.)

This home, which formerly stood on Pine Street in Arkadelphia, once belonged to merchant Joseph Columbus Saunders. His family had come to Clark County from Virginia around 1840. Following service in the Civil War, Saunders returned to Arkadelphia and opened a mercantile store. His father was one of the earliest schoolteachers in Arkadelphia, and Saunders supported education as well. Saunders provided a tract of land for the high school built in 1888 and worked tirelessly to raise funds for Ouachita Baptist College. (HSU.)

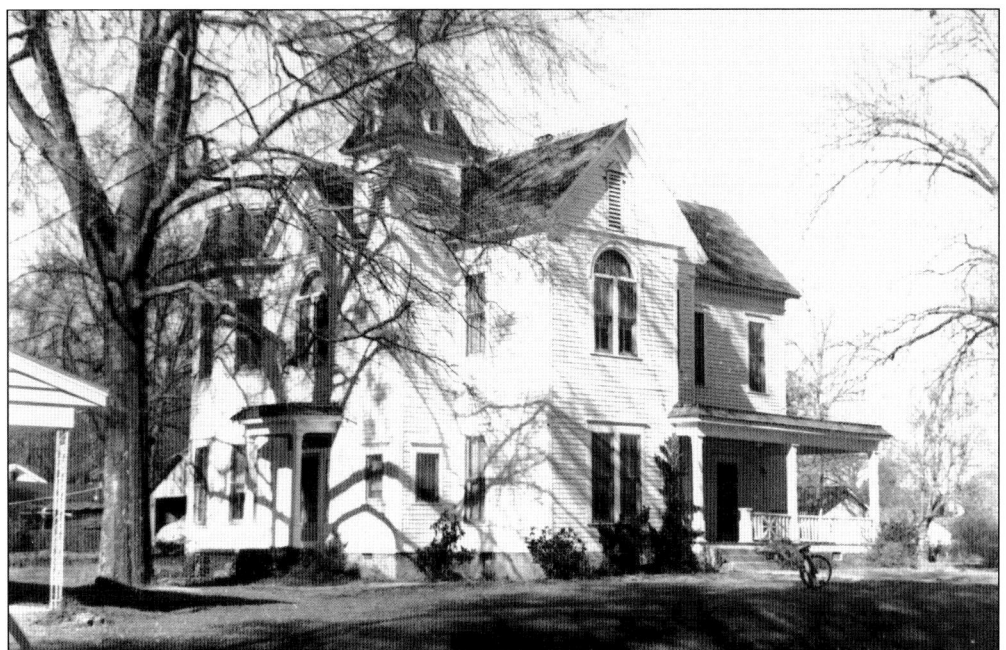

The Moles-Phillips house at 1050 Haddock Street in Arkadelphia was constructed around 1869 by Civil War veteran Col. J.C. Moles and his wife, Rebecca. Following the Civil War, Moles settled in Arkadelphia where he ran a dry goods establishment and farmed a considerable amount of land on the Ouachita River. The home was later owned by the Charles Phillips family and continues to serve as a private residence. (HSU.)

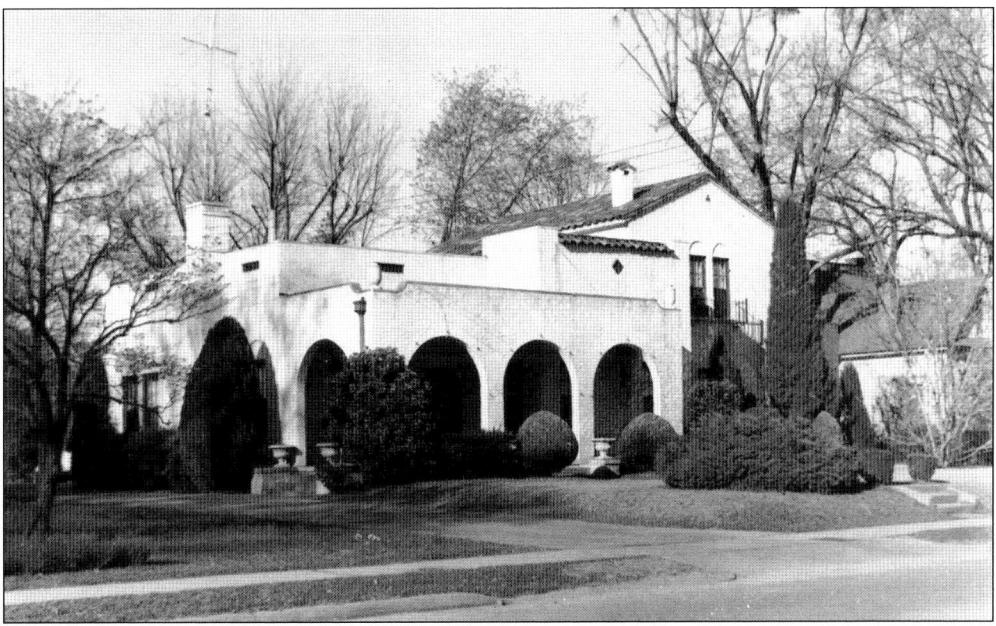

This distinctive stucco and Spanish tile-roof residence, which still stands at 1036 Caddo Street, was at one time the home of attorney J.H. Lookadoo and his wife, Caledonia. Built around 1928 by Alice McNutt, wife of Samuel Ralston McNutt, the home also served as a parsonage for Arkadelphia's First Methodist Church at one time. (HSU.)

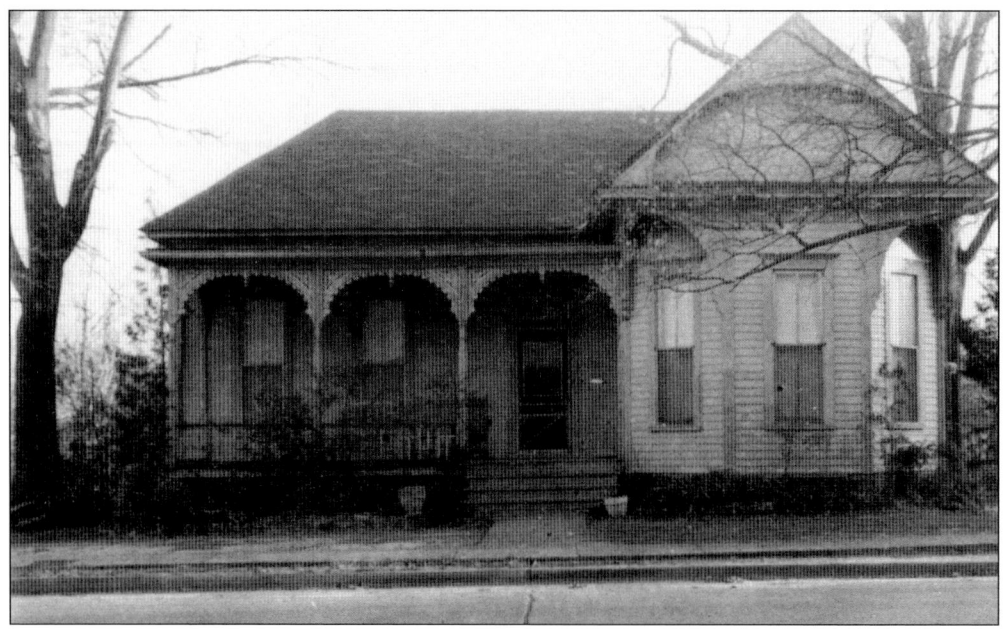

The James B. Garrett house, which once stood at 1027 Henderson Street in Arkadelphia, originally was built by Charles C. Henderson in early 1903. Later that year, Henderson sold the home to Garrett and his wife, Mary (Moles). James, a master carpenter, was employed in 1901 as superintendent of buildings and grounds of the Arkadelphia Methodist College, where students affectionately called him "Dad" Garrett. (HSU.)

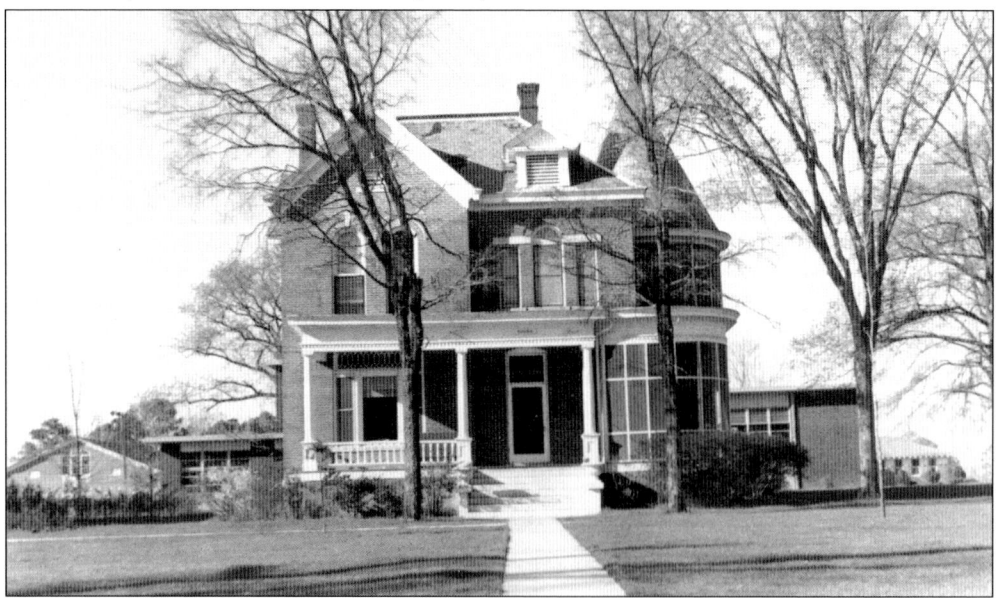

Ouachita College president Dr. John Conger and his wife, Tennie, built this two-story brick home on the western edge of campus in 1904. When Conger resigned in 1907, the Congers sold the home, valued at $10,000, to the college for $7,000 to be used as the president's home. The structure served that purpose through the mid-1950s but was razed around 1958. Berry Chapel and a classroom building were erected on this site and dedicated in 1962. Riley Library, the gymnasium, and the Fine Arts Building are visible in the background. (HSU.)

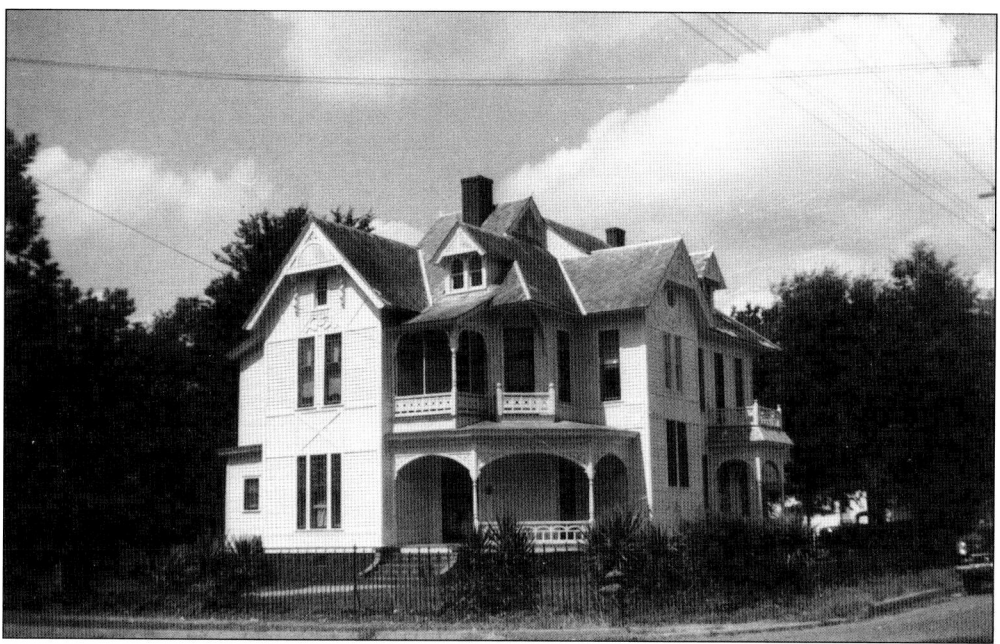

The Housley House once sat at 1327 Ouachita Street on the corner of the Ouachita Baptist University campus near the current site of the Maddox Hall dormitory. Built around 1918, in later years, the residence served as a boardinghouse for students. (HSU.)

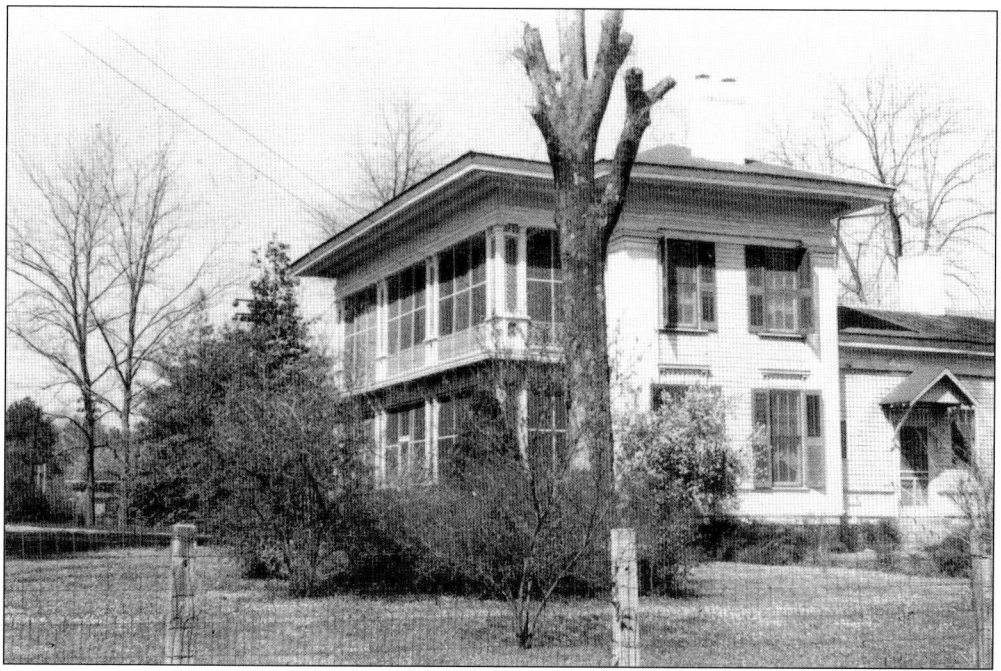

The Barkman Home, completed around 1860, was built for James E.M. Barkman, the son of pioneer settlers Jacob and Rebecca Davis Barkman. Henderson College acquired the property on North Tenth Street in 1968 for $65,000. Over the years, the home has served the university as an office for sororities, development, alumni services, and communications and marketing. The Barkman Home was added to the National Register of Historic Places in 1974. (HSU.)

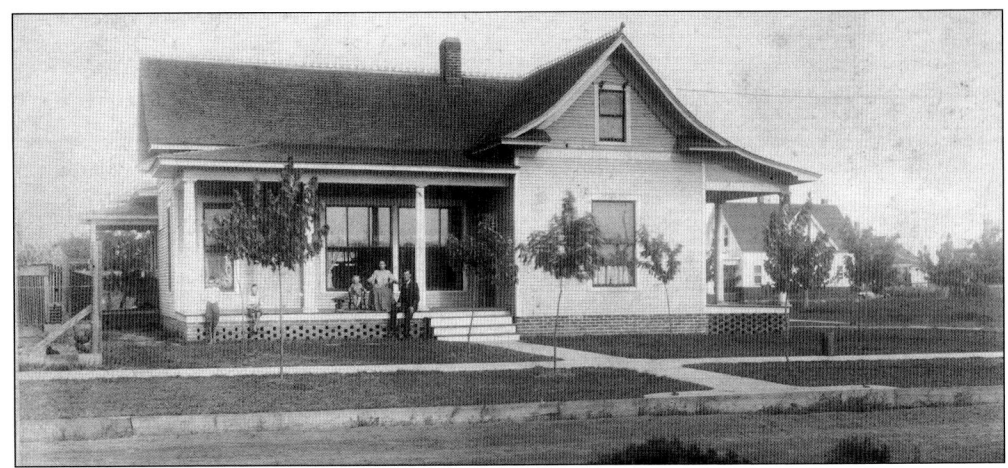

This house, identified as 239 Cherry Street, was the home of Herbert and Lucile Ray Stanford around 1925. Herbert was an Arkadelphia native and World War I veteran who was employed at the J.W. Patterson and Sons Department Store before opening his own shoe store on Main Street. The Stanfords had one son, Herbert Stanley, born in 1922. The three people seated on the porch are likely the three members of the Stanford family. (OBU.)

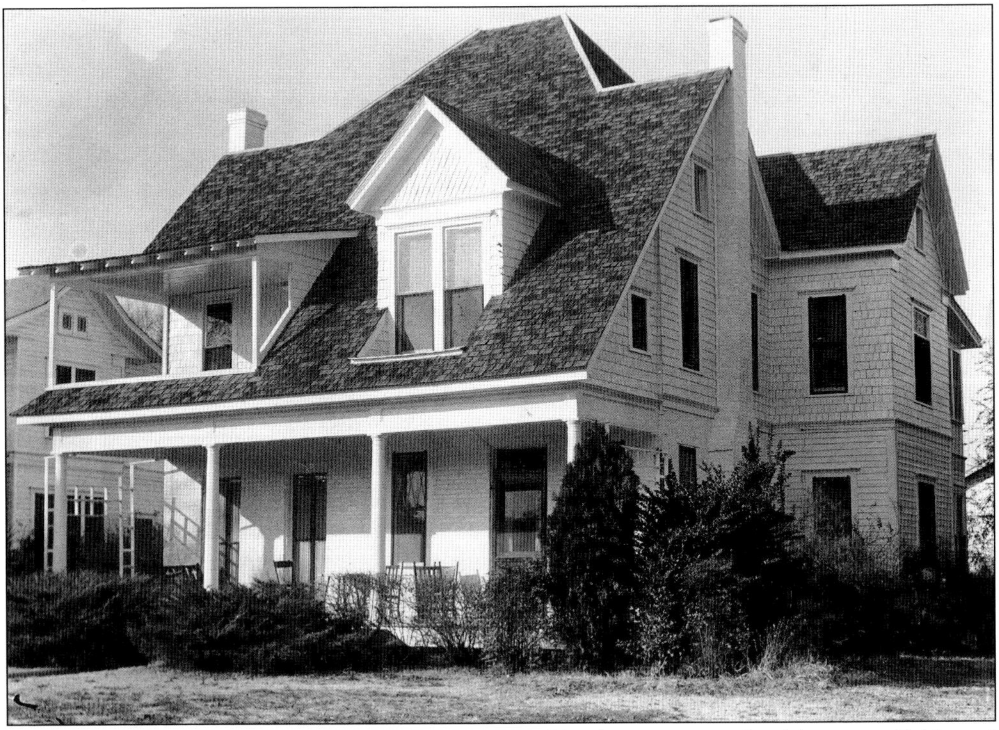

In February 1967, Arkadelphia razed the 117-year-old Thompson-Rowland house at Fifth and Caddo Streets. The original home was a one-story structure built in 1850 by Thomas Sloan Sr., an early sheriff of Clark County. When Harry Anderson purchased the property in 1907, he added a second story and attic. Dr. Noble R. Townsend purchased the house around 1912. In 1917, he sold the house to fellow physician Dr. W.T. Rowland, who lived there with his family until his death in 1939. Rowland family members continued to own the home until it was torn down. (OBU.)

The home place of Capt. Thomas Robertson Tennyson and his wife, Jane Hamilton Anderson Tennyson, was once located in Arkadelphia in the area of West Pine Street. Tennyson was a steamboat captain, running ships on the Ouachita River. One of Tennyson's boats, the *Arkadelphia City*, a 53-ton stern wheel paddleboat suffered a disastrous boiler explosion about 12 miles below Arkadelphia on April 25, 1863, killing six people. (OBU.)

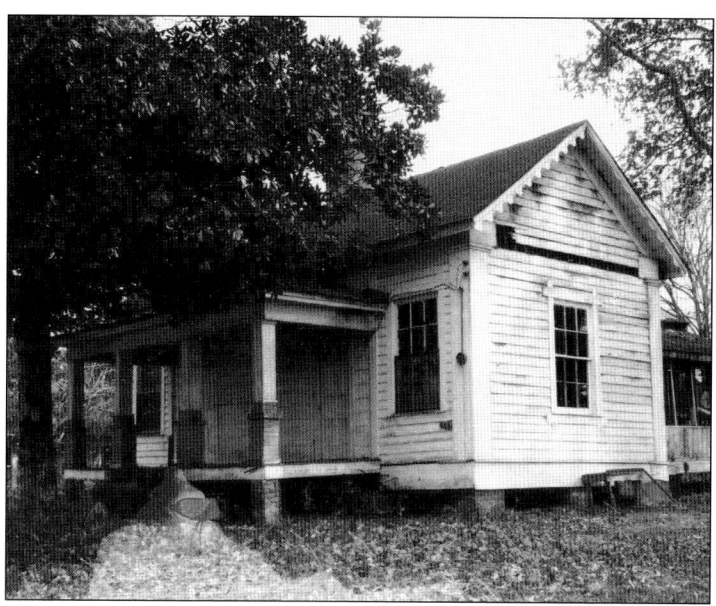

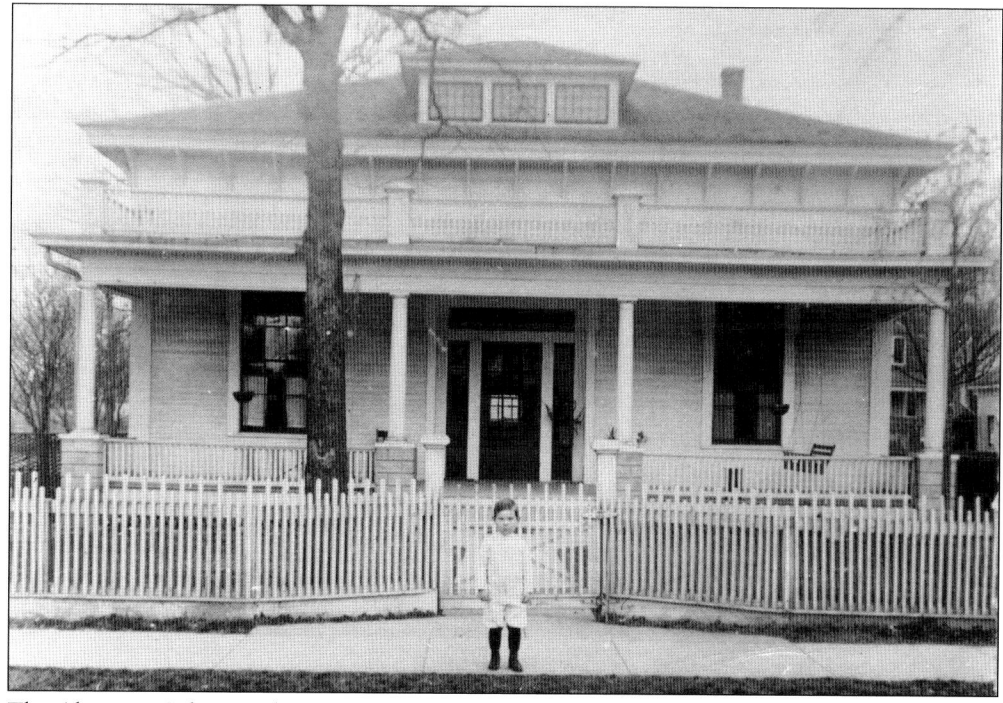

The Algernon Sidney Bailey Greene House was once located at Eighth and Barkman Streets, a site now occupied by the First United Methodist Church. Greene built this home in Arkadelphia shortly after returning from the Civil War. He was the grandfather of Amy Jean Greene, who taught history at Arkadelphia High School and later education at Henderson. The Greene home was razed sometime in the 1960s. The young child standing in front is unidentified. (OBU.)

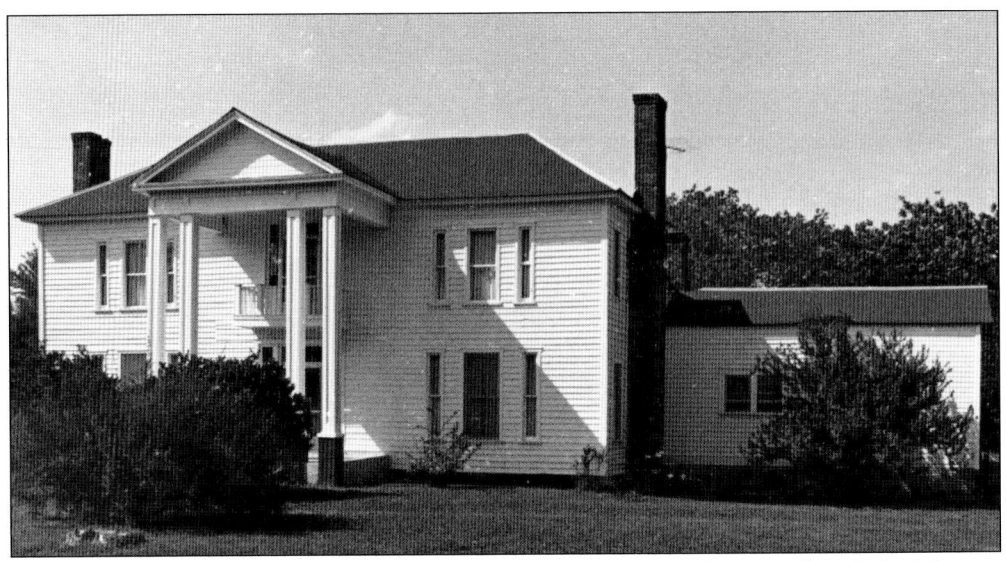

The Hudson-Jones House in the Manchester community was built around 1840 by Thomas Hudson, a member of the Tennessee-based Somerville Land Company, which acquired the land that is now Manchester in 1836. In 1859, Hudson sold the property to Nat Kimbrough Jones, another member of the land company. Nat's son and Arkansas legislator, James Kimbrough Jones, lived in the house from 1859 to 1867. The home was added to the National Register of Historic Places in 1982 and today is privately owned. (OBU.)

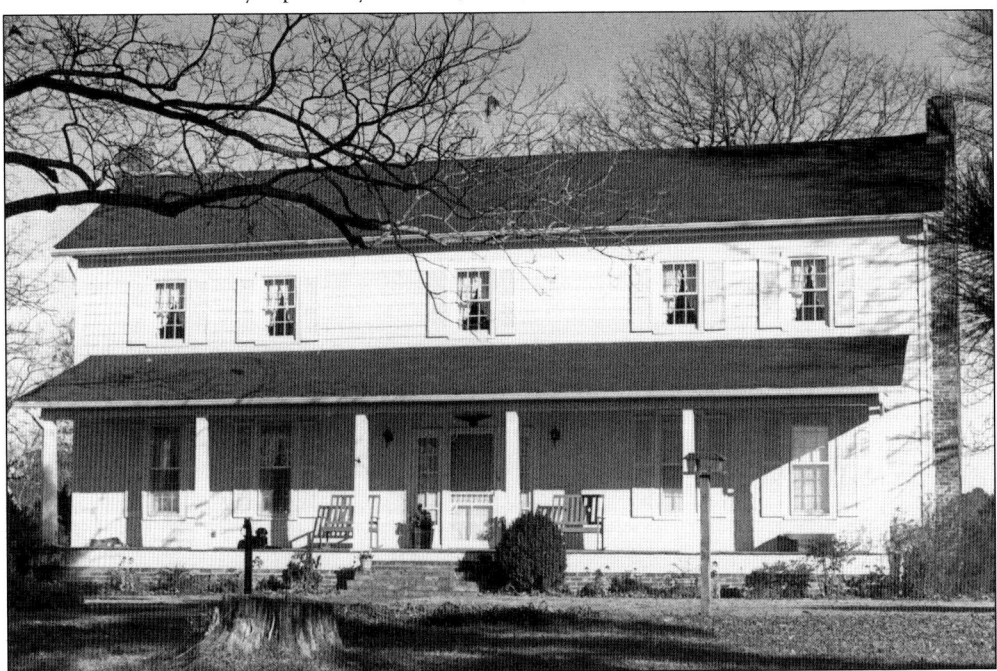

The Strong house on Highway 8 West in Manchester was built by planter Nathaniel "Nathan" Strong around 1854. Strong arrived with his family in Clark County in 1837. He settled on a 640-acre tract of land acquired for him in 1836. The two-story frame house of six rooms with a 12-foot-wide hall down the center is one of the county's oldest homes. Strong died in 1863 and is buried in the nearby Strong Cemetery. (OBU.)

Five

RIVERS, ROADS, AND RAILS

The DeSoto Bluff, just west of Arkadelphia on US Highway 67, was named after Spanish explorer Hernando de Soto, the first European explorer in Arkansas. Local legend says that de Soto and his men camped on the bluff, but this is not supported by historical evidence. However, the William Dunbar and George Hunter expedition in 1803–1804 did visit the bluff as part of Pres. Thomas Jefferson's Grand Expedition of Discovery. Today, the bluff trail and overlook is a popular spot for hiking and taking in a view of the Ouachita River. (OBU.)

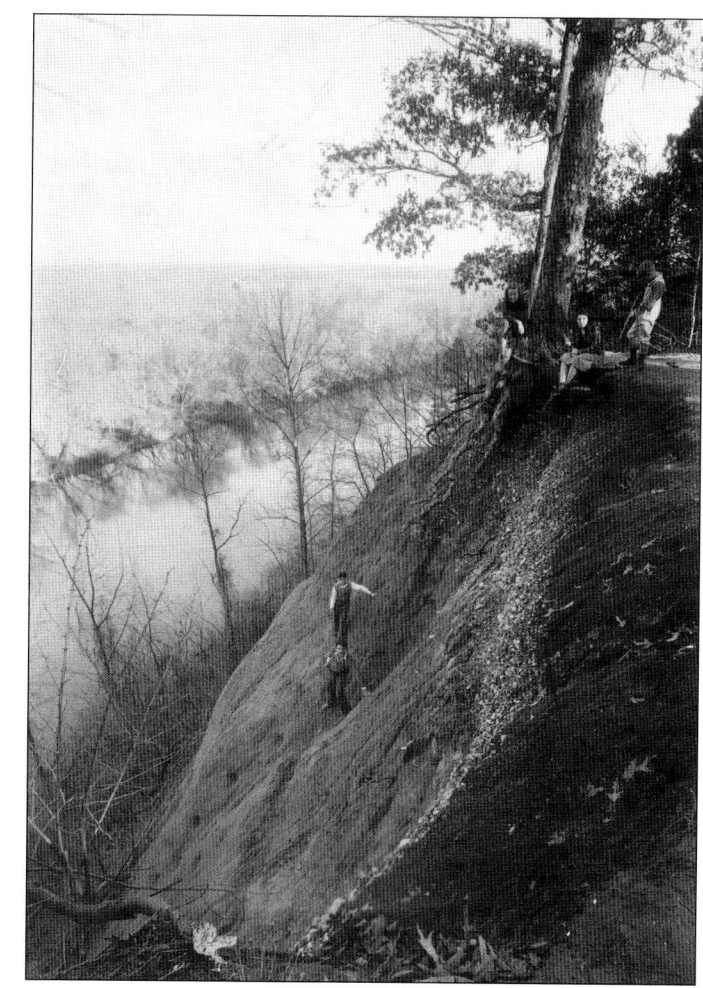

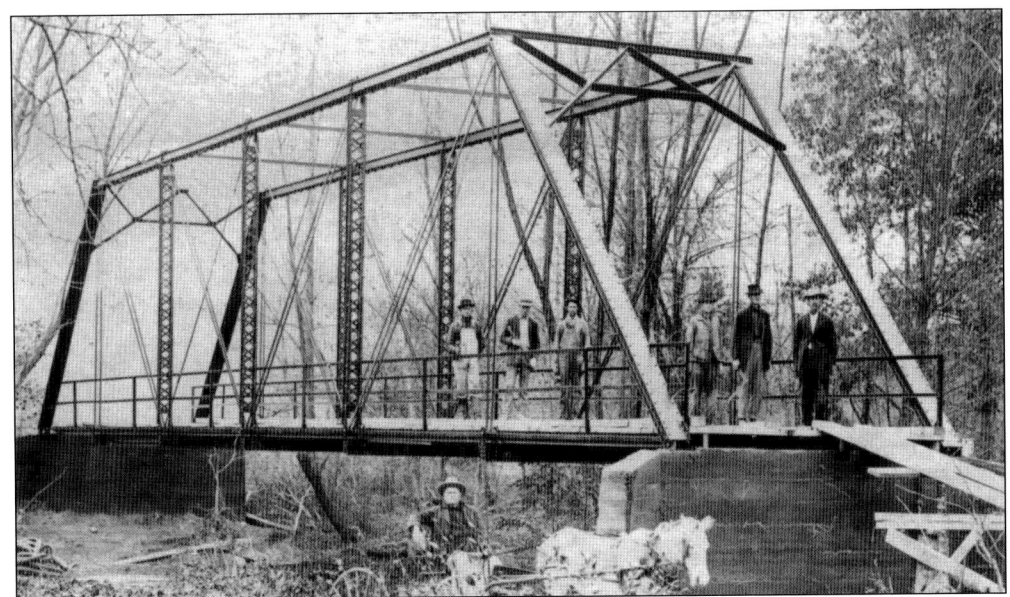

Construction on the Gentry Creek Bridge on Highway 26 between Halfway and Clear Spring was completed in late November 1916. The steel structure replaced a wooden bridge erected in 1912. Henry Meeks, a resident of Halfway, is shown here seated in a buggy below the bridge, and the men on the bridge are identified as Claud Rollins, Clib Golden, Sol Rollins, Floyd Payne, Oscar Hignight, and J.W. Sorrells. (OBU.)

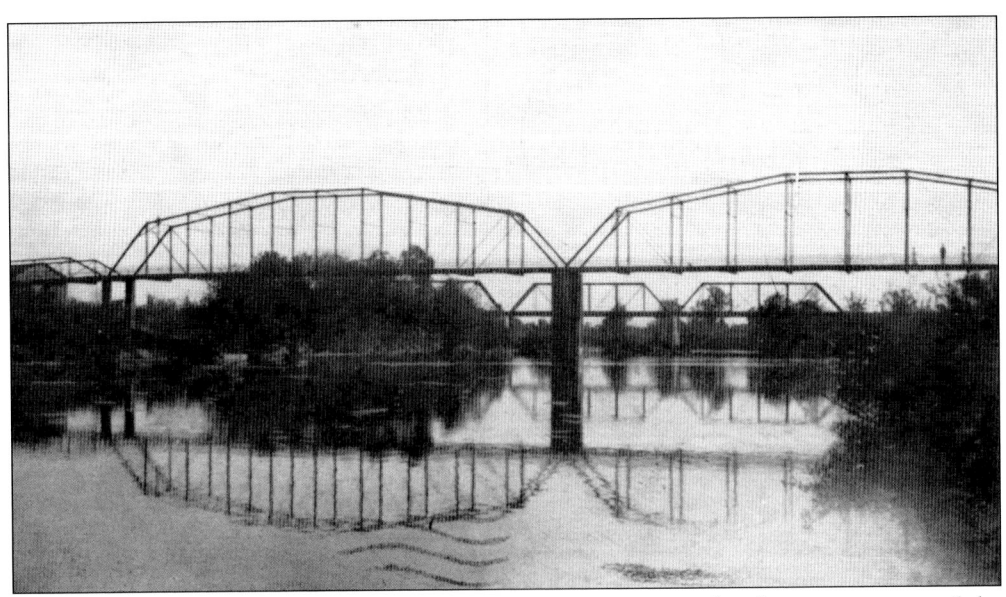

This postcard, mailed as a New Year's greeting in 1908, captures the elegant symmetry of the Ouachita River and Missouri Pacific Bridges as well as their reflections in the tranquil waters. The railroad bridge was constructed by the Cairo & Fulton Railroad in 1873. The Ouachita River traffic bridge opened in 1903 and was added to the National Register of Historic Places in 2006. (OBU.)

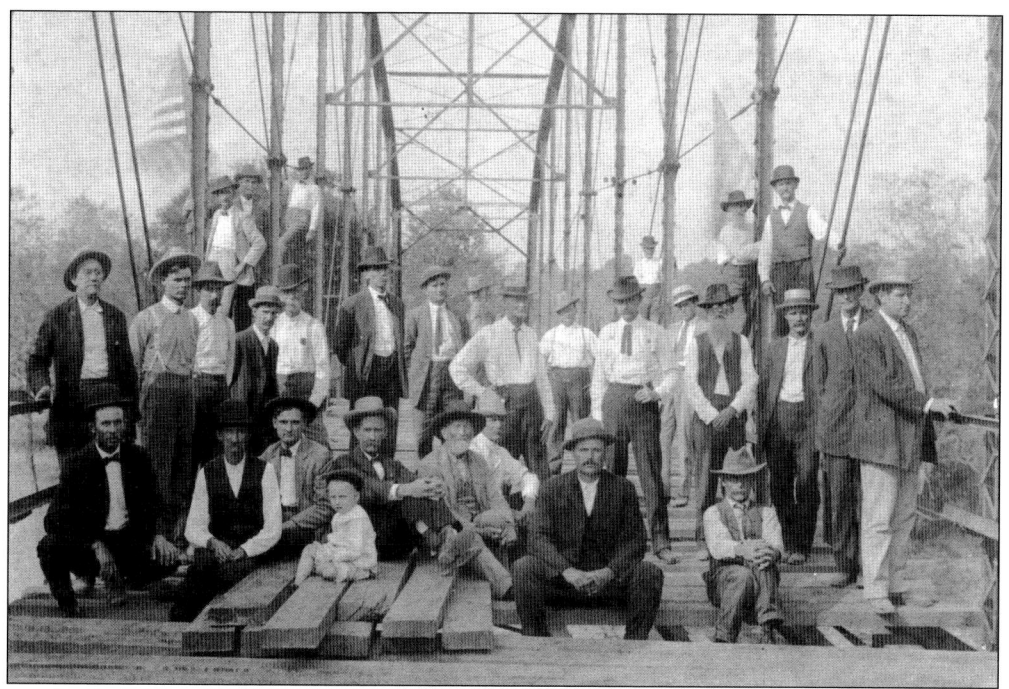

Above, a group of local men and boys pose on the new free bridge over the Ouachita River at Arkadelphia in October 1903, near the end of construction. Prior to the bridge's opening, the only eastern access across the river was by ferry. No toll or fee was charged to cross the bridge, thus the moniker "free bridge." Stupp Brothers Bridge and Iron Company of St. Louis, Missouri, secured the construction contract for $29,975. Thirteen companies from seven states attended the public bidding in Arkadelphia, with each company wishing to bid posting a $2,000 deposit at Elk Horn Bank. Among those pictured at the opening are members of the Quorum Court, including Tom Tennyson, B. Meador, Paul Davidson, Joe Greeson, Mack Shackleford, John Allen, Asa Townsend, and Isaiah D. Ellis. The bridge served the community and region until it was replaced in 1960. (Above, HSU; below, OBU.)

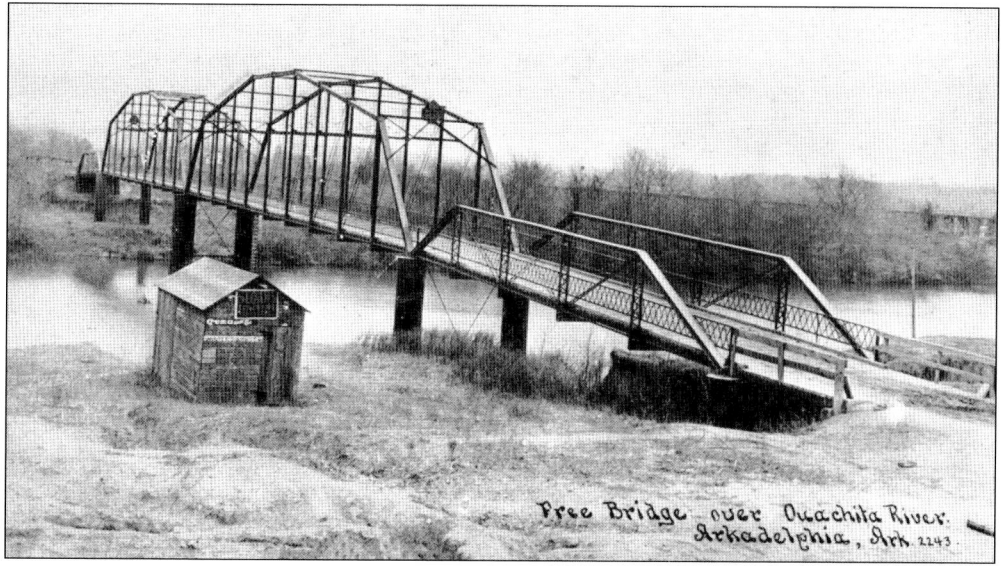

Free Bridge over Ouachita River. Arkadelphia, Ark. 2243.

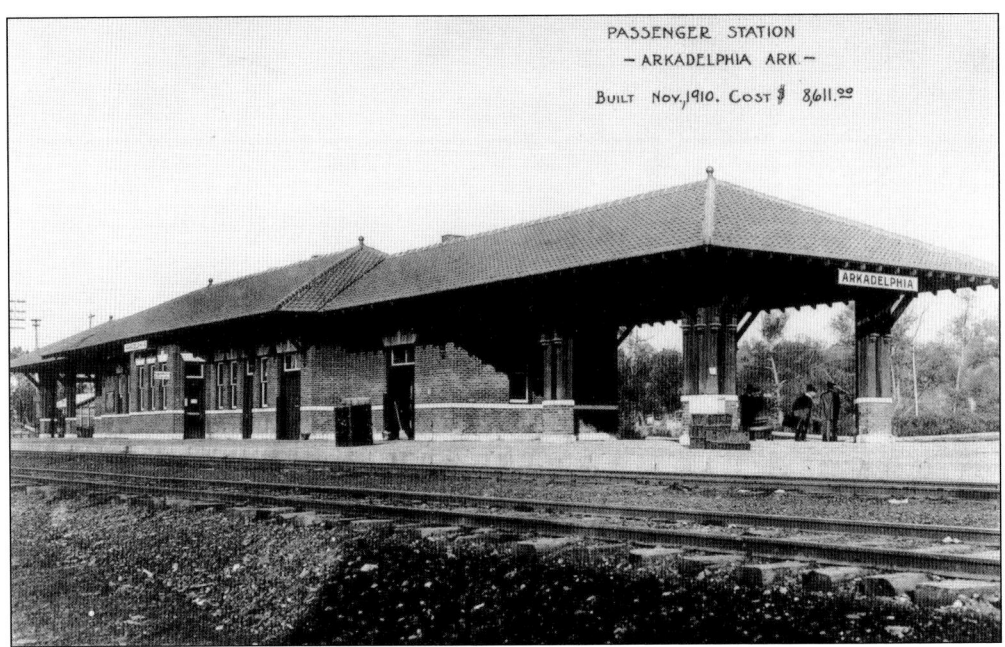

The St. Louis, Iron Mountain & Southern Railway passenger depot was constructed in Arkadelphia in 1910. The new station replaced a depot that burned in September 1909. The Railroad Commission approved plans for the station, freight depot, and cotton platform. The St. Louis, Iron Mountain & Southern was merged with Missouri Pacific in May 1917. Today, the Clark County Museum occupies most of the station, with Amtrak operating an office on one end. The depot was added to the National Register of Historic Places in 1992. (OBU.)

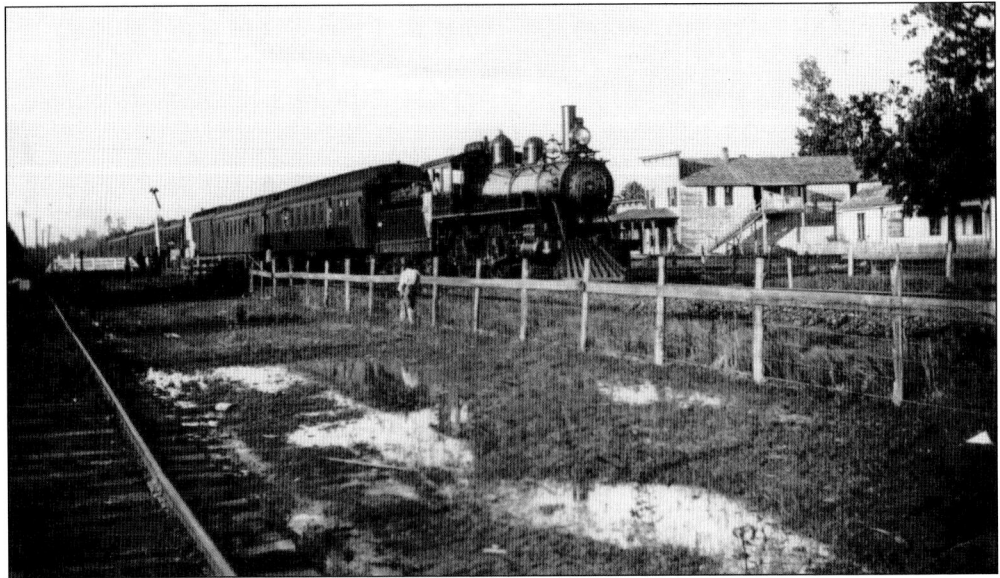

The No. 5 train, known as the "Cannon Ball," stopped at the station at Smithton, an unincorporated community about two miles northeast of Gurdon. Smithton was named for James A. Smith, an Irish-born construction worker on the Iron Mountain Railroad who came to Clark County in the 1870s. The original Smithton Lumber Company commissary, which served as a grocery and post office in later years, is shown at right. (OBU.)

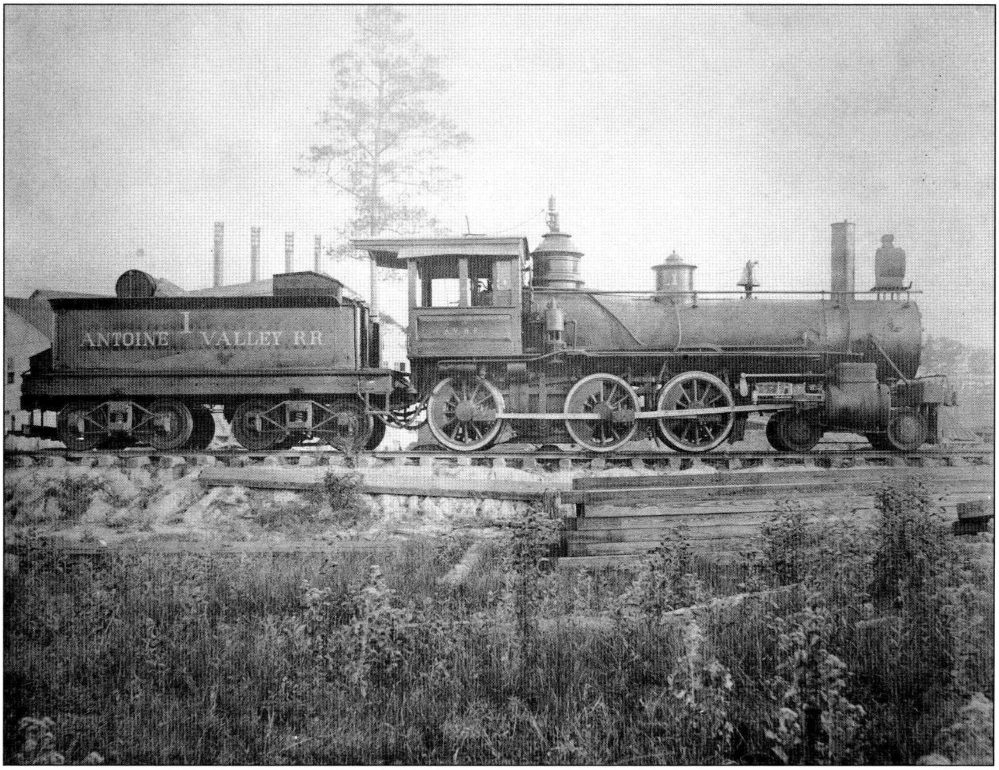

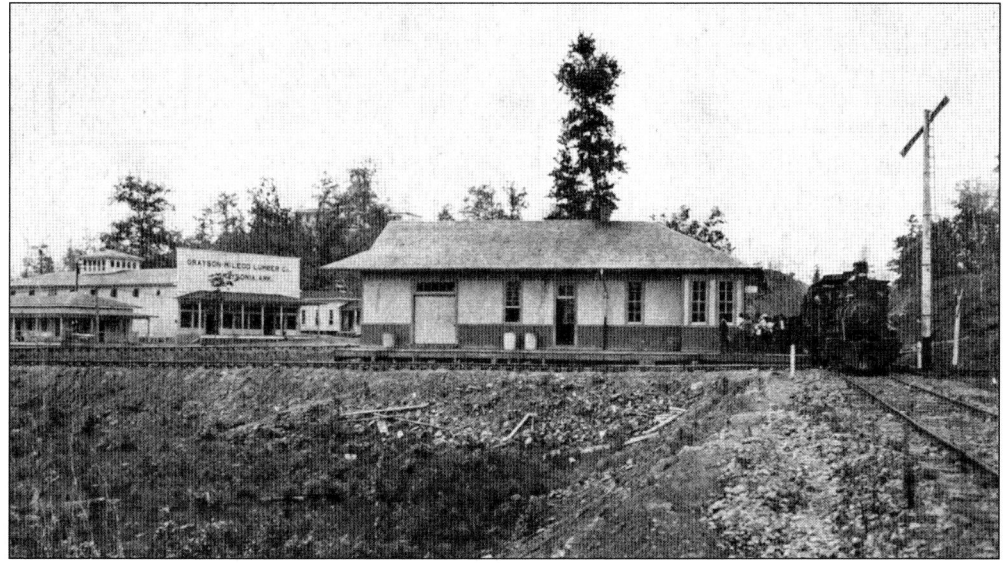

The Antoine Valley Railroad was incorporated in April 1907 by shareholders in the Graysonia Lumber Company. The rail line lay entirely within the county's borders, extending from the mill town at Graysonia, situated on the Gurdon & Fort Smith Railroad, to Arkadelphia, a distance of about 27 miles. In 1910, the Memphis, Dallas & Gulf Railroad Company, under general manager Charles C. Henderson, took ownership of the Antoine line, along with the Ultima Thule, which ran 25 miles from Arkadelphia toward Pine Bluff. The offices of the Grayson-McLeod Lumber Company are visible at left behind the depot in the image below. (Above, HSU; below, OBU.)

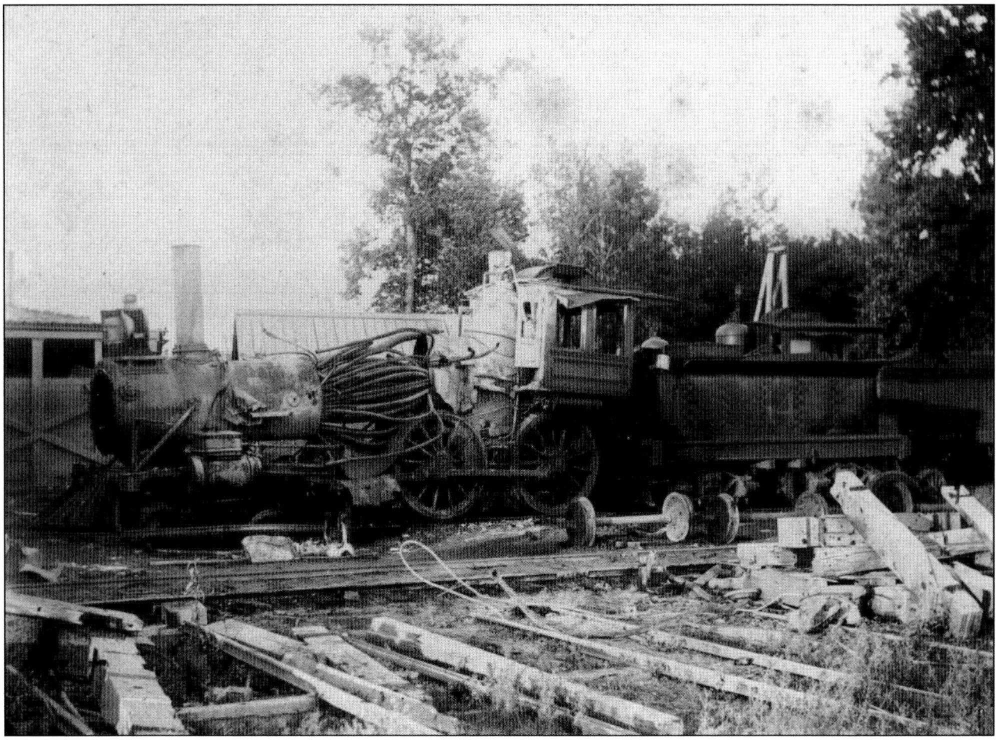

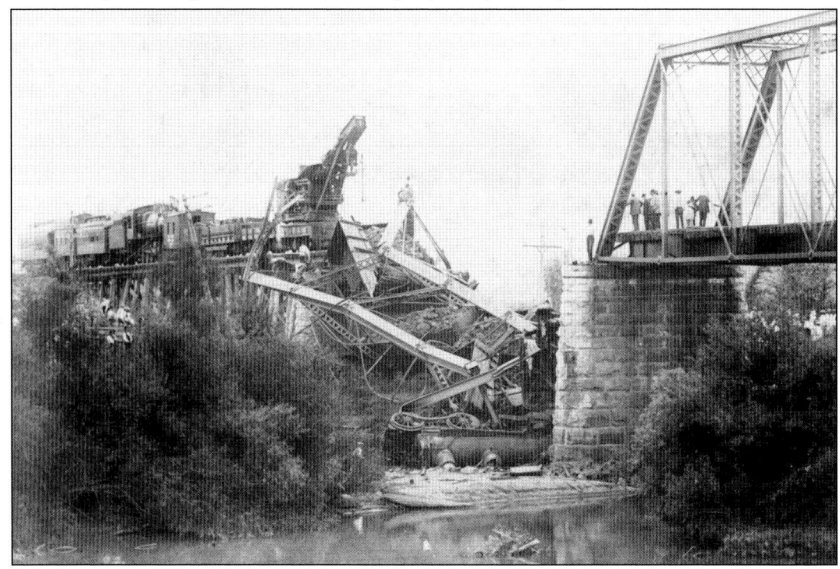

This spectacular train accident on the Ouachita River bridge at Arkadelphia occurred on Sunday, September 11, 1904, when a "dead engine" jumped the tracks about 50 yards from the bridge. The engine, which was not being used to power the train, was in the middle of about 60 cars. After it left the tracks, the engine violently smashed into both sides of the heavy steel bridge, causing the structure to break loose from its pier. When the bridge gave way, the engine and eight coal cars were pulled into the dry riverbed below. While no one was injured in the wreck, a foreman, L.H. Inman of Bald Knob, Arkansas, died from injuries sustained while cleaning up the wreckage when he was crushed by a falling section of the bridge. (Both, OBU.)

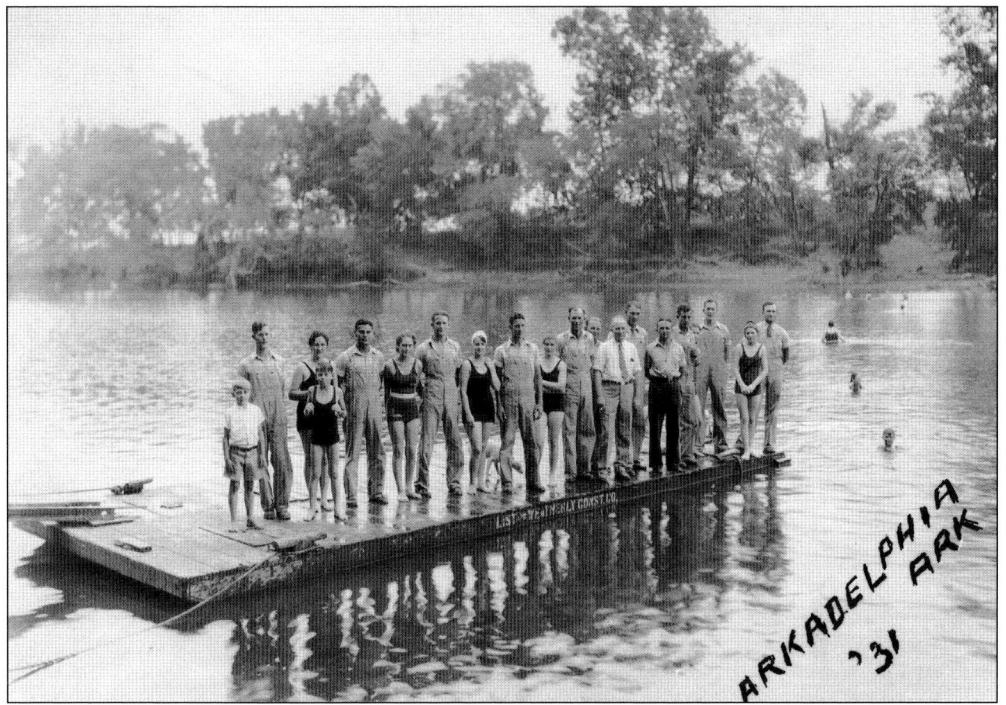

Starting in 1931, the Arkadelphia Rotary Club sponsored a supervised swimming hole immediately south of the Ouachita River Bridge on Highway 8. A local newspaper noted that the swimming hole was "a considerable distance above the point where the sewer empties." The swimming hole was free to residents of Arkadelphia and available to others for a small fee. This photograph may have been taken on opening day, although the occasion is not known. (OBU.)

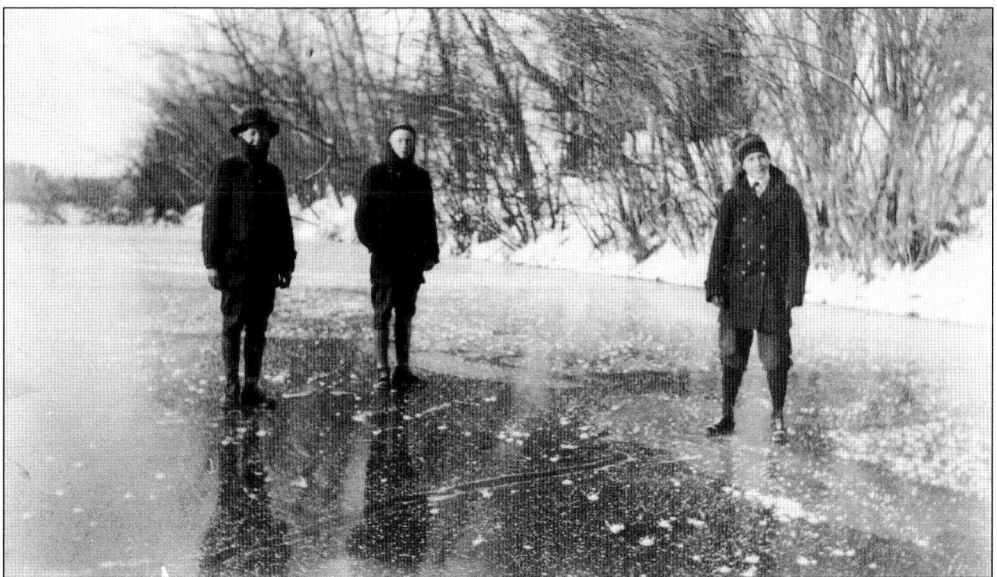

Three unidentified men test the ice on the partially frozen Ouachita River at Arkadelphia in January 1918. On January 17, the *Southern Standard* newspaper reported that Clark County experienced unusually cold temperatures, with the thermometer hovering at negative 10 degrees Fahrenheit for several days. Seven inches of snow accompanied the cold snap. (OBU.)

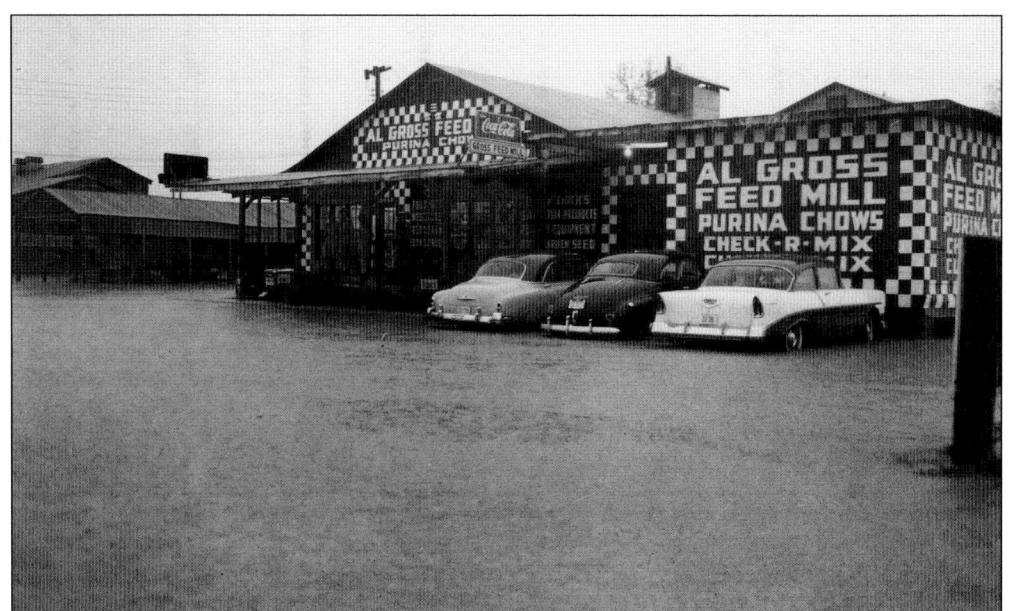

Floodwaters in Arkadelphia surrounded Al Gross Feed Mill (above), the Arkadelphia Rolling Mill, and the Missouri-Pacific Passenger Station (below) around the 1950s. This low-lying area south of town is affected by periodic flooding. Flash floods in July 2019 and April 2025 inundated the Humane Society of Clark County, forcing the emergency evacuation of animals and resulting in the death of one dog in 2019. (Both, OBU.)

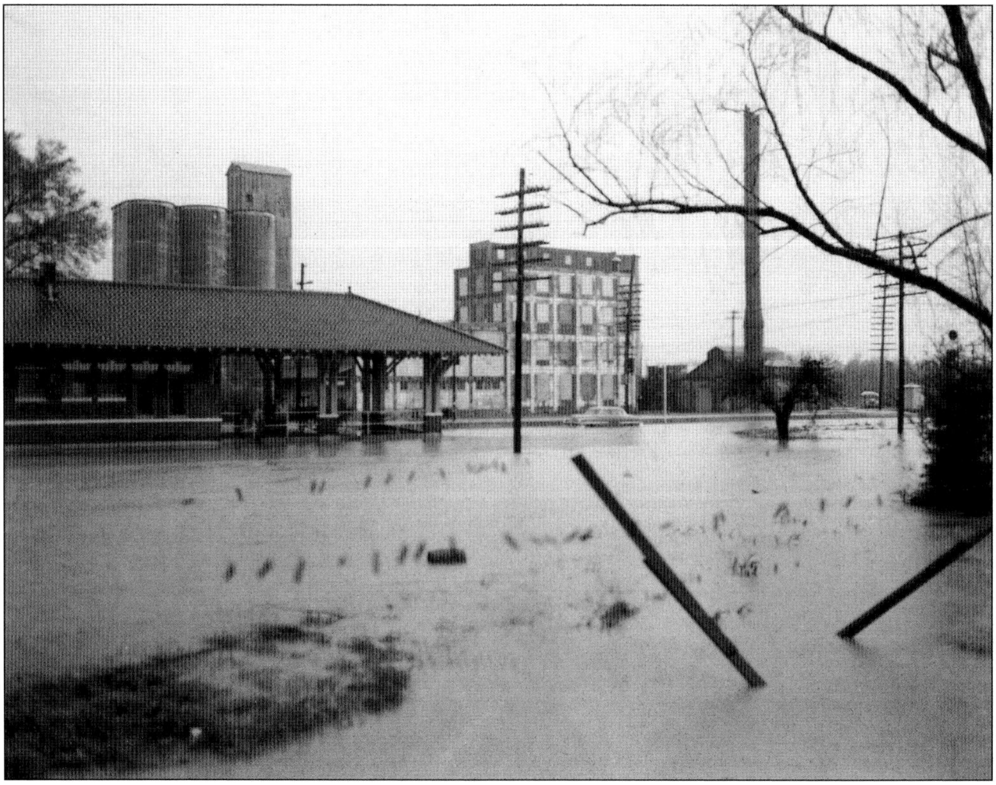

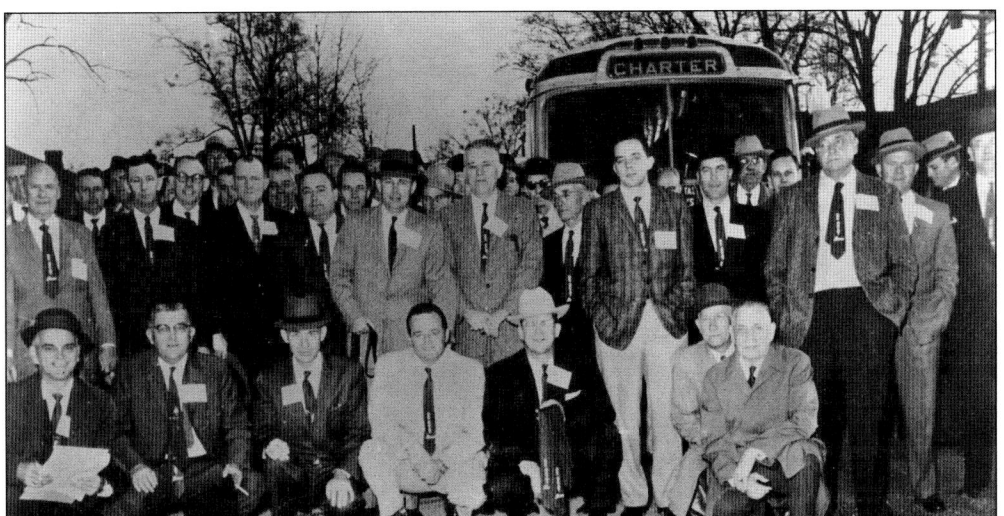

In 1959, seventy-four men representing Clark County and adjacent Hot Spring County traveled by bus to El Dorado, Arkansas, for a meeting of the Ouachita River Valley Association to show support for the DeGray Dam construction project. The group wore maroon ties featuring the words "DeGray Dam." The Trailways charter bus on which the men rode was decorated with signage that read, "Uncle Sam, We Want DeGray Dam." (OBU.)

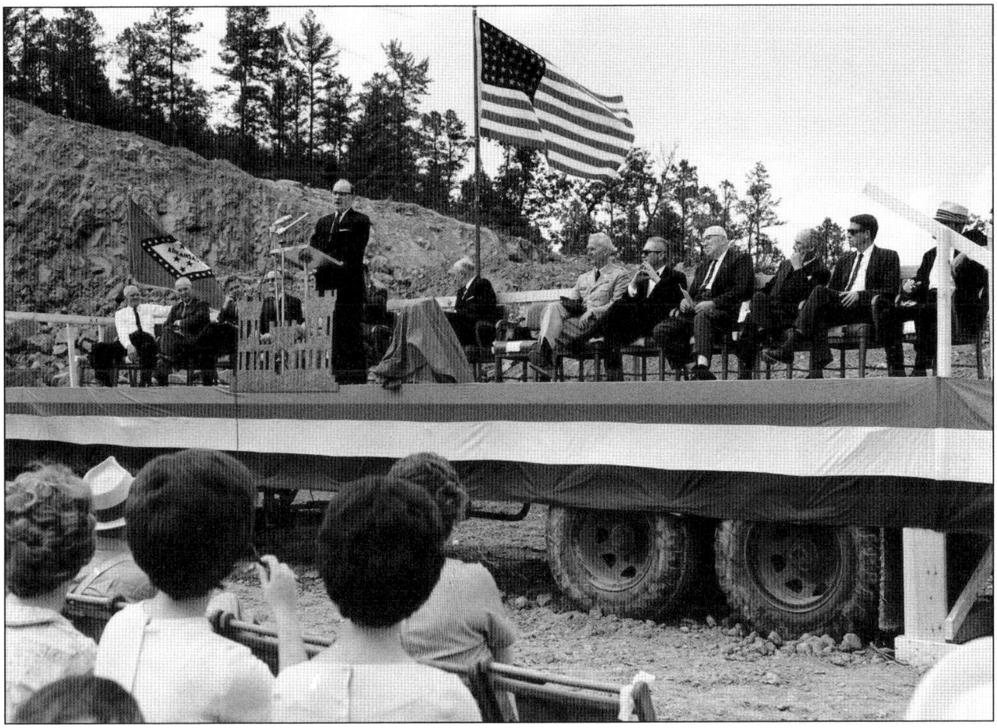

US senator from Arkansas, John L. McClellan, addresses the audience at the June 6, 1964, ground breaking for DeGray Dam. Dignitaries in attendance included members of the Arkadelphia Chamber of Commerce, representatives from the US Army Corps of Engineers, members of the Ouachita Valley Association, and local, state, and national officials. McClellan, along with Rep. Oren Harris, also of Arkansas, lobbied hard for support for the dam. (OBU.)

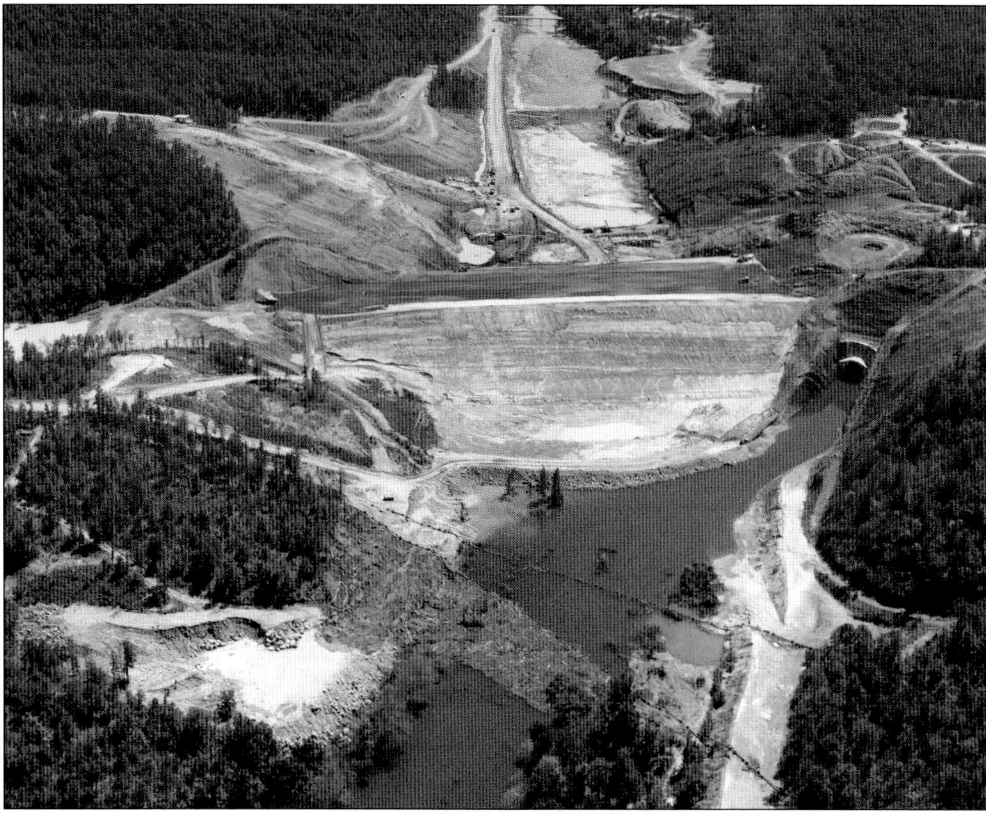

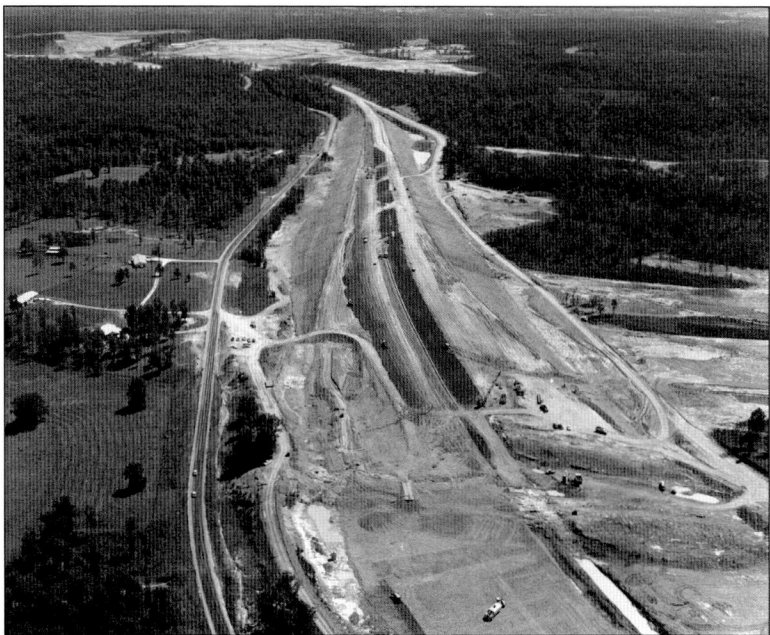

These two aerial views show the construction of the elevated earthen dike that runs along the north side of DeGray Lake. US Highway 7 now runs along the top of the dike, providing a spectacular view of DeGray Lake. The original path of the highway is shown below on the left. (Both, OBU.)

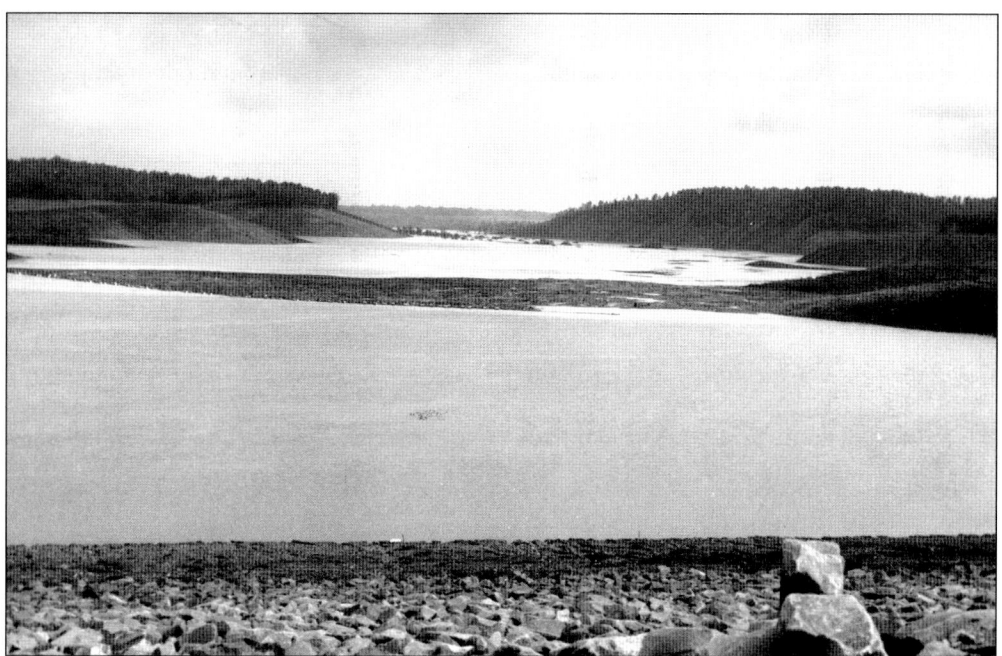

This photograph of the rain-swollen Caddo River at the DeGray Dam and Reservoir construction site was taken on May 14, 1968, by the US Army Corps of Engineers, Vicksburg District. Upstream at the top center is a log boom, a barrier designed to collect or contain floating logs. (OBU.)

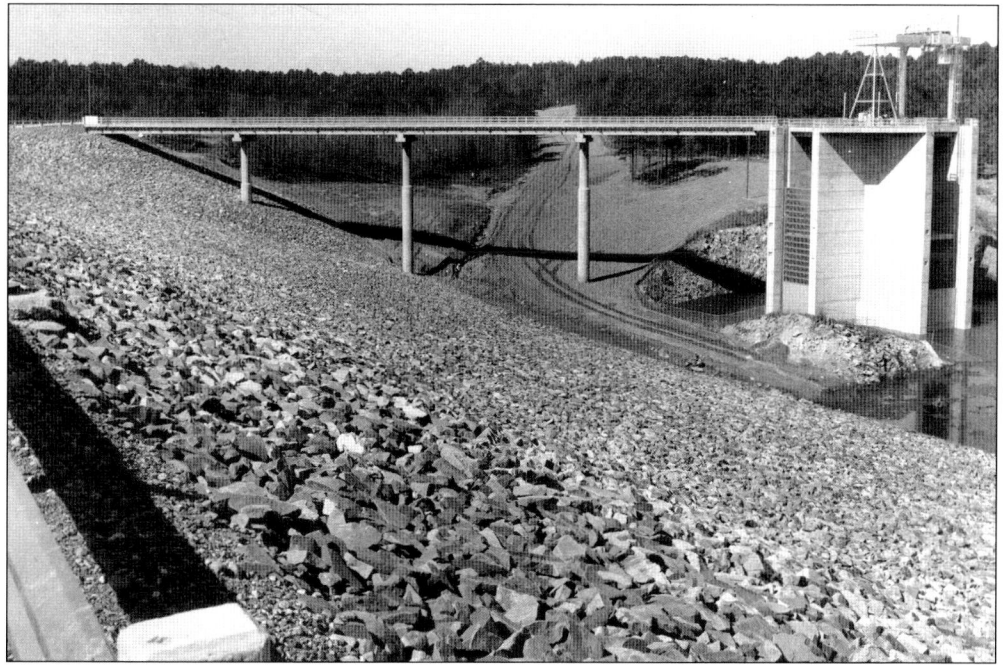

This view of construction on the DeGray Dam power plant looks upstream at the intake structure and service bridge during the initial filling of the reservoir on March 9, 1970. The contractor for this portion of the work was the Martin K. Eby Construction Company of Wichita, Kansas. (OBU.)

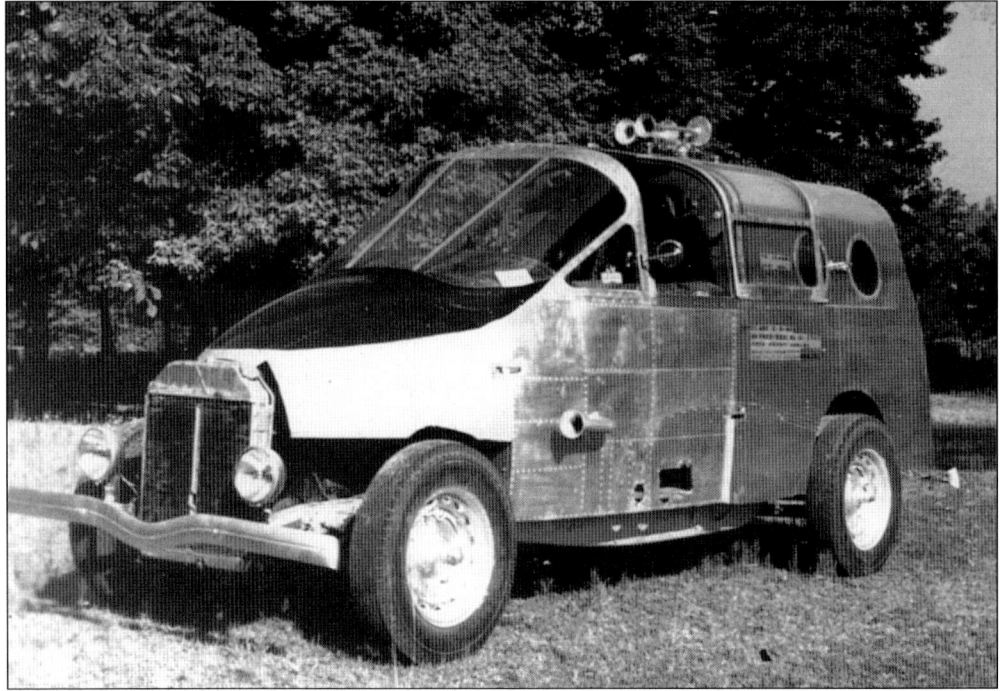

The "airplane car" was owned by Billy Joe Greeson and Lowden Simonson and built by a group of Arkadelphia friends, including Simonson, in the 1940s. The body of the car was from a surplus World War II advanced trainer—a Beechcraft AT-15—and the chassis was a 1936 Ford with a V-8 engine. In 1947, Simonson and Rush drove the car to the Indianapolis 500 and round-trip to California from Arkansas. (OBU.)

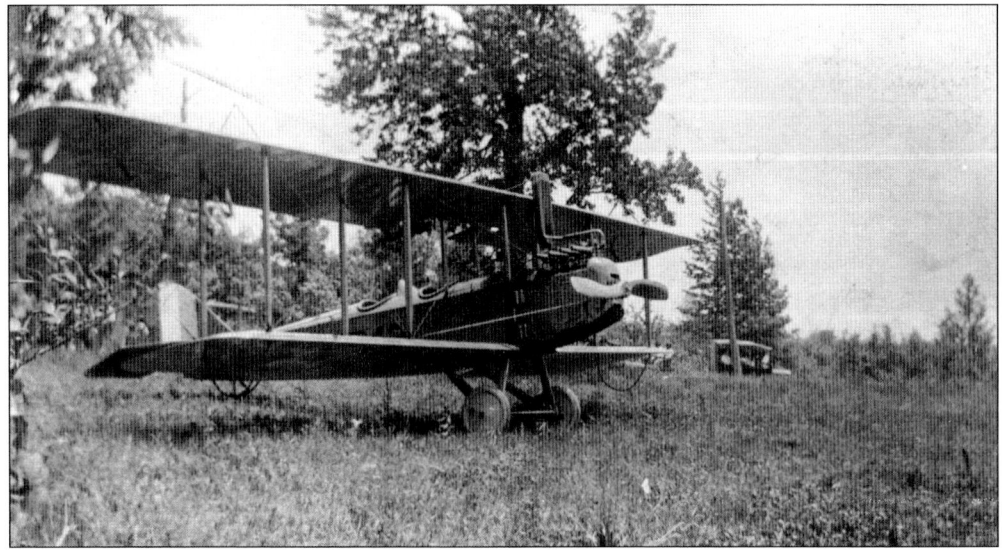

The first airplane to fly to Arkadelphia arrived around 11:00 a.m. on Saturday, May 25, 1918. The airplane, piloted by Lieutenants Pendleton and Harvey from the Air Force training school at Lonoke, landed in Meador's pasture by the Arkadelphia Milling Company. The *Southern Standard* newspaper reported that the aviators delighted "one of the largest crowds which has ever assembled in our city" with somersaults and barrel rolls, "revolving like a whirligig." (OBU.)

Six

LEISURELY PURSUITS

William "Bill" McMillan (left) and William Edger "Bill" Nowlin (right), both members of prominent Arkadelphia families, played tennis for Ouachita Baptist College in 1929. After college, Nowlin ran a local business, and McMillan became an attorney. Tennis was first played as an organized sport at the college in 1923. The *Ouachitonian* yearbook noted that while tennis did not "arouse the enthusiasm and 'pep' of the student body to such an exalted pitch as does football," enough interest existed to form a team in the spring. (OBU.)

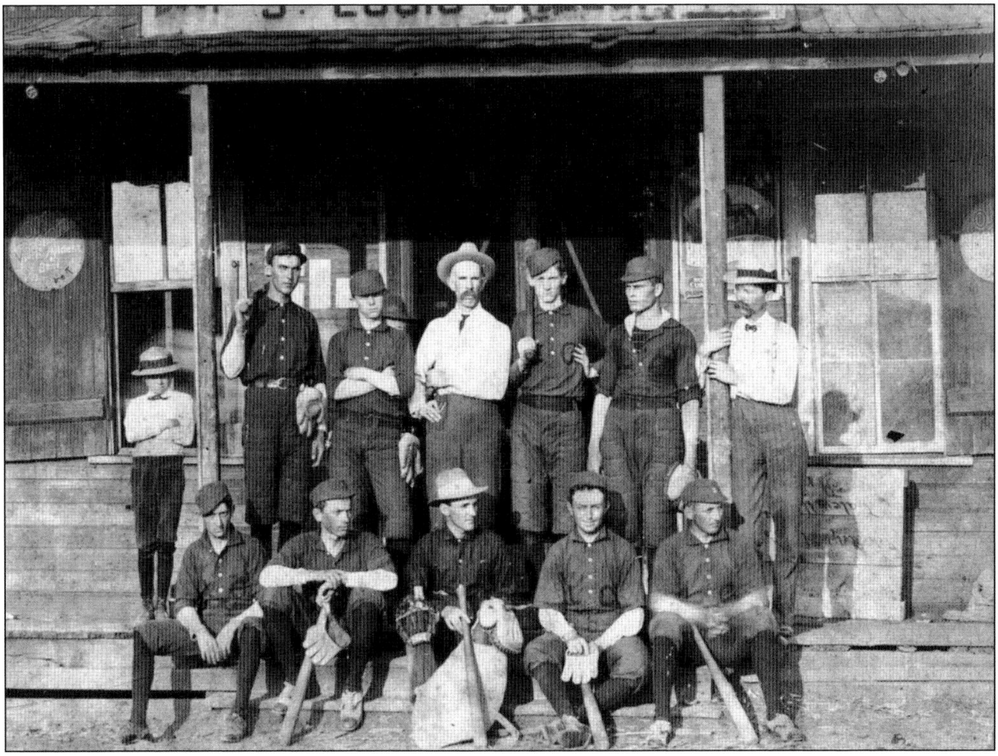

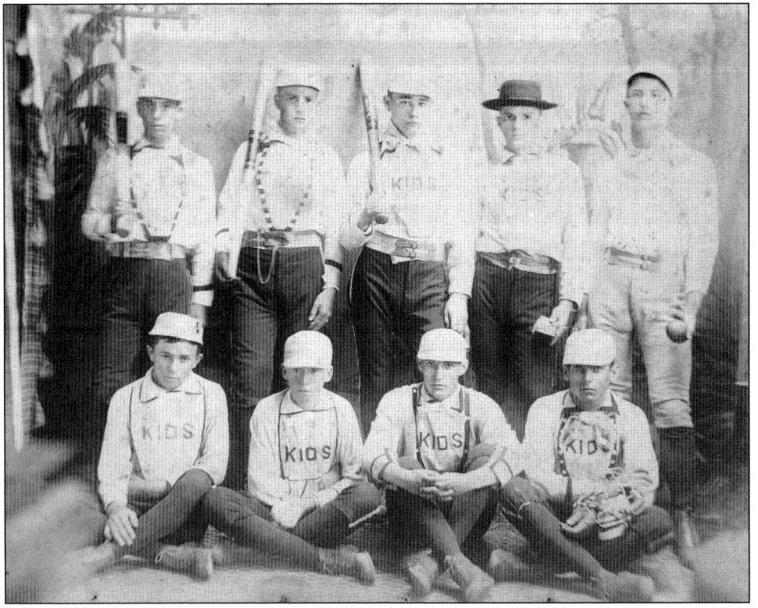

Daleville, located just across the Ouachita River from Arkadelphia, was the site of one of the largest lumber mills in Arkansas. The baseball team pictured here around 1900 may have been composed of men who worked at the mill. Pictured are, from left to right, (first row, seated) Charles Atkinson, Jim Callaway, Irvin Rudolph, Carl McDaniel, and Ed Jordan; (second row, standing) John Brown Jr., Cy Hudson, Cy Brown, C.G. Carpenter, Dan Finger, Fred Meyers, and C.C. Jackson. (HSU.)

The Arkadelphia Kids baseball team was a junior team that played against other juvenile teams between around 1886 and 1903. Shown here around 1890s, this team included players J. Williamson, R. McDaniel, Frank Obaugh, Joe Thomas, Albert Crow, Doug McMillan, Harvey Spenser, and Wallace Cossart. (HSU.)

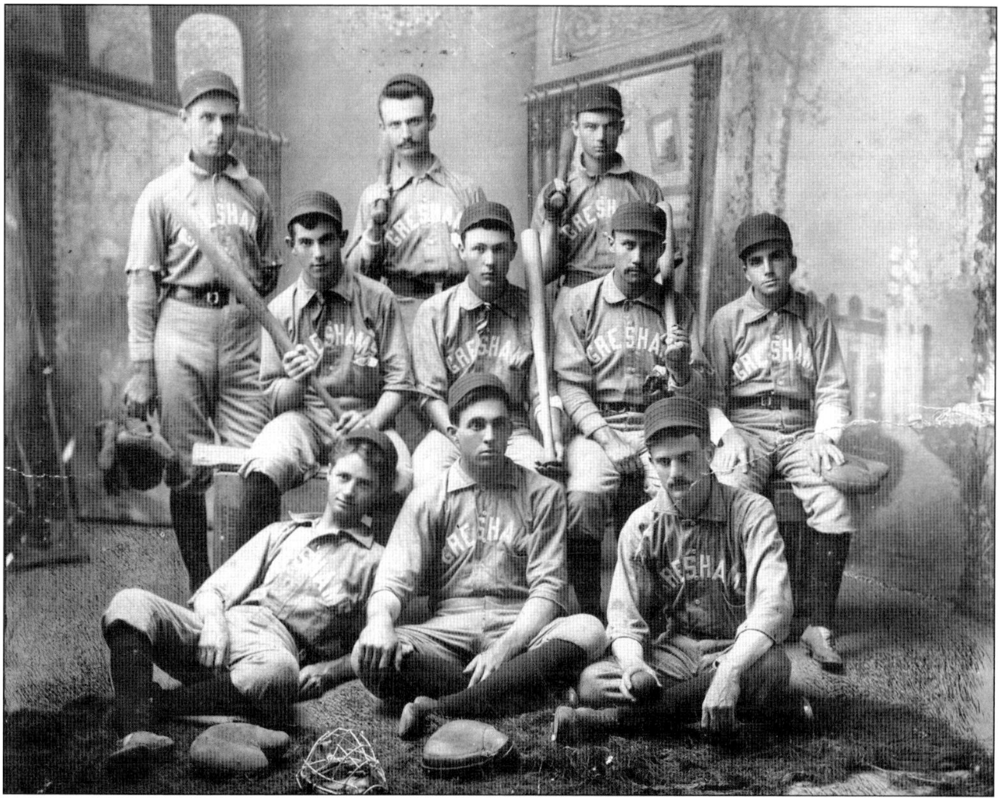

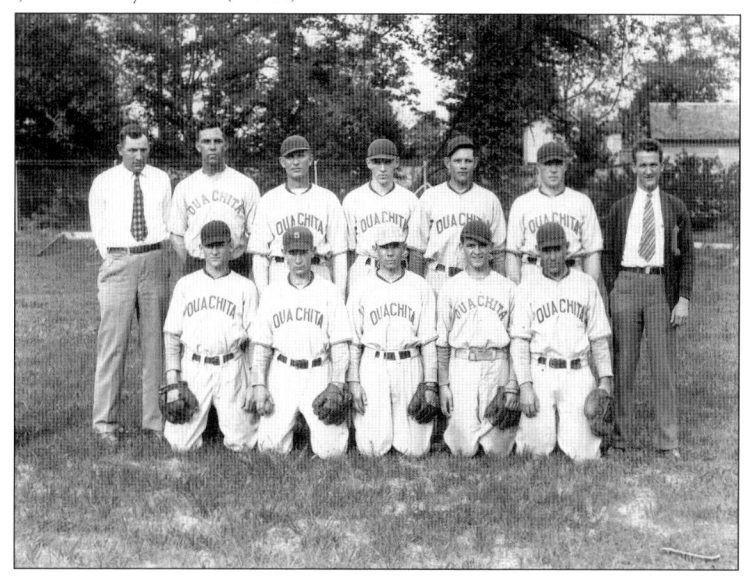

The Greshams was an early baseball team in Clark County, formed around 1895 and named for Arkadelphia merchant William Wadley Gresham. Gresham was owner and founder of the Gresham Mercantile Company and Gresham's Opera House as well as a store in Benoit, Mississippi. Gresham likely outfitted the baseball team named in his honor. Players are identified as Lou McCorkle, John A. Williamson, Charles Crow, T.T. Rudolph, Pat Dawson, John B. McDaniel, Fred Kaufman, Dick Reed, and Henry Green. (HSU.)

The 1929 Ouachita baseball team was coached by Foy Hammons, standing at left, and assistant coach Bill Brasher, standing at right. Ouachita had won the state championship in baseball for the previous 14 consecutive years. Standing fifth from left is "Mert" Hill, who was offered a contract with the Cleveland Indians. (OBU.)

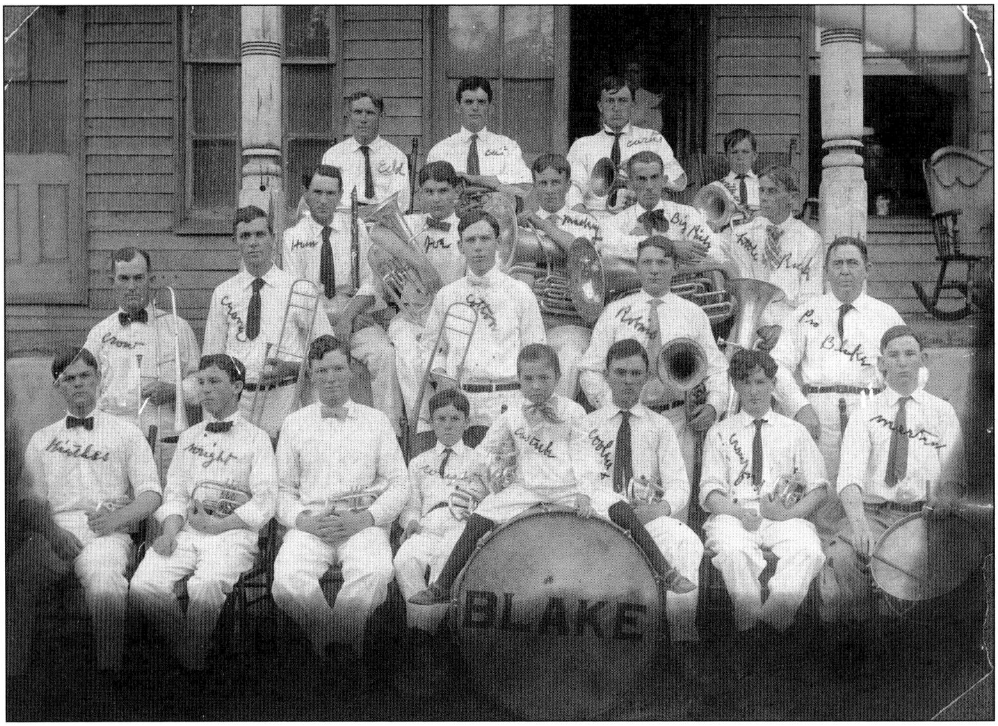

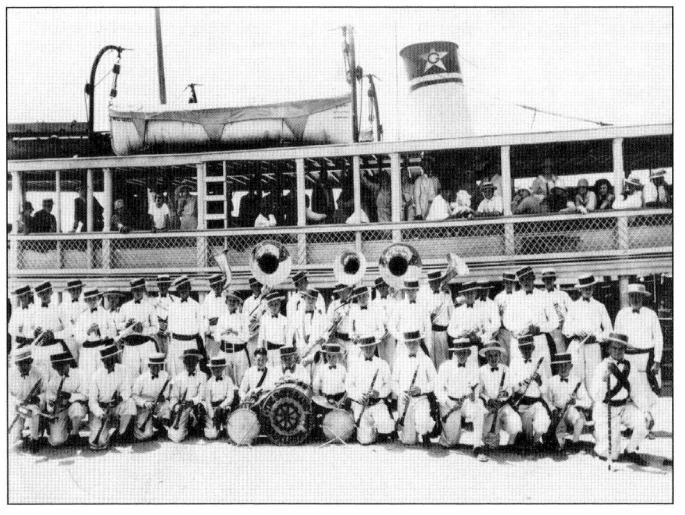

While Arkadelphia was home to numerous bands over the years, none was more popular than Blake's Brass Band under the direction of Prof. Dwight Blake. Born in 1870, Blake began his music career in Arkadelphia at the age of 19, becoming one of the state's best-known band directors. Bands under his direction played for events around Arkansas and outside of the state. In 1892, Blake's Band played in Little Rock at a celebration for the election of presidential incumbent Grover Cleveland. Blake's musical career spanned more than 50 years. (HSU.)

The Arkadelphia Boys' Band was organized in November 1916 under the directorship of J.F. Steindall, a chemist for the Arkadelphia Milling Company. Boys were required to purchase their own instruments, and 30 lads joined initially. The band was still performing into the 1920s, when this photograph was likely taken. In May 1924, the band won second place at a District Rotary Convention competition held in Hot Springs. (OBU.)

The Top Hatters band was organized around 1937 by Louis Ohls and performed in and around Arkadelphia until the American entry into World War II. This 1938 photograph was taken at an Arkadelphia County Club function and includes Audrey Ballard, Flave Carpenter, Jack Chitwood, Bill Laster, Alvin Allison, Fuzzy Winburn, Dick McFarland, O.G. Crum, Louis Ohls, Vascoe Carson, Hank Thompson, and Wayman Ballard. (OBU.)

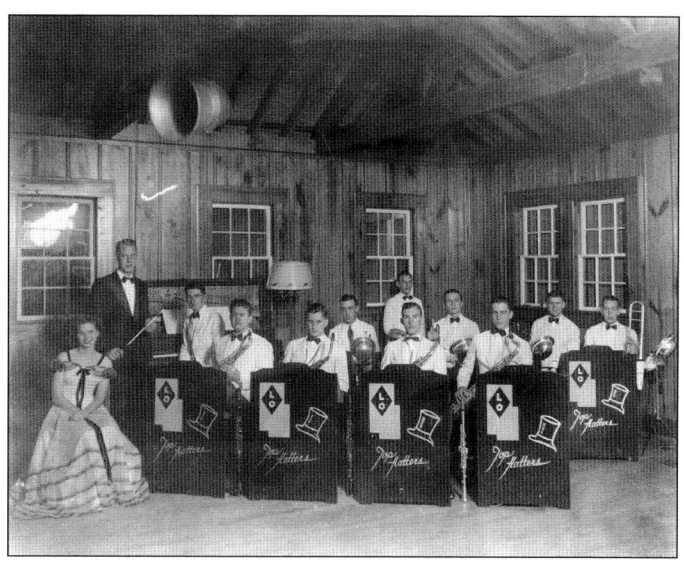

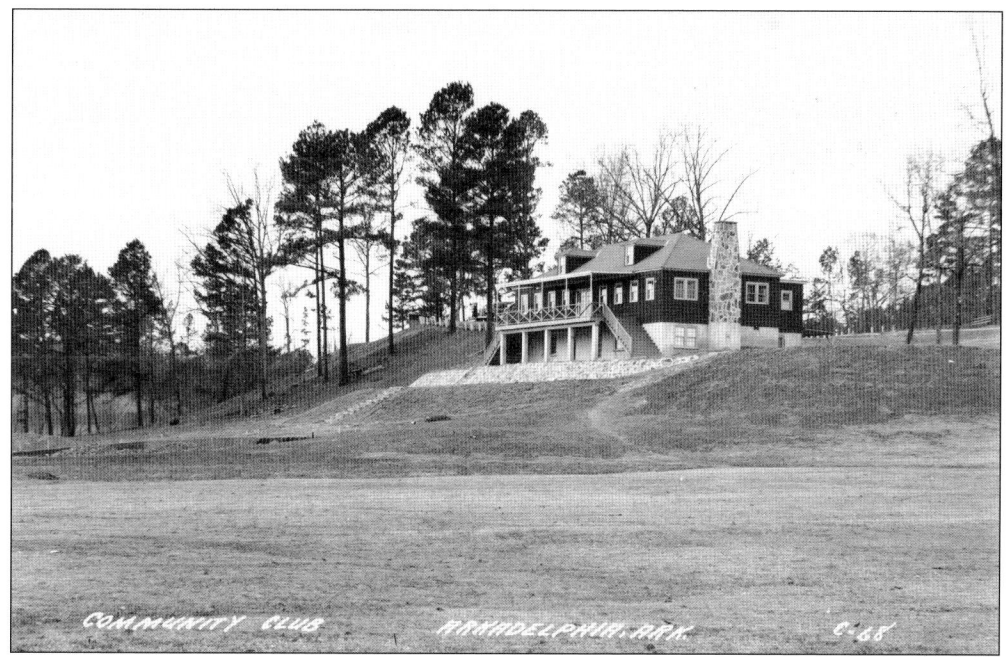

The Arkadelphia Country Club started as just a golf course in the 1920s. In 1936, the Young Businessmen's Association began promoting the idea for a clubhouse. With a $12,000 loan from the Works Progress Administration, the organization acquired a site bordering Mill Creek and constructed a clubhouse, which opened with a New Year's Eve party in 1937. In 1965, the property was sold to Henderson, and the club relocated three miles northwest of Arkadelphia. The old clubhouse burned in January 1976. The land where the clubhouse sat is now part of Henderson's athletic complex. (OBU.)

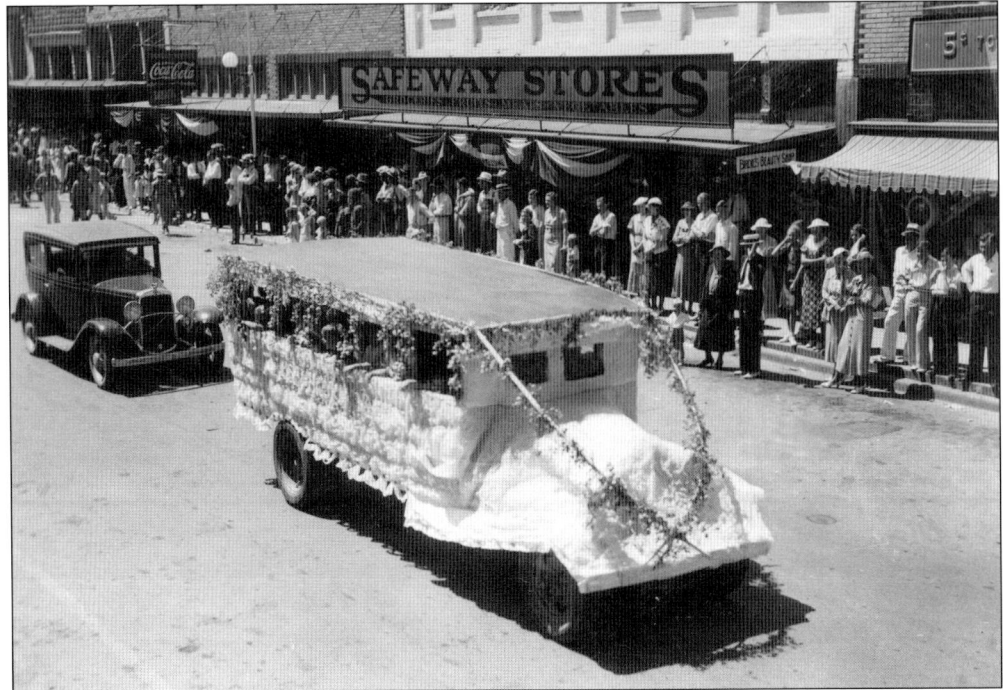

On May 15, 1936, Clark County celebrated the centennial anniversary of Arkansas statehood. Part of a coordinated statewide effort to mark a century of statehood, citizens held a lavish parade in Arkadelphia, reportedly one mile in length; elected a centennial queen—Edna Earle Epperson of Amity; and held an elaborate historical pageant, written and directed by Arkadelphia High School history teacher Amy Jean Greene at Ouachita's A.U. Williams field. Taken during the parade, these photographs show the Works Progress Administration Nursery School float (above) and crowds milling about in downtown Arkadelphia after the parade (below). (Both, OBU.)

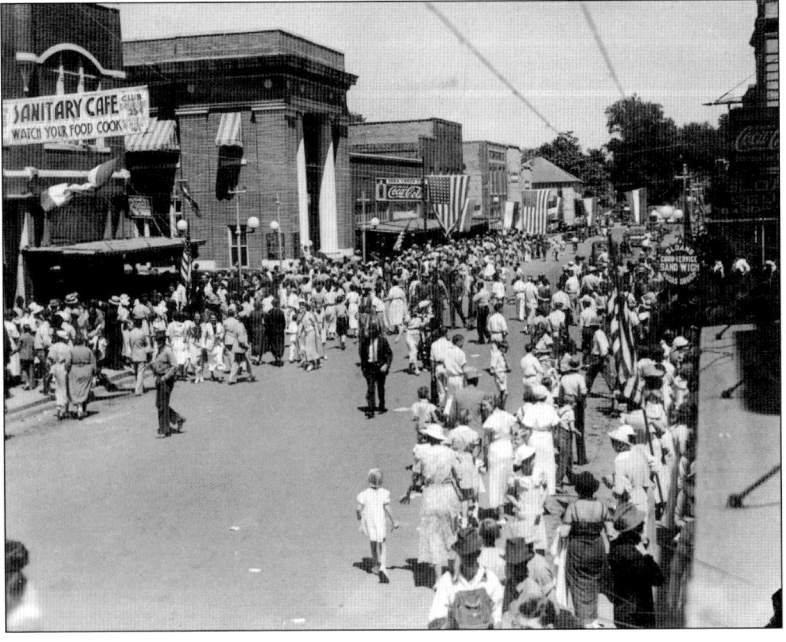

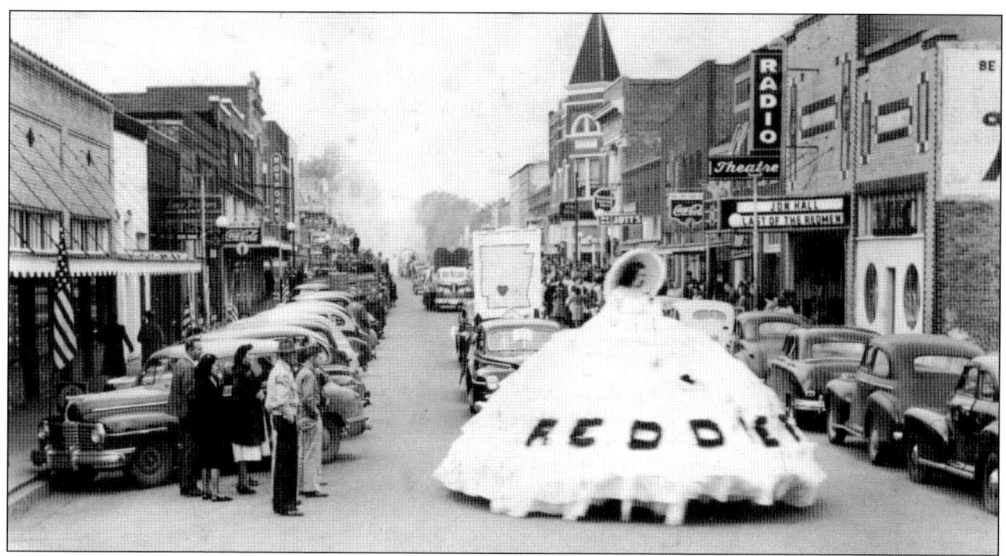

Henderson homecoming queen Jimmy Neal Tweedle of Arkadelphia rides atop the "Reddie" float in the 1947 Thanksgiving Day parade down Arkadelphia's Main Street. The parade preceded the annual football game between local college rivals Ouachita and Henderson, which unfortunately ended in a scoreless tie. (OBU.)

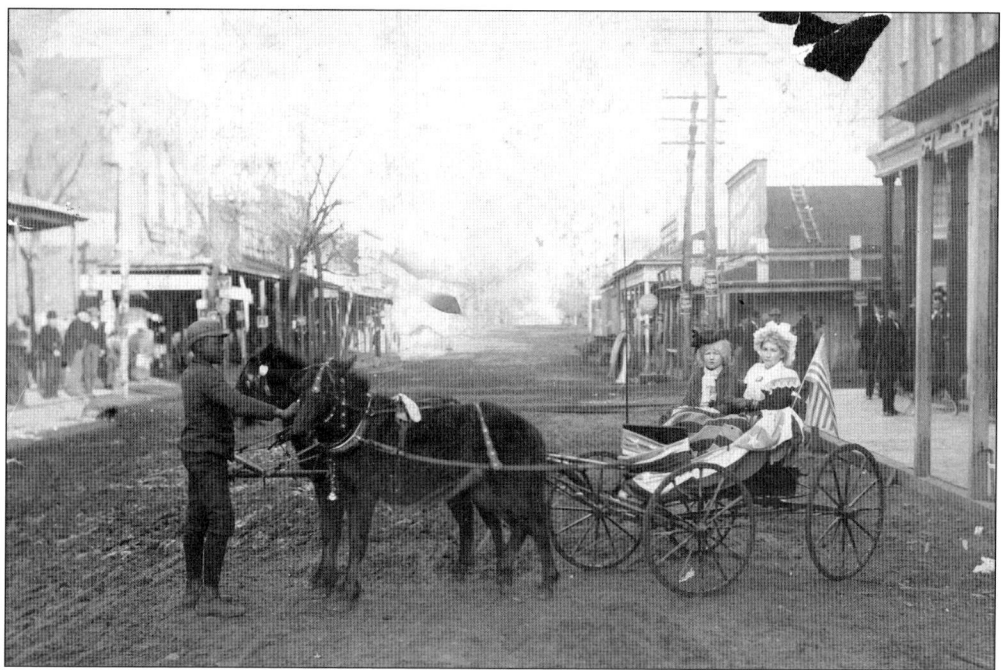

Dwight Crawford and Louis Dale (seated in a carriage) are dressed as George and Martha Washington, Main Street, Arkadelphia, 1898. This photograph was taken just west of the intersection of Sixth and Main Streets, looking east. The young man presumably leading the ponies is unidentified. The photograph may have been taken in observance of Presidents' Day, officially Washington's birthday, a federal holiday established by Congress in 1879. Dwight Crawford became a lawyer in Arkadelphia. Lois may have been the daughter of Robert and Ada Dale, who later married Donald Blakeney. (OBU.)

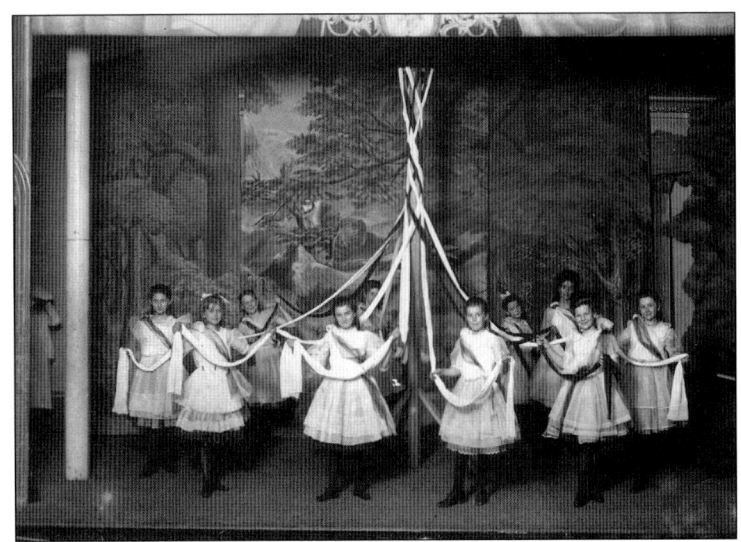

A maypole dance was one of the festivities planned by the Women's Library Association of Arkadelphia to celebrate the retirement of the debt on the town's first public library on May 16, 1913. The 1913 celebration also included a parade, reception at the library, burning of the banknote, musical performances, and a basket supper. (OBU.)

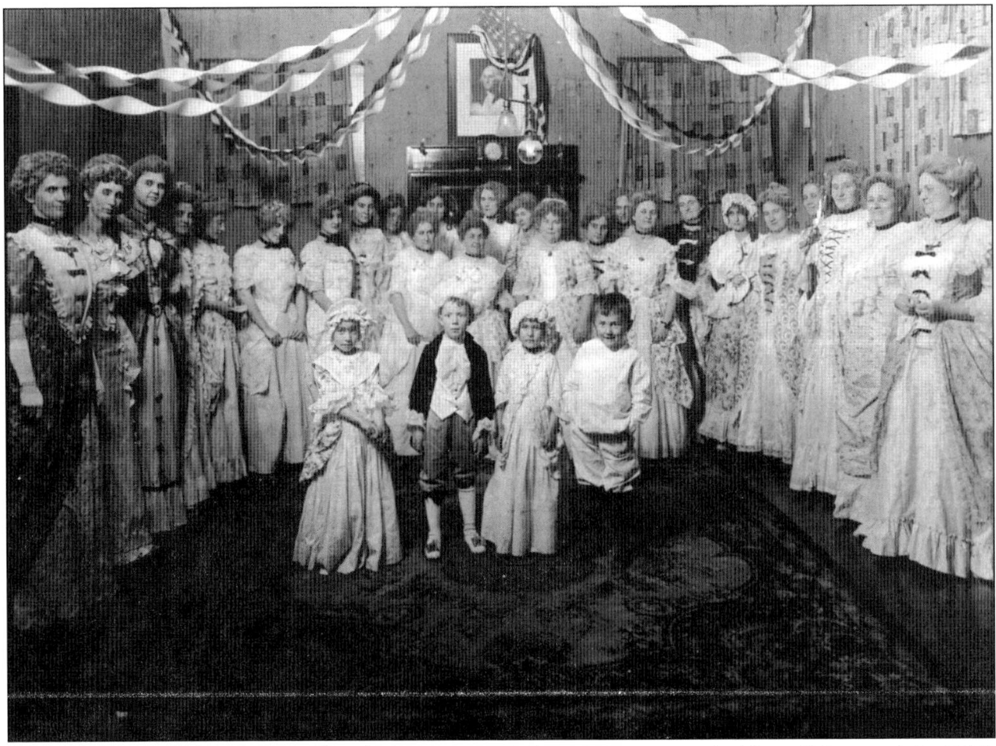

The occasion for this costumed gathering was a Colonial Dames tea held on February 20, 1914, and hosted by Mary Francis Meador and Georgia Ann Greene. The gathering at 1012 West Main Street in Arkadelphia included over 200 guests commemorating President's Day. The tiny George Washington (center) was played by Dougald McMillan, while the two tiny Martha Washingtons were played by Martha Greene and Martha Virginia Stuart. The other boy is unidentified. (OBU.)

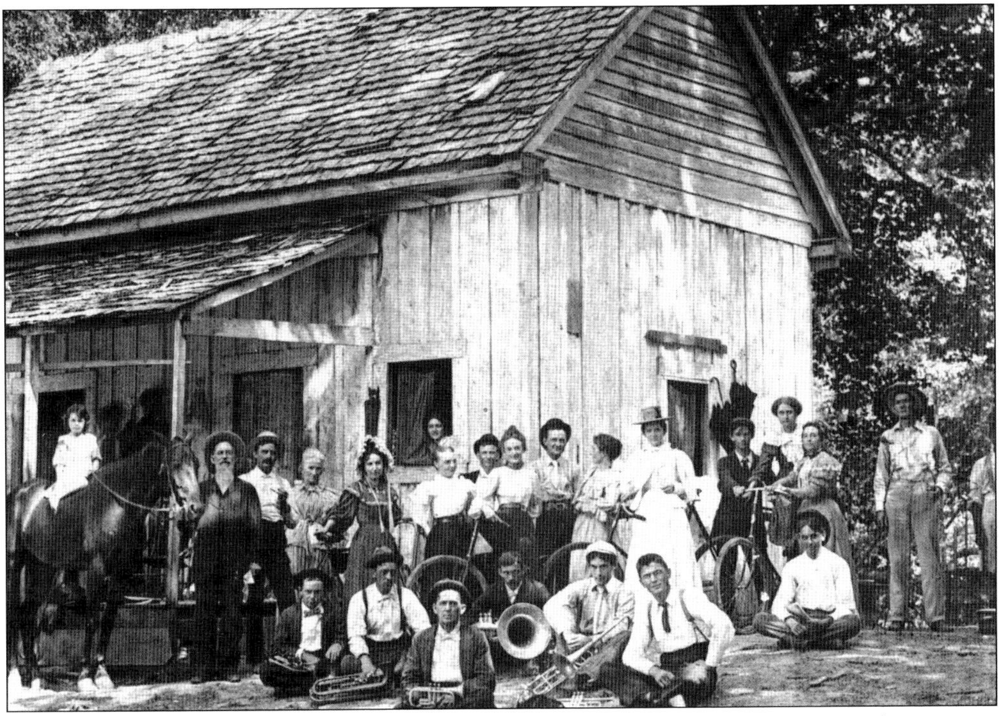

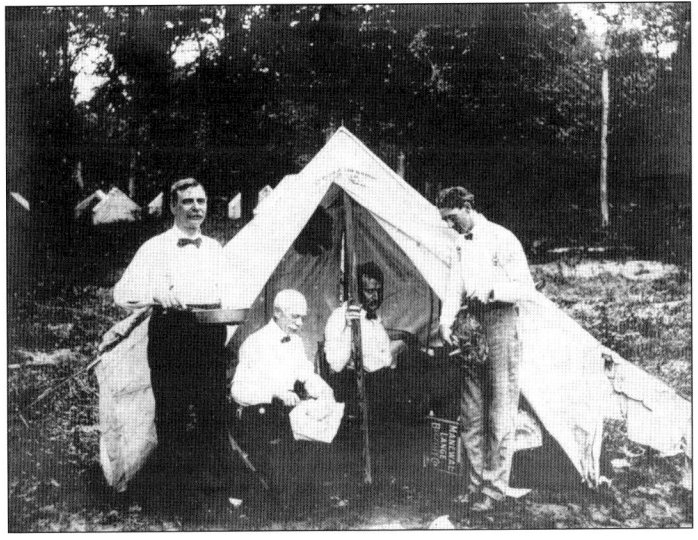

Brown Springs, located about 11 miles northeast of Arkadelphia on Highway 51 and just across the Hot Spring County line, was a popular summer vacation spot for residents of Clark County. Dotted with mineral-rich springs, the community was named for an early settler, H.L. Brown. "Camping at the springs" was a popular activity, while cottages and a hotel provided alternative lodging for families requiring more amenities. An annual Fourth of July picnic brought visitors from all over the area, as did Methodist and Baptist camp meetings. Above, the family of A.M. Crow of Arkadelphia vacations at the springs around 1900. Seated in front are members of Blake's Band, which frequently entertained at the springs. Below, Ouachita Baptist College professor Frederick D. Baars, seated in front of the tent, prepares supper for friends attending the Baptist Assembly around 1905. (Both, OBU.)

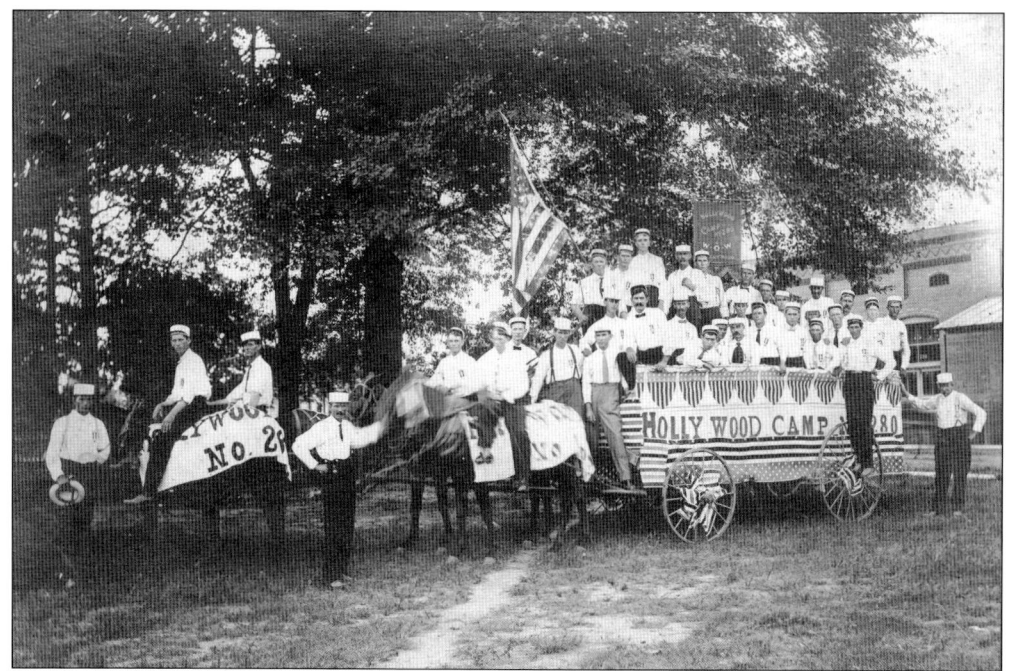

While the occasion for the above gathering of the Hollywood Chapter No. 280, Woodmen of the World (WOW), is not known, the national fraternal benefit society was active in Clark County as early as 1895. Founded in 1890 in Omaha, Nebraska, the WOW is a philanthropic organization known for the distinctive tree-stump-shaped headstones they provide to members. The photograph below was taken at a Hollywood WOW annual picnic in either 1906 or 1907. (Both, OBU.)

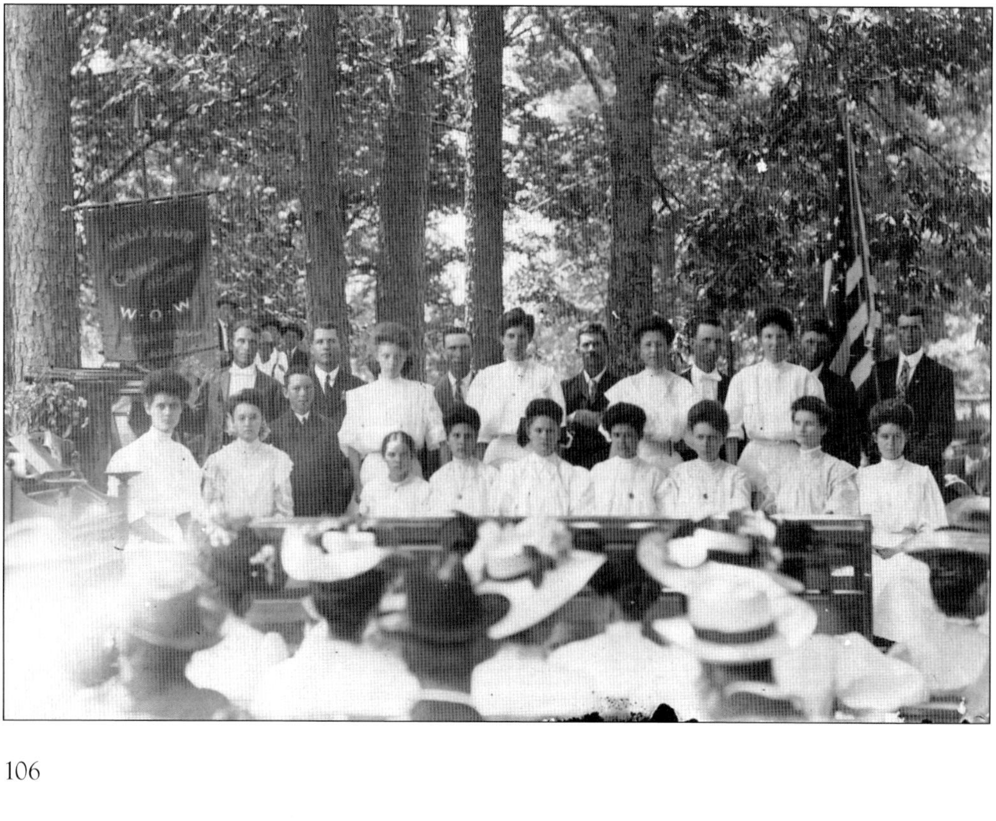

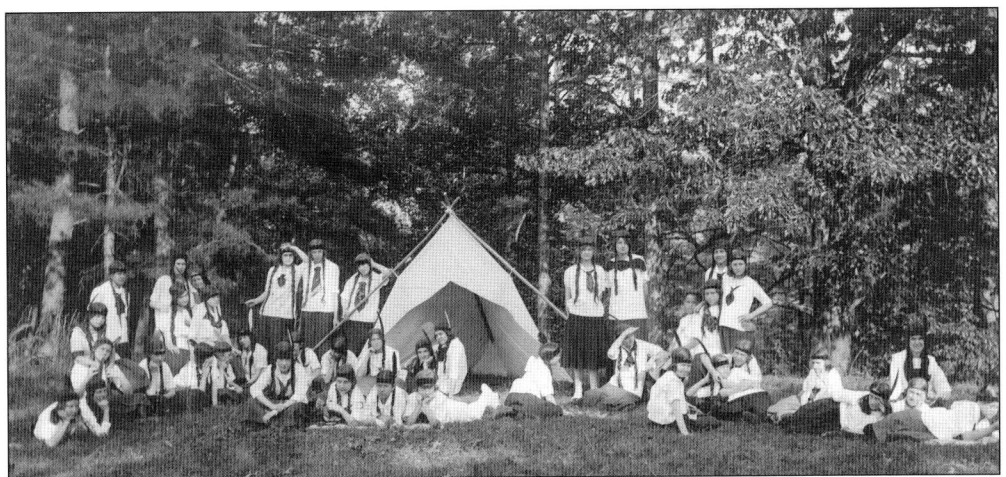

The Camp Fire Girls, a sister organization to the Boy Scouts of America, was incorporated in 1912. This group of Clark County members was among the between 7,000 and 8,000 girls who held membership in the group. The location of the 1913 expedition is not identified. (OBU.)

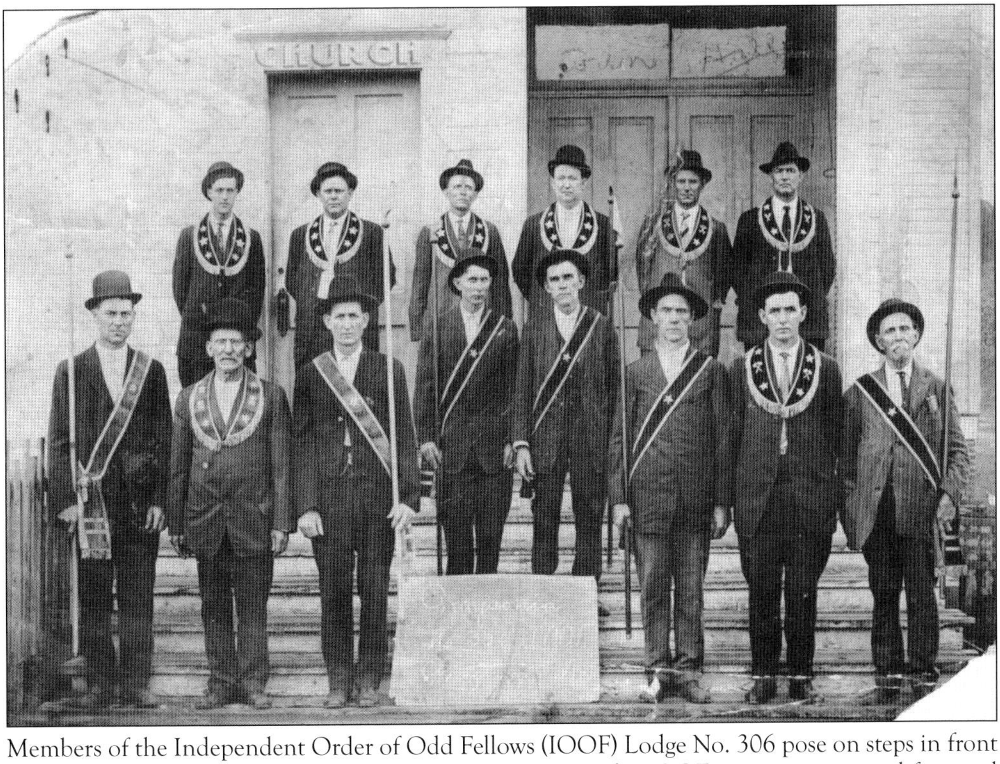

Members of the Independent Order of Odd Fellows (IOOF) Lodge No. 306 pose on steps in front of Graysonia Town Hall and church around 1907–1917. The IOOF is an international fraternal organization founded in 1819 in Maryland. The IOOF became the first fraternity in the United States to admit women in 1851. (OBU.)

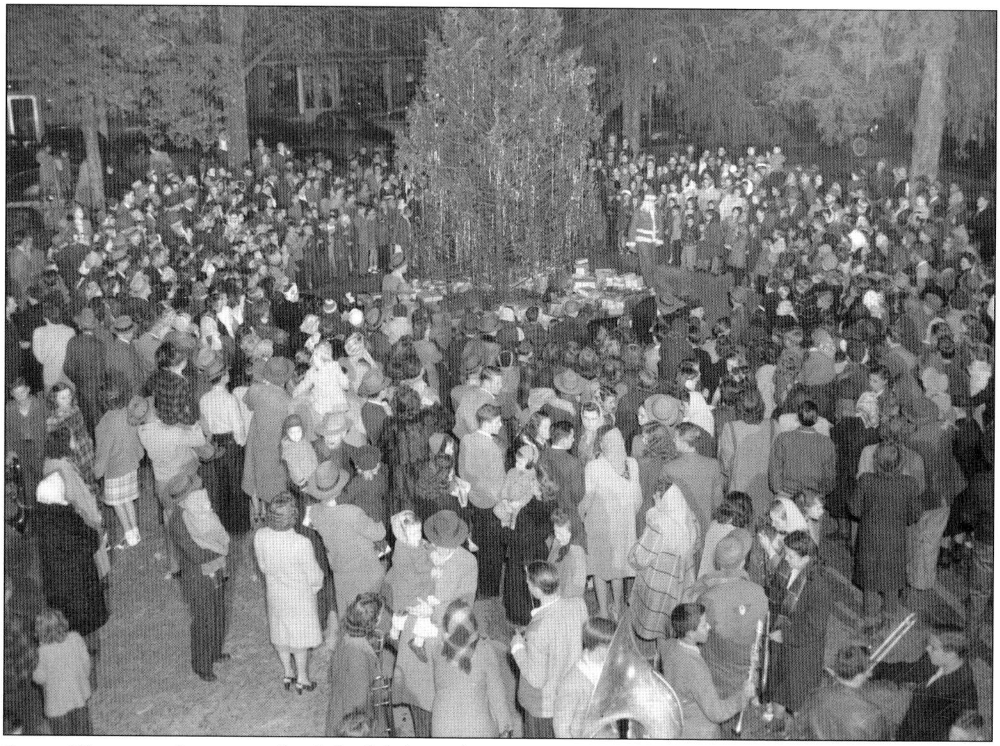

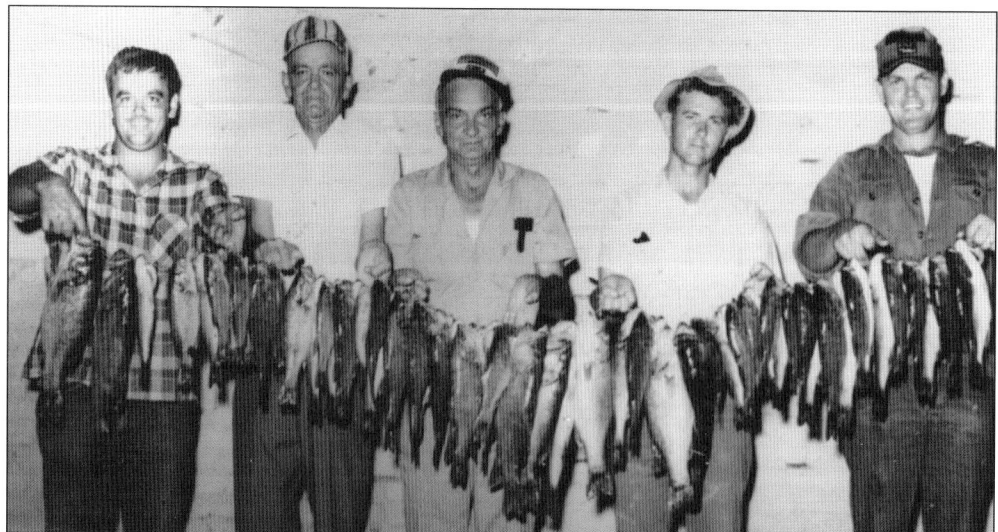

Santa Claus stands next to the Arkadelphia Christmas tree around the late 1940s. The community Christmas party, sponsored by the Junior Chamber of Commerce, was an event celebrated for a number of years in Arkadelphia. The event included music by the high school band, the singing of carols, a visit by Santa, and the presentation of gifts to all children between the ages of three and eight who sent in postcards to "Santa." (OBU.)

With five rivers and a lake, Clark County has long been a popular spot for all types of recreation involving water, as illustrated in this image of five men with their large haul of fish from the Ouachita River around 1973. From left to right, they are Jimmy Lemons, Olen Lemons, Monroe Lemons, Johnny Adair, and Glenn Scott. (OBU.)

Seven

A RESILIENT CITY

The March 1, 1997, tornado damaged the roof and clock tower of the 1899 courthouse, blew out windows, and toppled the memorial to Confederate soldiers on the lawn. In the days immediately after the tornado, county government officials raised the possibility of demolishing the courthouse and building a new, modern structure in a location closer to what had been downtown. Public pressure from historic preservationists and other interested parties eventually led the county to scrap plans to relocate the courthouse. While awaiting restoration, a temporary courtroom was set up in the nearby National Guard Armory building, and courthouse workers relocated to the Blackmon building at Third Street Baptist Church. Eventually, the county purchased modular buildings to house county offices, and these were set up in a nearby parking lot. The courthouse was rededicated, following renovation, two years to the day after the tornado. On that day, the tower bell tolled six times in solemn remembrance of those who died in Clark County. (HSU.)

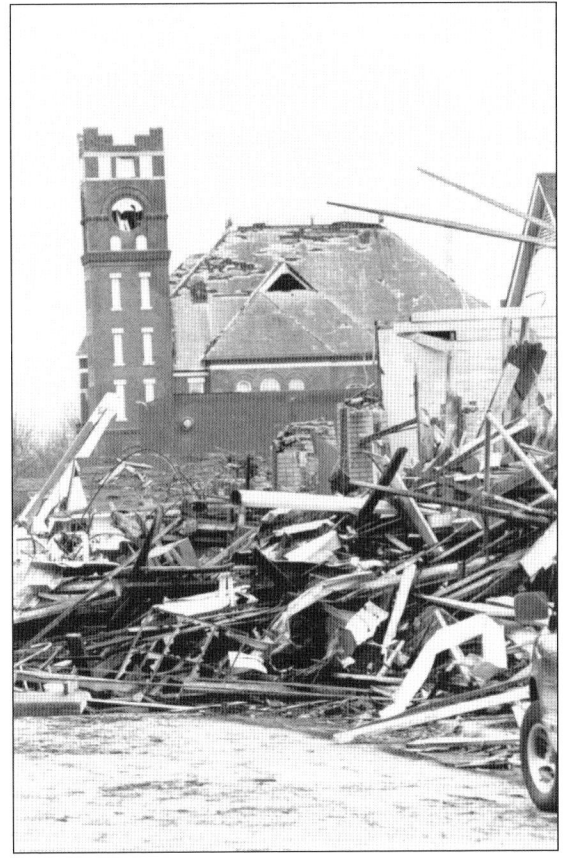

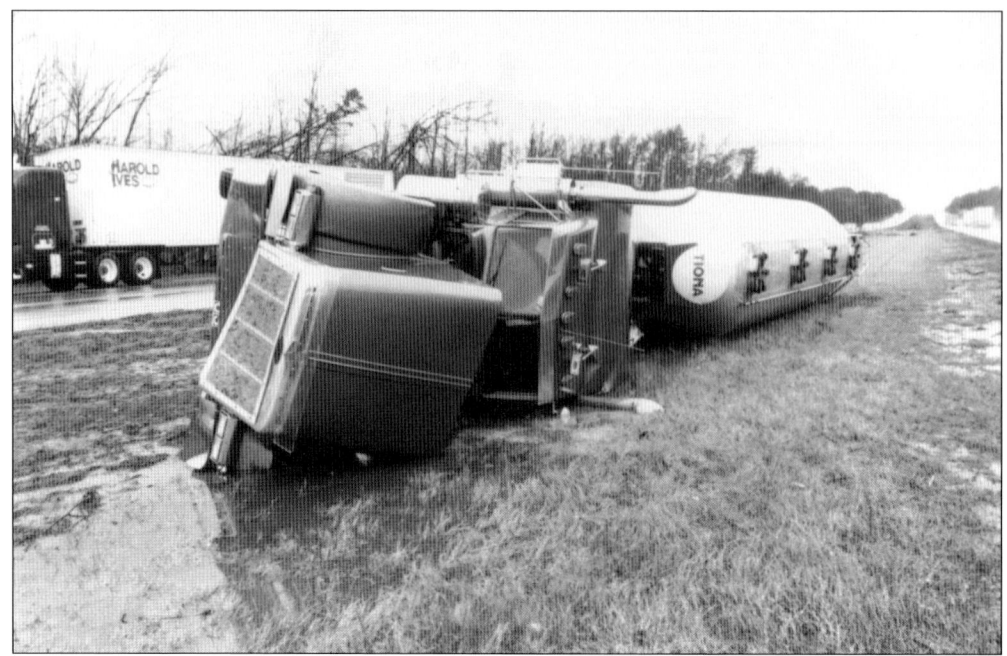

The F-4 tornado, which cut a 20-mile path across Clark County, was spotted about 2:15 p.m. southwest of Arkadelphia. The storm first developed in the Okolona area and was on the ground much of the time. The storm passed through Centerpoint and Southfork, ripping down hundreds of trees and damaging a few homes. The Arkansas Forestry Commission estimated that around 2,500 acres of timberland were impacted. At the 68-mile marker, the tornado blew vehicles off the road, including a tractor-trailer rig (above). One person—Michael Lumpkin—died in a car that was blown off the interstate. Honky's Truck Stop and Deli at Gum Springs (below) was destroyed. No one was injured at the truck stop. From Gum Springs, the tornado approached Arkadelphia from the south, running parallel to US Highway 67. (Both, HSU.)

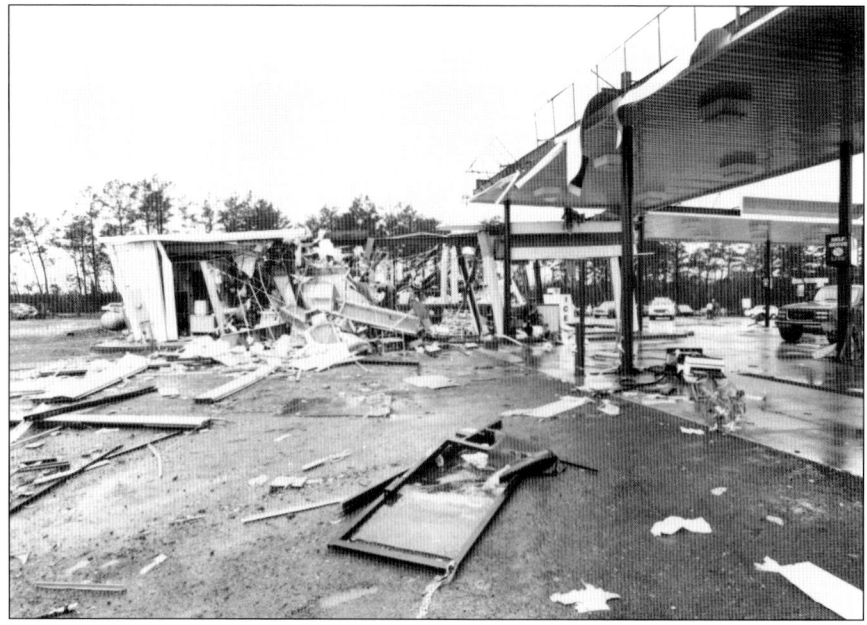

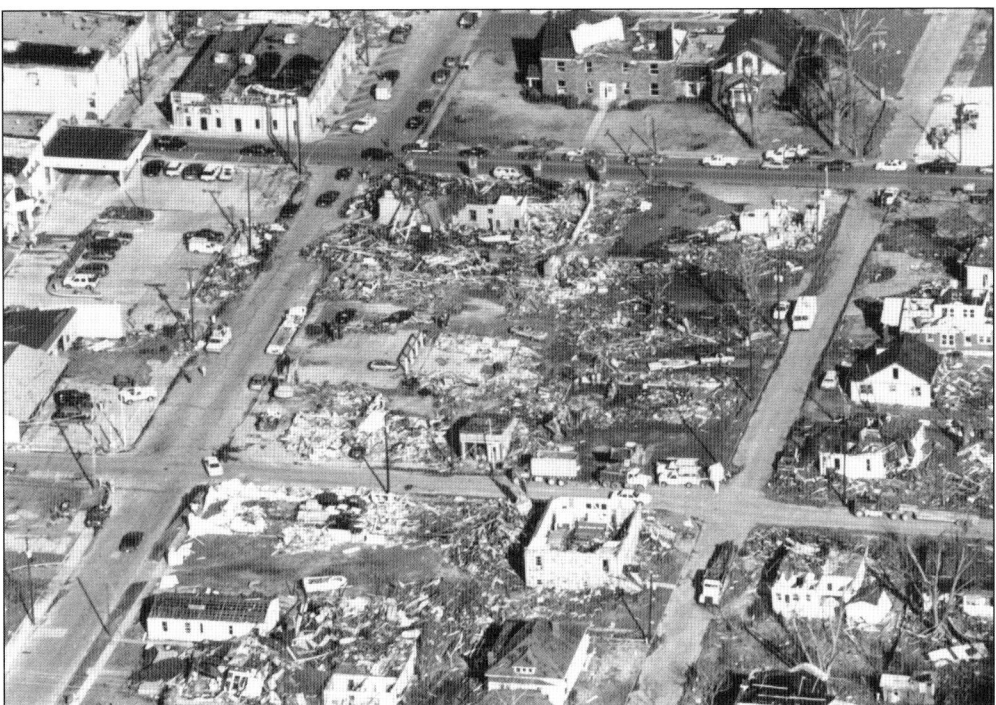

The area around Clay and Crittenden Streets (above) was one of the areas hardest hit in Arkadelphia. Murry-Ruggles Funeral Home is visible at the top right and below. Funeral director Tim Welch was at work when the tornado struck. Welch later told an interviewer that the tornado "sounded like a hundred freight trains." The National Weather Service estimated that the massive tornado was three-quarters of a mile wide with wind speeds up to 260 miles per hour. A total of 45 businesses, 16 public buildings, and approximately 120 residences were destroyed, with countless others heavily damaged. In describing the scene to reporters, Arkadelphia mayor Mike Kolb said, "It's like a bomb that's gone off, but there's no crater." Gov. Mike Huckabee, who flew over by helicopter, declared Arkadelphia a disaster area by 6:00 p.m. on March 1. (Both, HSU.)

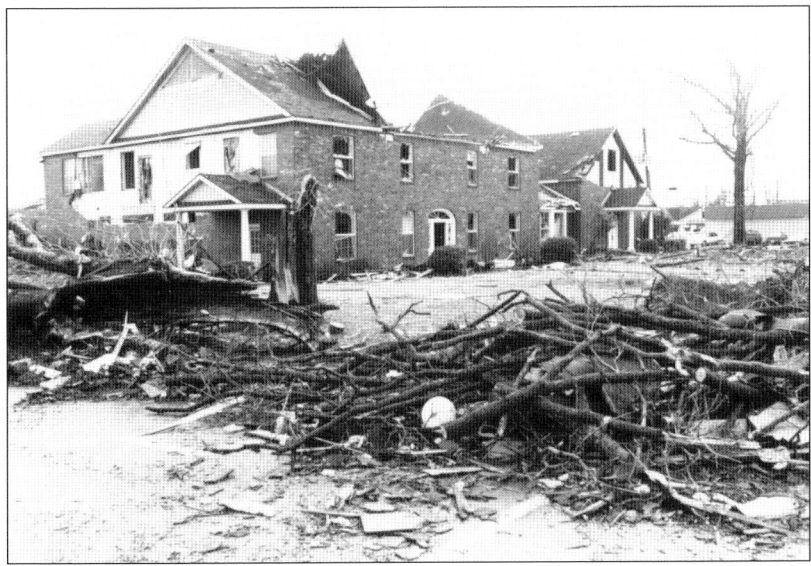

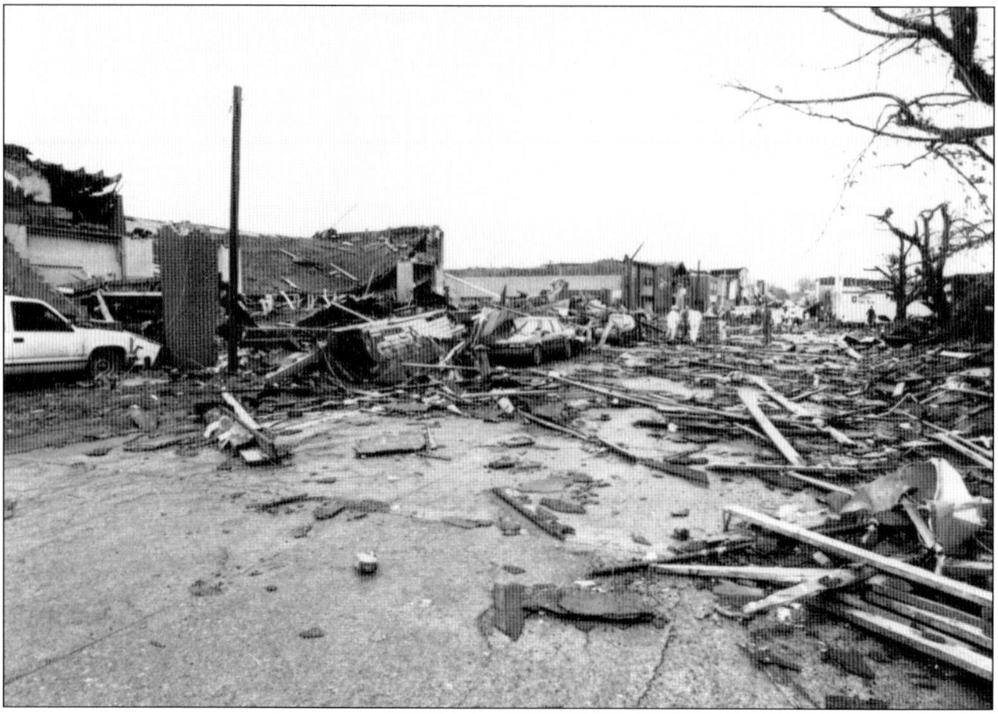

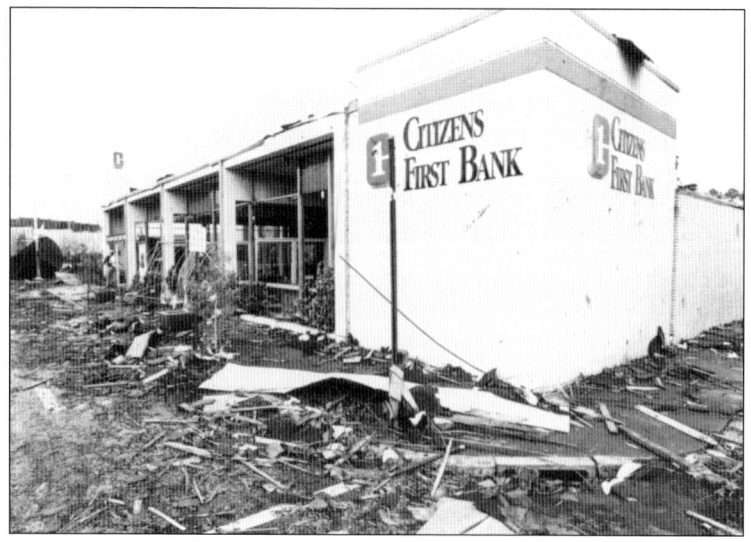

Along Main Street (above) and in other parts of downtown, the storm destroyed numerous businesses, including All-Care Pharmacy, Conine's Coast to Coast appliances, Arkadelphia Custom Carpets, Wells Discount Shoes, Quality Shoe Store, the Honeycomb Restaurant and Bee Hive Industries, the Salt Shoppe Christian Books & Music, the office of Dr. John Balay, and others. At Wells Discount Shoes, an employee was trapped when the roof collapsed on him. Emergency personnel took about 30 minutes to extricate him from the wreckage. He was not seriously injured. Several Arkadelphia banks were heavily damaged or destroyed, including Elk Horn, Horizon, and Citizens First State Bank, visible at the top right and below. Because the tornado struck on a Saturday mid-afternoon, many local businesses had already closed for the day, avoiding a greater number of deaths and injuries. (Both, HSU.)

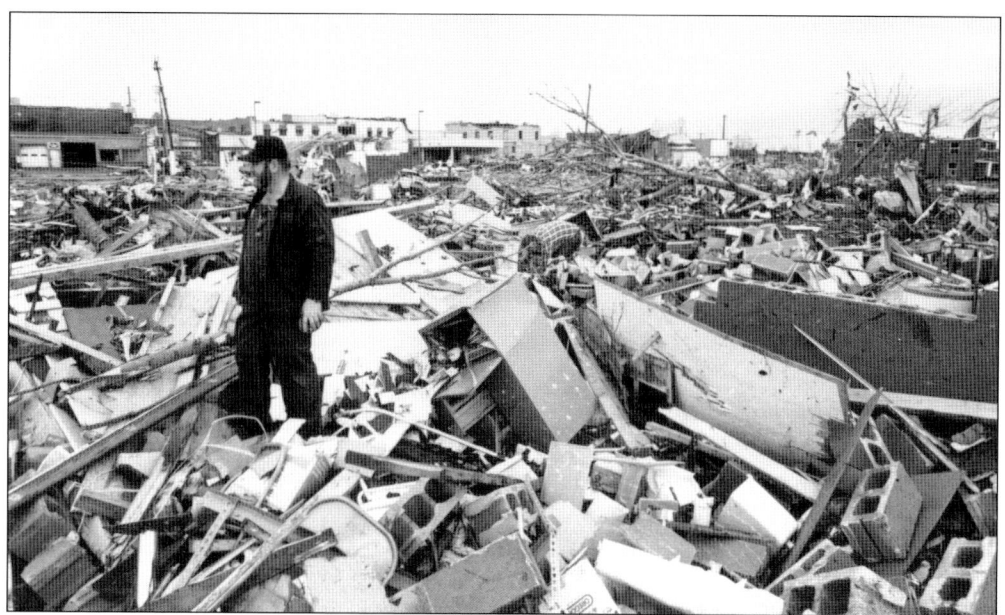

Dwight Kirkpatrick stands amid the rubble of his business, Williams Saw Company, at 408 South Seventh Street (above). Randy Gaither (below, standing) sorts through the rubble of Juanita's Candy Kitchen on South Twelfth Street. Other businesses destroyed included Troy Keeton Garage; the Buckelew's Bed and Breakfast; Adair's Automotive; Deaton Barbershop; Precision Automotive; Barbara's Photography; the office of Sanders & Hill, attorneys; Andy Berry's accounting office—where one person, Donna DuBoise, died—Bob's Bail Bonds; Summerhill Carpet; Paula's Beauty Salon; and others. Surveying the complete devastation of the downtown Arkadelphia area, Mayor Mike Kolb said, "Downtown's gone. It's all gone." Kolb also told reporters, "It's going to be extremely difficult to rebuild, but we will because this is a resilient city." (Both, HSU.)

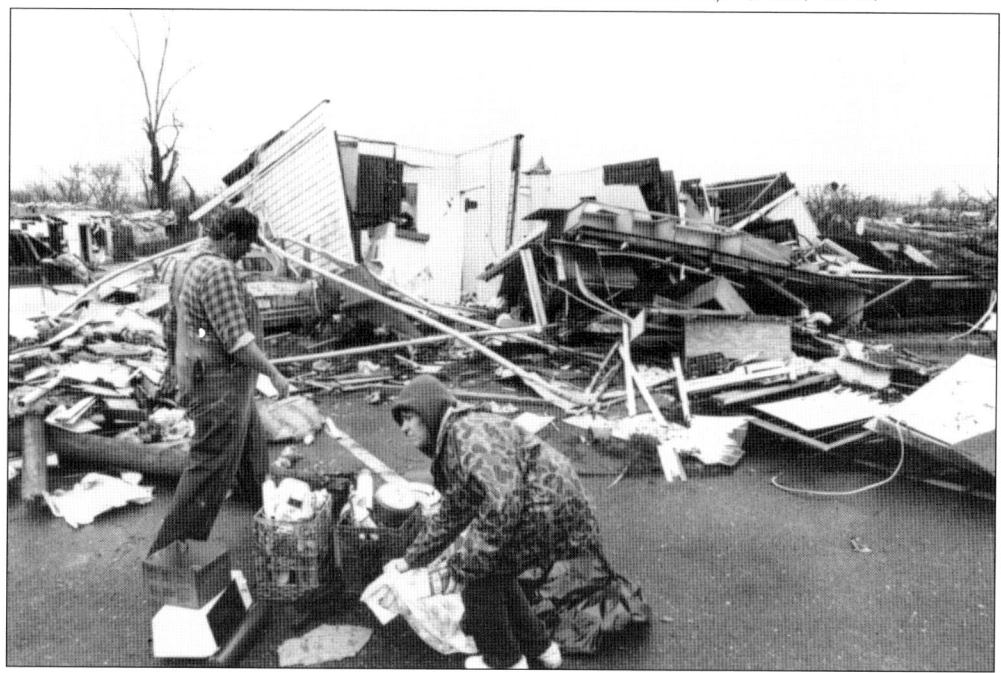

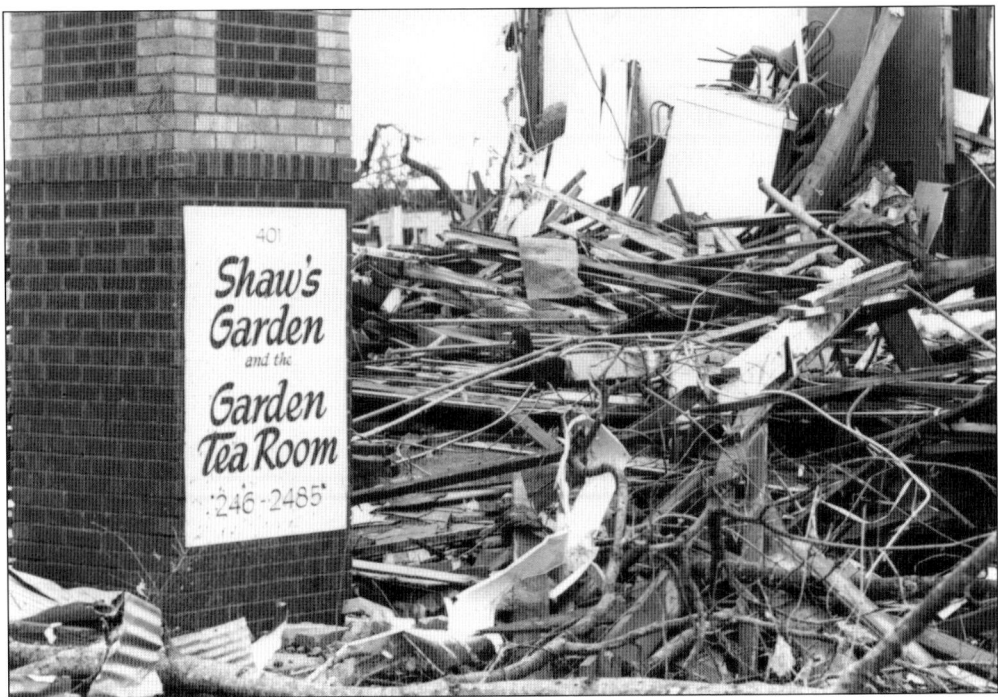

Shaw's Garden and the Garden Tea Room at 401 South Sixth Street (above), just across from Murry-Ruggles Funeral Home, was leveled by the tornado. Owner Judy Sligh was at work when the tornado hit. A call from an employee warning her to take cover gave her seconds to find shelter under the worktable that likely saved her life. Below, Sligh points to where she was trapped in the wreckage. Murry-Ruggles funeral director Tim Welch heard Sligh's cries for help and went to her assistance. Some National Guardsmen passing by helped to free her from the wreckage. She was not seriously injured. Sligh told reporters at the time, "I don't have my shop, but I do have my life." (Both, HSU.)

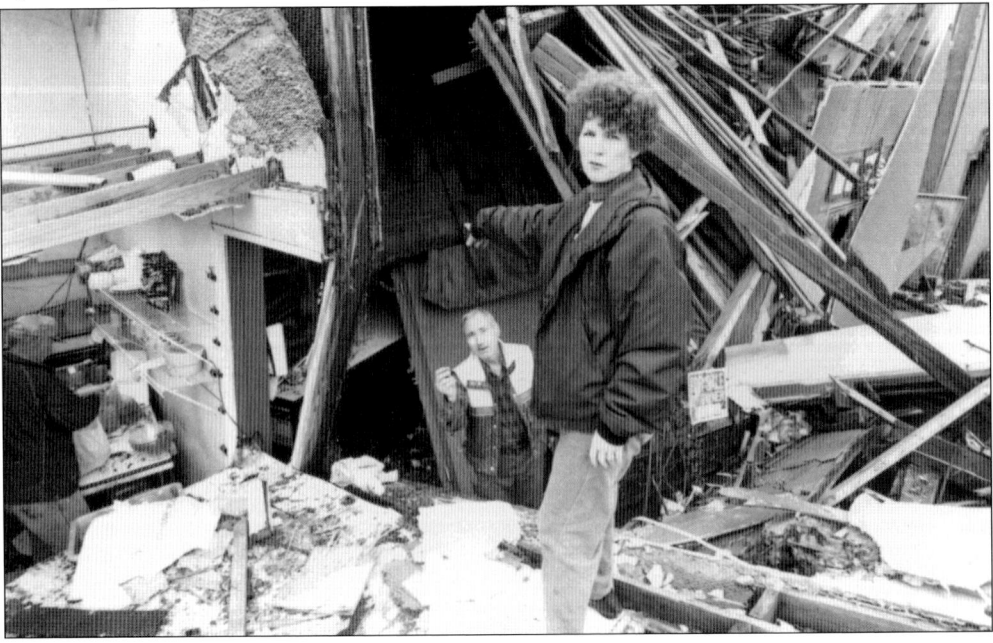

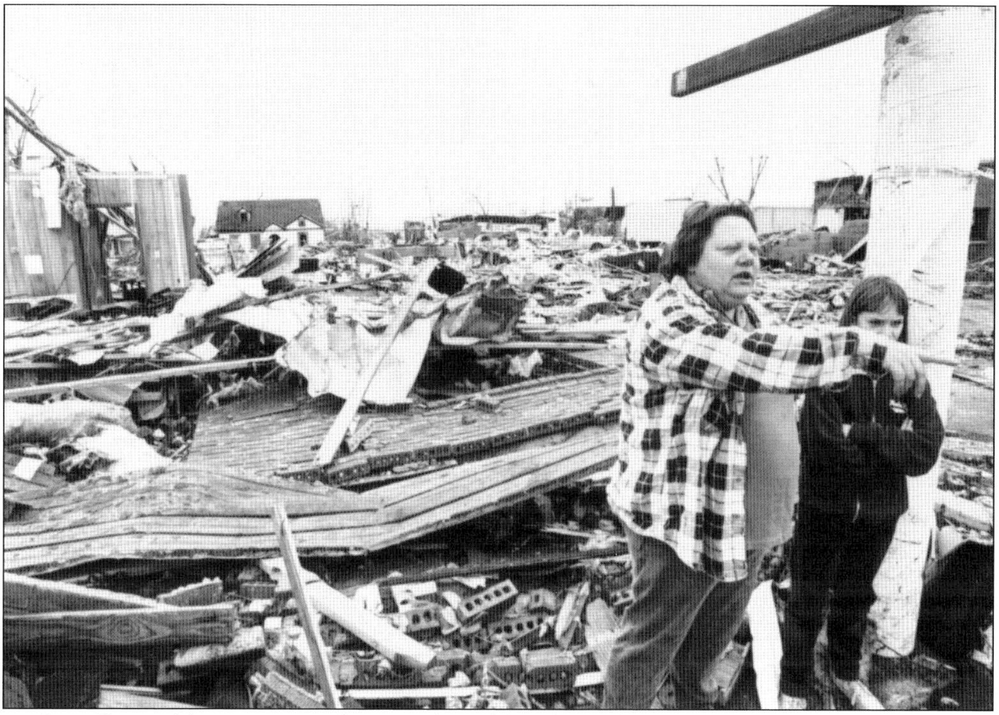

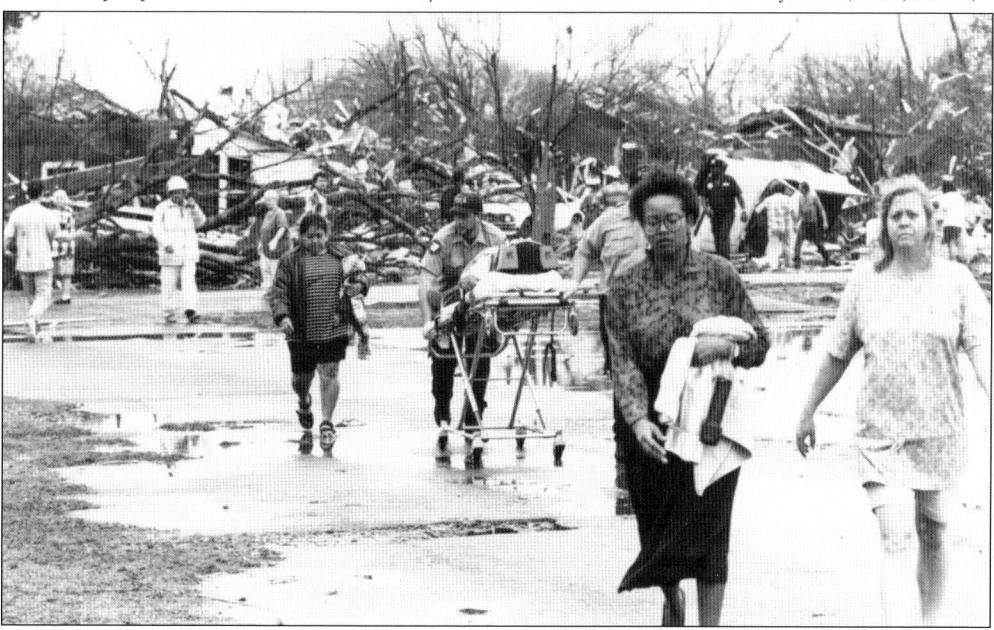

Linda Miller and her niece Stephanie Hebert (above) stand in front of the destroyed Arkansas Revenue Department Office on Clay Street. Miller was local manager at the time of the tornado. The Revenue Department Office temporarily relocated to Pine Street, across from Andy's, until a new facility was constructed on Clay Street. The Cutler Street area (below) was another hard-hit area where 56 out of 57 trailers in a mobile home park were destroyed. Four people died in the mobile home park: John Christman, DeMorris Ann Christman, Abby Bryant, and Reita Coffey. In all, six people died in the Clark County storm. A hundred others were injured. (Both, HSU.)

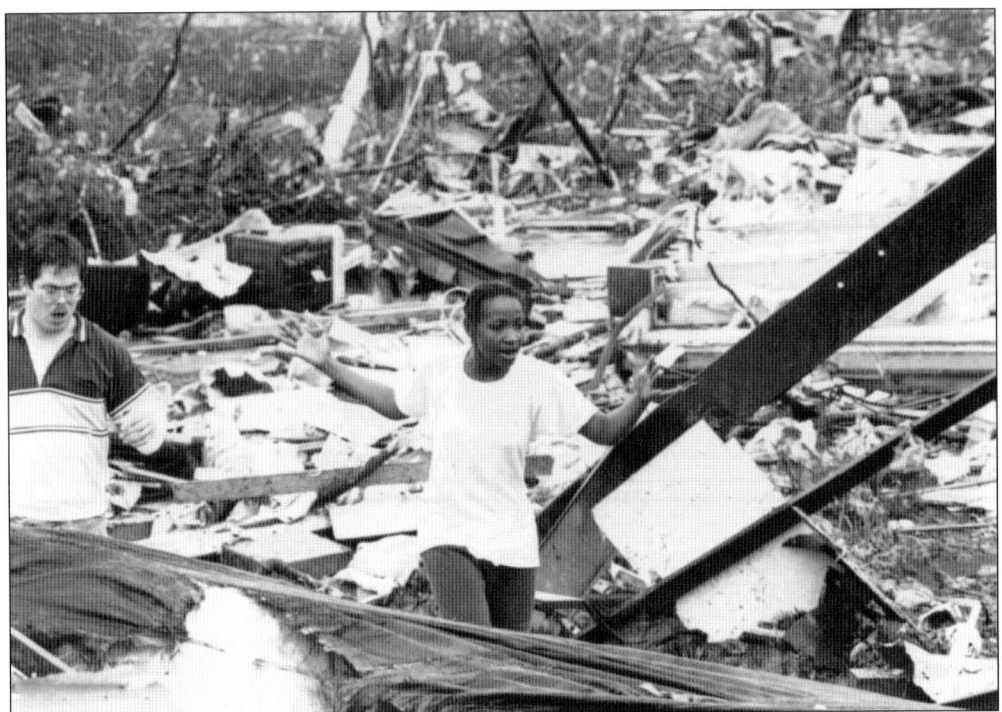

Cora Watson (above) searches through the rubble of her home in the Cutler Mobile Home Park for her son Stefone Buckley. National Guardsmen help Watson remove her son from the wreckage (below). He was not seriously injured. By nightfall, approximately 50 ambulances and rescue vehicles were on scene in Arkadelphia. Rescue personnel searched for survivors in the rubble of businesses and homes throughout the night. (Both, HSU.)

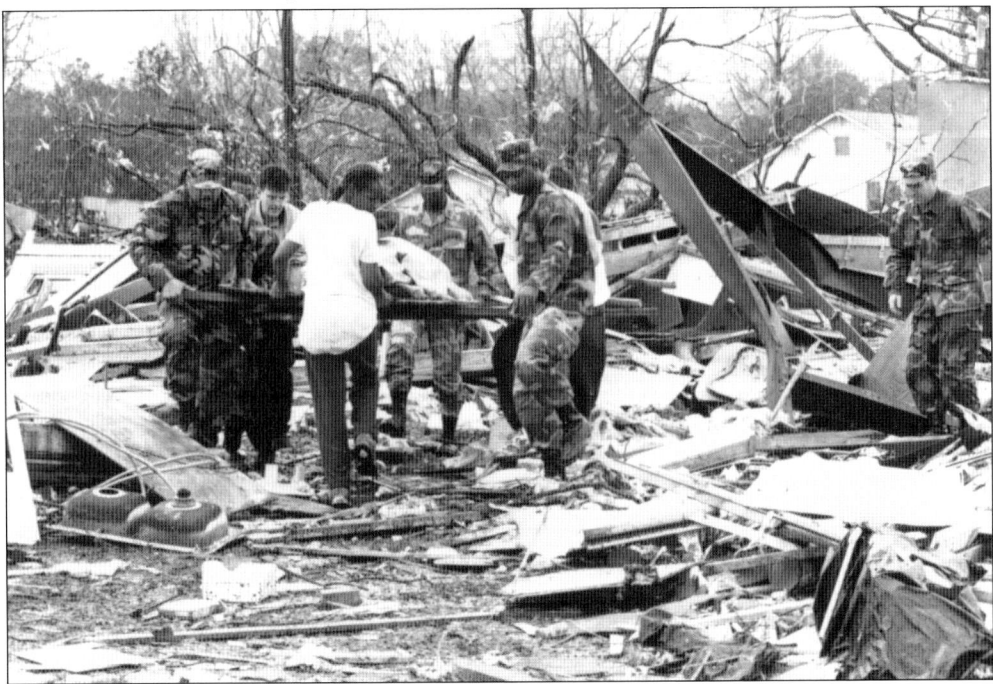

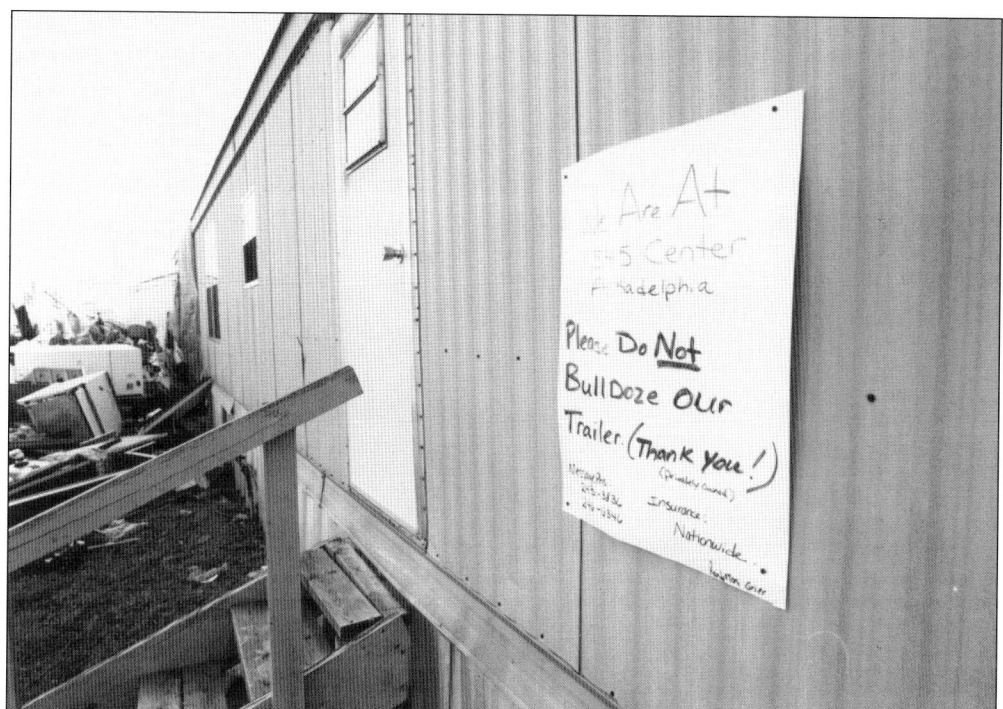

Randy and Toni Grier, occupants of the single trailer left standing in the Cutler Mobile Home Park, affixed a notice to the outside wall of the home, imploring cleanup crews not to bulldoze their home. In Arkadelphia, 67 mobile homes were destroyed, and another 12 were damaged. The Arkadelphia City Board contracted with the US Army Corps of Engineers to clean up tornado debris. FEMA covered 75 percent of the cost of cleanup, while the state split the remaining 25 percent with the city. (HSU.)

Many houses along Caddo Street were reduced to splinters. Shelters were set up at several local churches, including Park Hill Baptist, Third Street Baptist, and First Methodist, and in two Henderson State University dormitories. (HSU.)

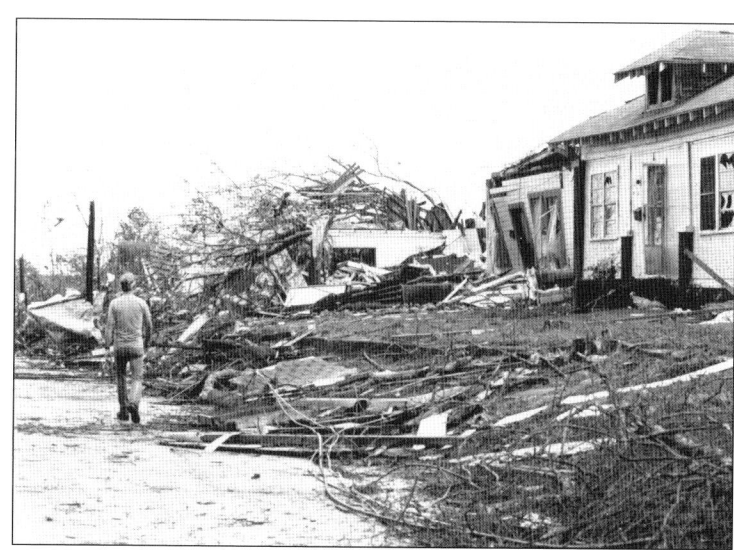

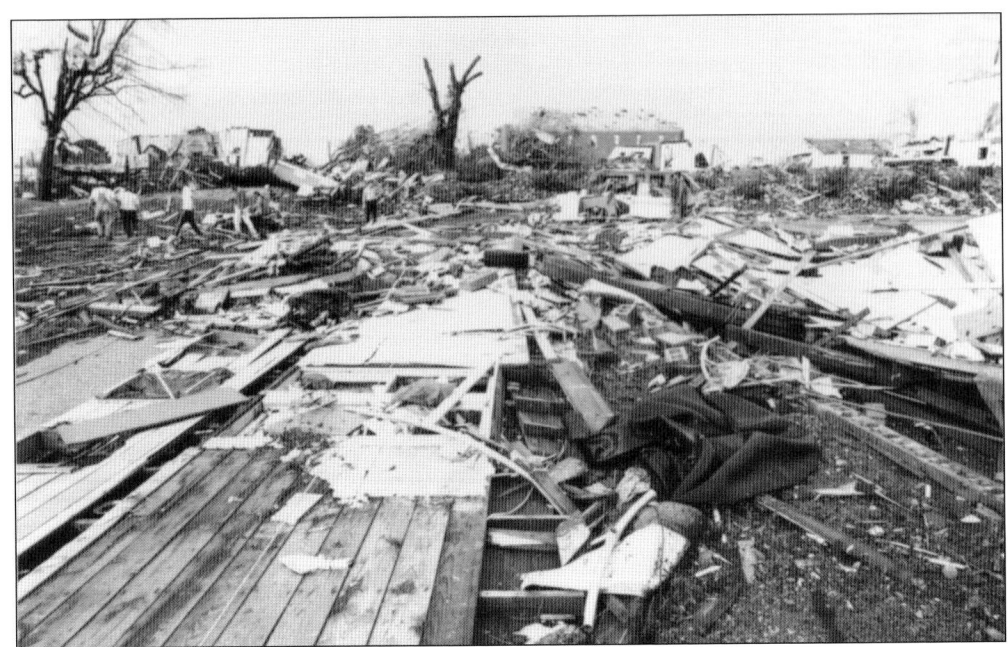

Homes along Cutler and Twelfth Streets (above) and South Tenth Street (below) were leveled or heavily damaged. Faintly visible in the background of the image below is the county courthouse clock tower. The winds from the storm cell, which tracked northeast from Clark County, deposited items from Arkadelphia in Mayflower, 83 miles away. In the weeks following the tornado, the local newspaper, the *Daily Siftings Herald*, announced it would hold and publicize items lost in the storm. Some of the items the newspaper held in an attempt to locate owners included pages from a baby book, photographs, a diploma, and a Special Olympics medal. (Both, HSU.)

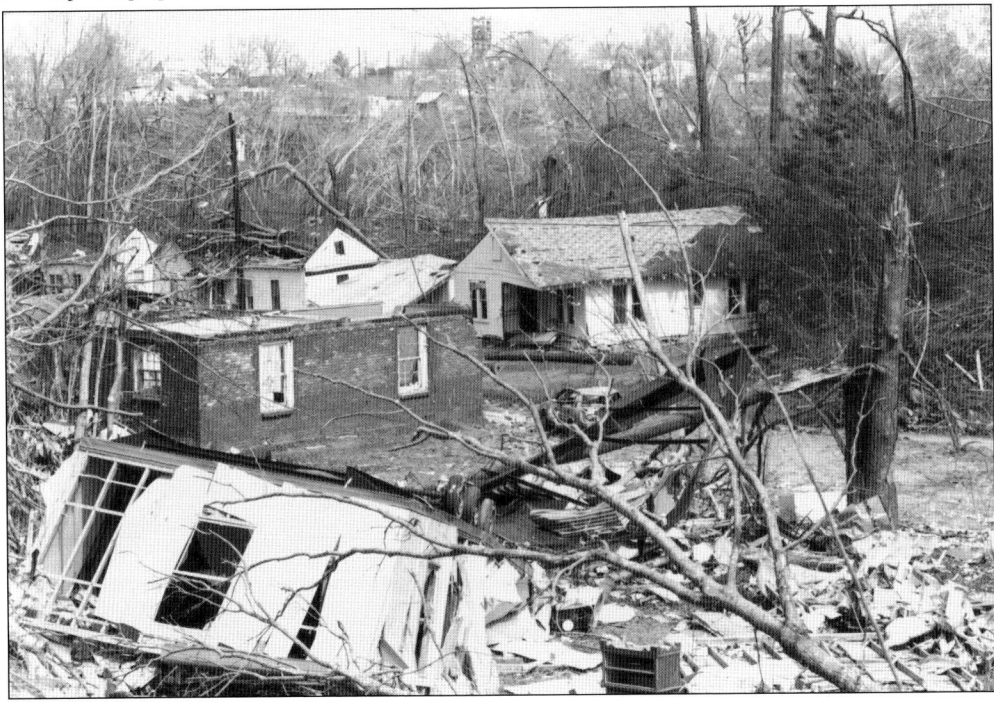

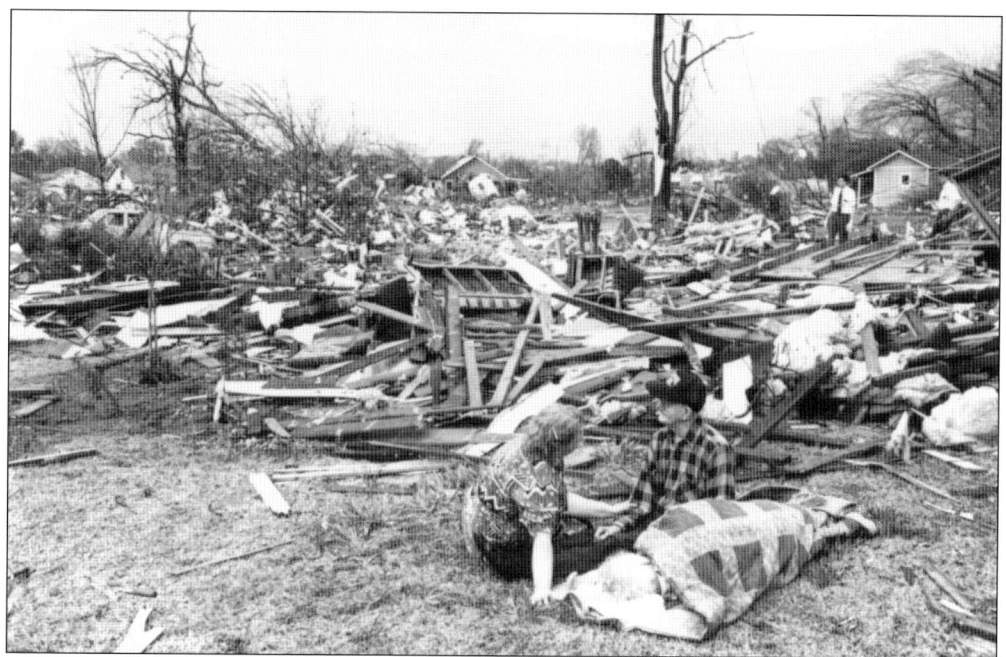

Mae Buck's home and day care on Twelfth Street near Cutler were destroyed. Had the tornado struck during a weekday, Buck's day care would have been full of children. Buck, seated on the ground with her father, Olen Huff, watches over her mother, Violet Huff, while they wait for assistance. (HSU.)

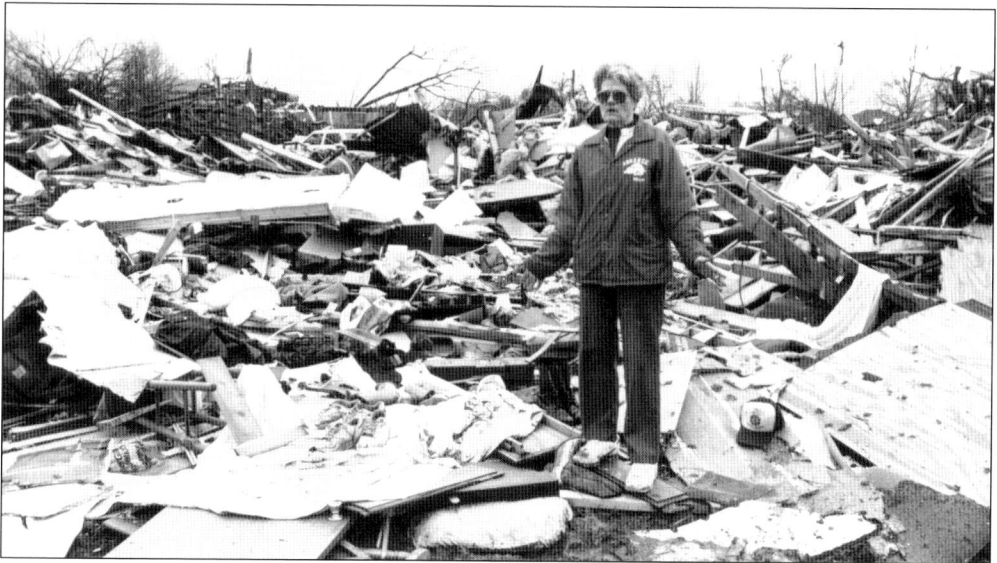

Billie Hill stands amid the rubble of Thelma Sparks's home on Cutler Street. Hill, a relative of Sparks, said five people were home when the tornado hit. In the hours immediately following the storm, help began to arrive from around the county and state. A total of 29 firemen from the Arkadelphia Fire Department responded, along with about 65 others from surrounding areas, including Amity and Alpine. State law enforcement, Search and Rescue, the National Guard, and the Red Cross also responded. Individual volunteers from Malvern, Sheridan, Pine Bluff, and Hope also came to Arkadelphia's assistance. (HSU.)

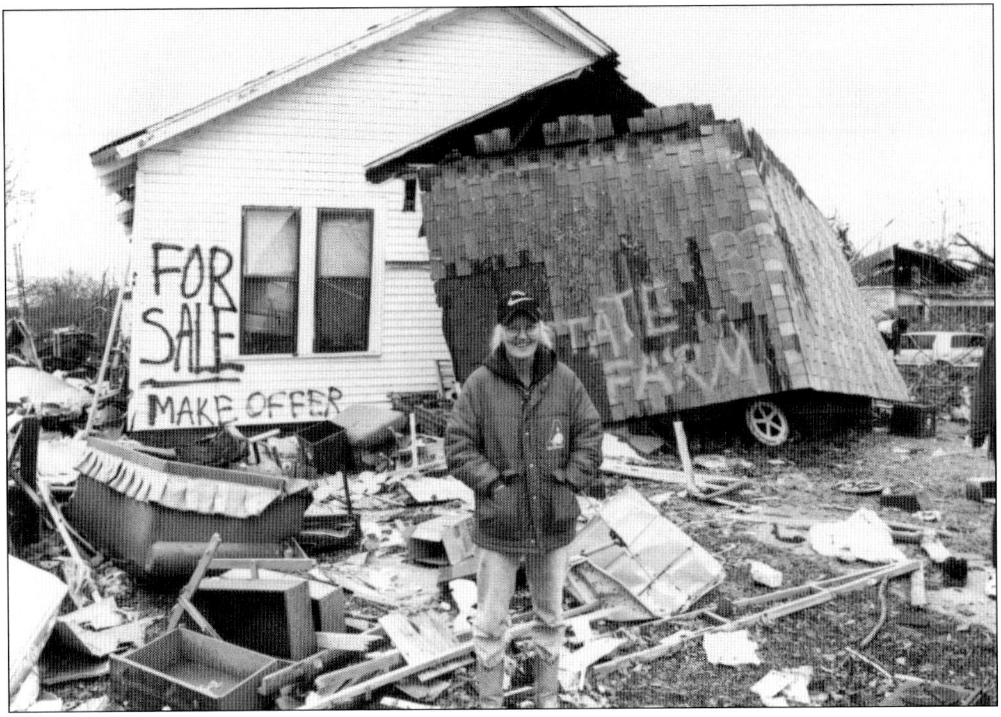

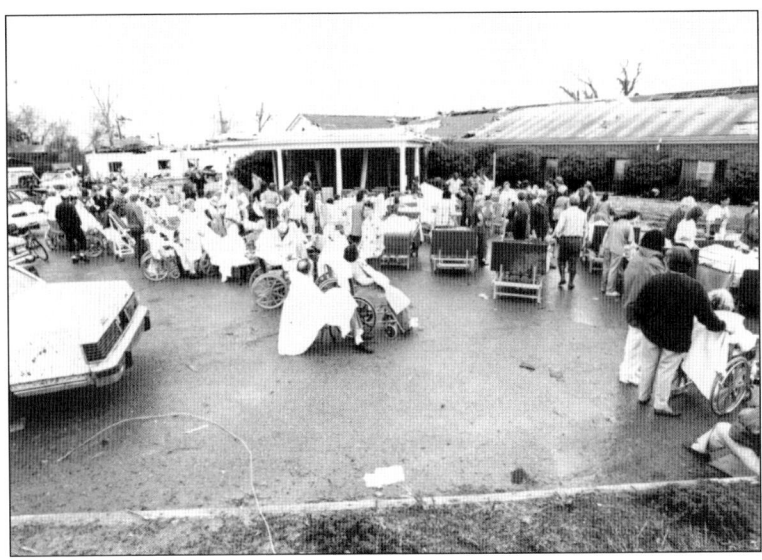

Joy McCarty stands in front of her family's heavily damaged home at 223 Clinton Street. McCarty told newspapers that when they heard the sirens, she and her husband ran into the bathroom and held onto the feet of an old cast-iron bathtub. The house imploded around them. When they emerged from the bathroom, she found a neighbor standing in the wreckage of their home. He had been blown out of his house and into the McCartys' home by the storm. (HSU.)

Residents at Beverly Health and Rehabilitation, formerly Riverwood Convalescent Home at 102 Caddo Street, await transportation to other facilities. Ninety residents in all were relocated to other facilities. (HSU.)

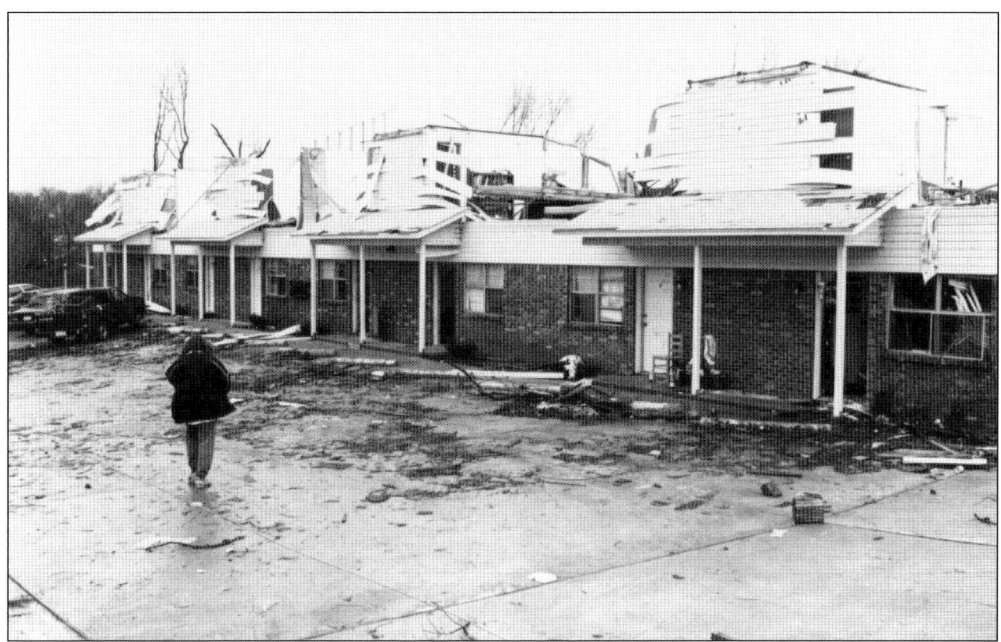

This apartment complex on Eleventh Street sustained heavy damage. In Arkadelphia, five apartments were destroyed, and another 28 were damaged. (HSU.)

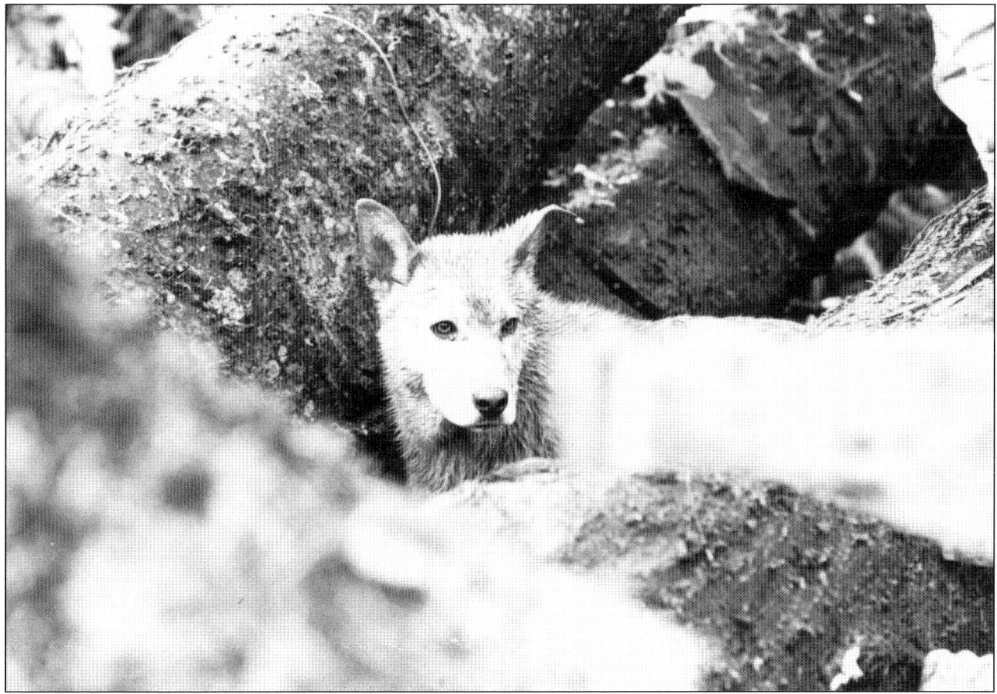

A disoriented dog stands among downed trees and rubble moments after the tornado hit. Human residents of Clark County were not the only ones displaced by the storm. The Humane Society of Clark County set up a temporary shelter for homeless pets at the county fairgrounds. At its height, the shelter housed 84 animals, mostly dogs. Some of the displaced pets were eventually reunited with their owners. (HSU.)

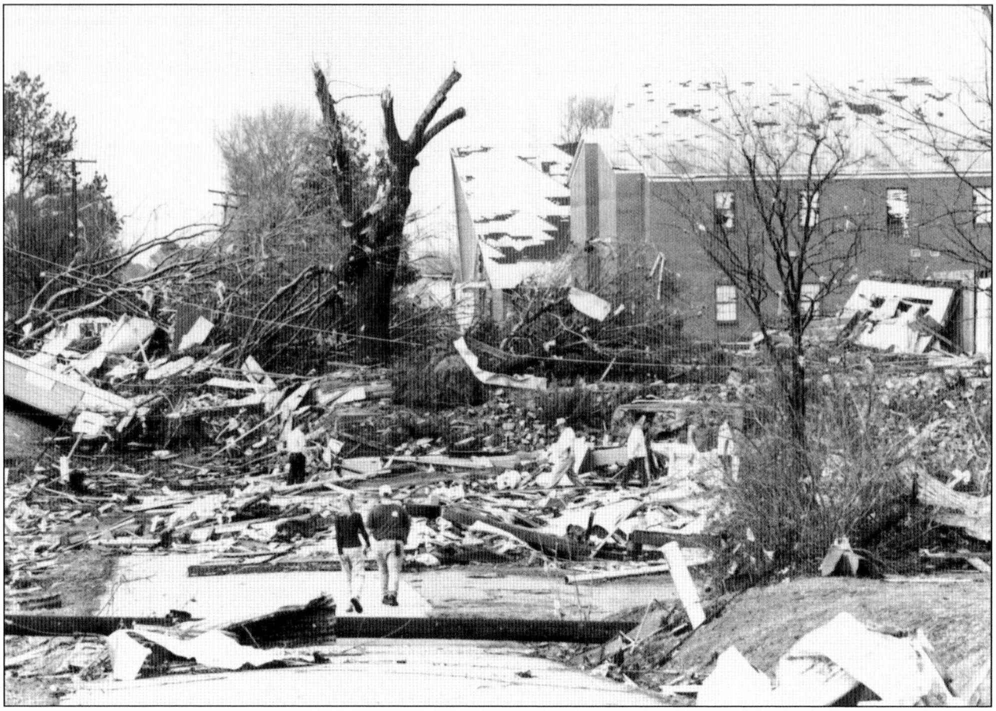

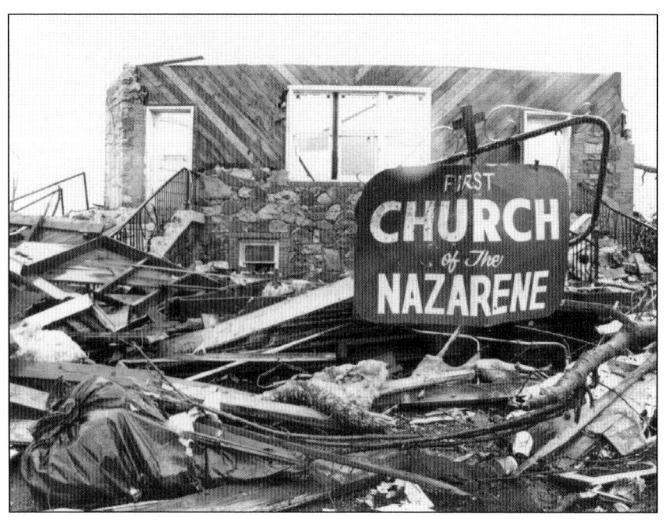

The southeastern portion of Arkadelphia, including Walnut, Fifth, Sixth, and Seventh Streets, was hard hit by the tornado. All four of Second Baptist Church's buildings, shown here, at right, were impacted. Windows were blown out, and the sanctuary roof was heavily damaged. Rain, following on the heels of the tornado, resulted in additional losses of furniture, hymnals, Bibles, and the church organ. Damage was estimated at $250,000. Until repairs could be completed, the congregation met for worship at Ouachita Baptist University's Baptist Student Union. (HSU.)

Only the sign remained at the First Church of the Nazarene at 414 South Seventh Street. Almost nothing from the church was salvageable. Rain destroyed the church's piano and organ and $1,000 worth of newly purchased hymnals. Until a new facility was constructed, the Nazarene congregation shared a facility with the New Hope Baptist Mission on Main Street. Eventually, the church built a new house of worship in Caddo Valley on a tract of land it owned. (HSU.)

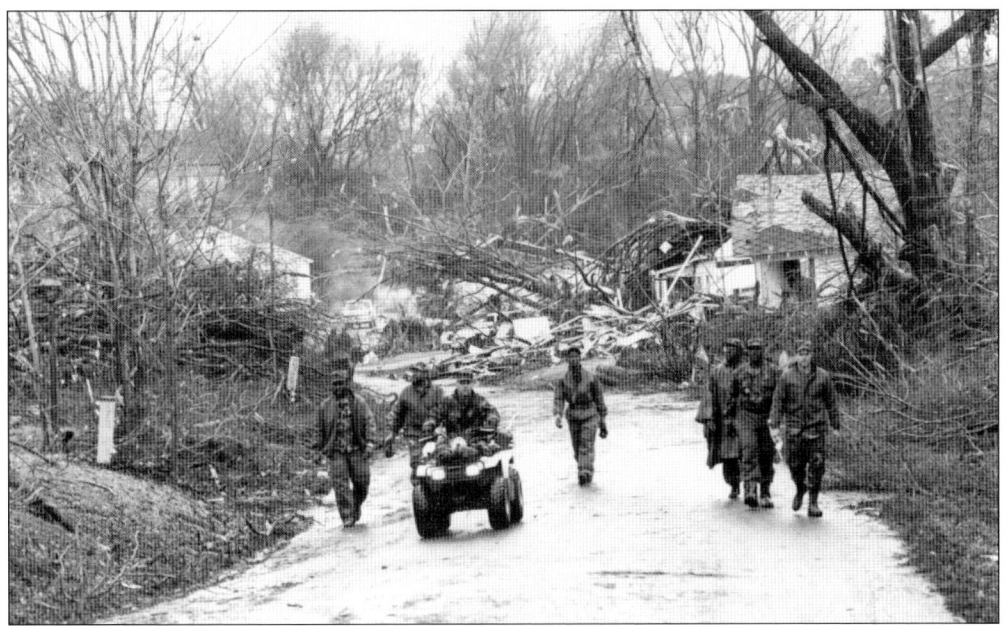

Members of the Army National Guard (ARNG) inspect the South Tenth Street area. The 153rd ARNG unit from Clark County had been training at Camp Robinson in North Little Rock on March 1. The unit returned immediately to Arkadelphia, where they assisted with search and rescue, securing properties, and enforcing the city's dawn-to-dusk curfew. Arkansas governor Mike Huckabee mobilized two additional units to aid Arkadelphia. By the time the ARNG pulled out of Arkadelphia on March 26, over 250 guardsmen had assisted with recovery efforts. (HSU.)

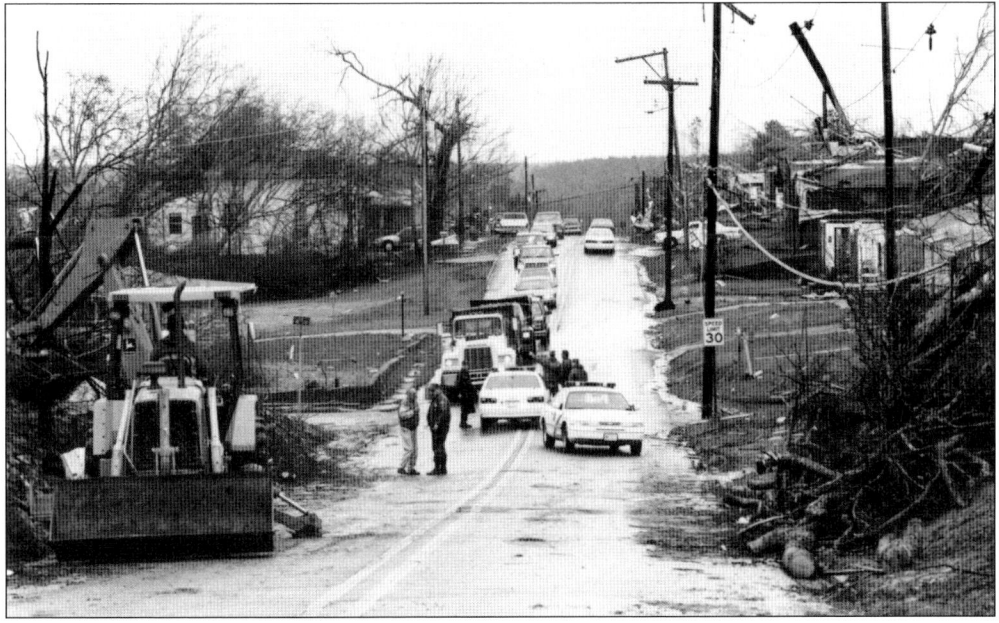

Two days following the tornado, traffic was finally allowed to pass through Arkadelphia on Caddo Street. Immediately following the storm, interstate exits to Arkadelphia were closed. To prevent unauthorized access and looting, Arkadelphia was divided into four travel zones, and individuals needing access were provided with zone-specific passes. (HSU.)

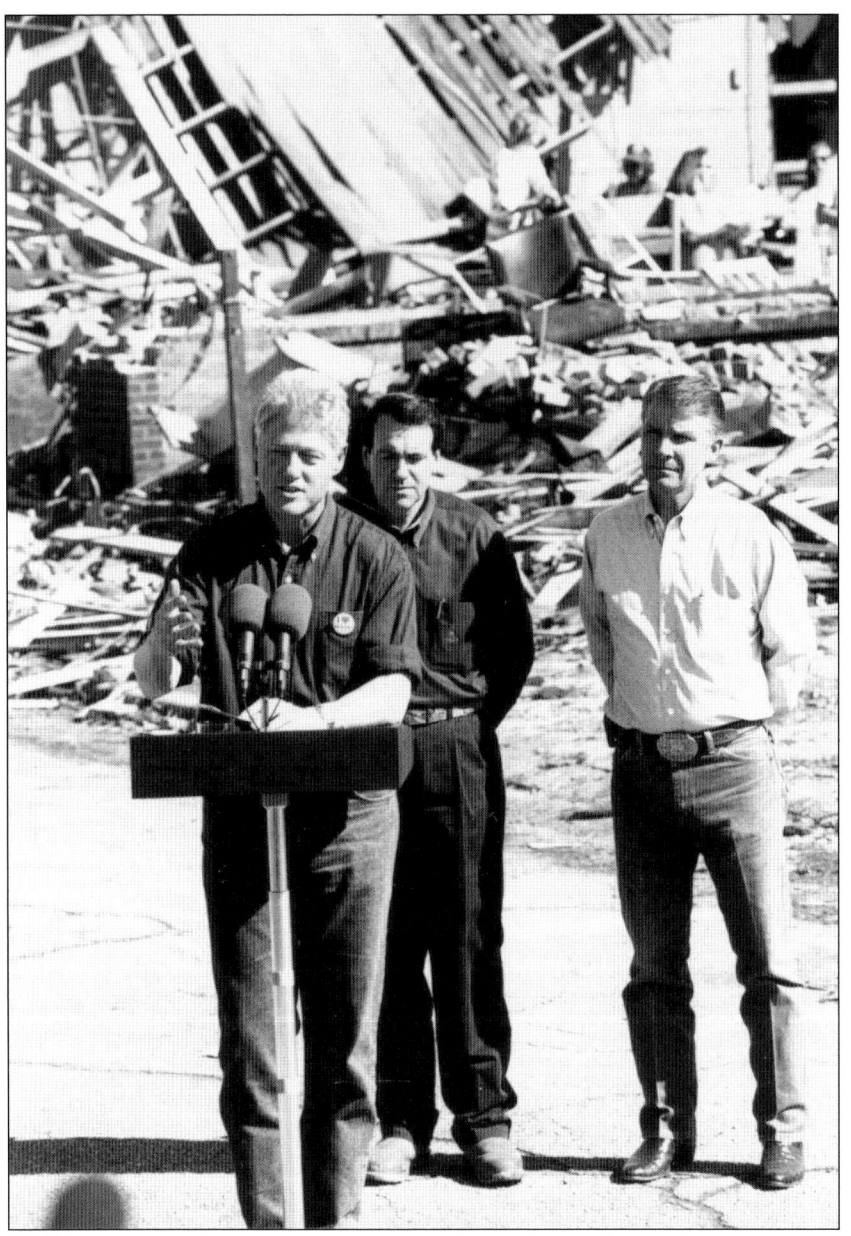

Pres. Bill Clinton, flanked by Arkansas governor Mike Huckabee (left) and FEMA director James Lee Witt (right), addresses reporters in Arkadelphia. President Clinton and other federal officials visited Arkadelphia, along with other towns in Arkansas affected by the tornado outbreak, on Tuesday, March 5. Clinton grew up in Hope, just a few counties down the road from Clark County. As a youth, he spent time in Arkadelphia and maintained friendships with town residents. While he noted that "Arkadelphia had been all but destroyed," he encouraged residents to focus on rebuilding. In conversation with Arkansas state representative Percy Malone, an Arkadelphia pharmacist whose business was impacted by the storm, Clinton suggested that, in rebuilding, Arkadelphians think about how they wanted the town to look in 30 years. Clinton's remarks spurred the formation of an Arkadelphia 2025 Commission that assisted in planning the town's rebuilding. (HSU.)

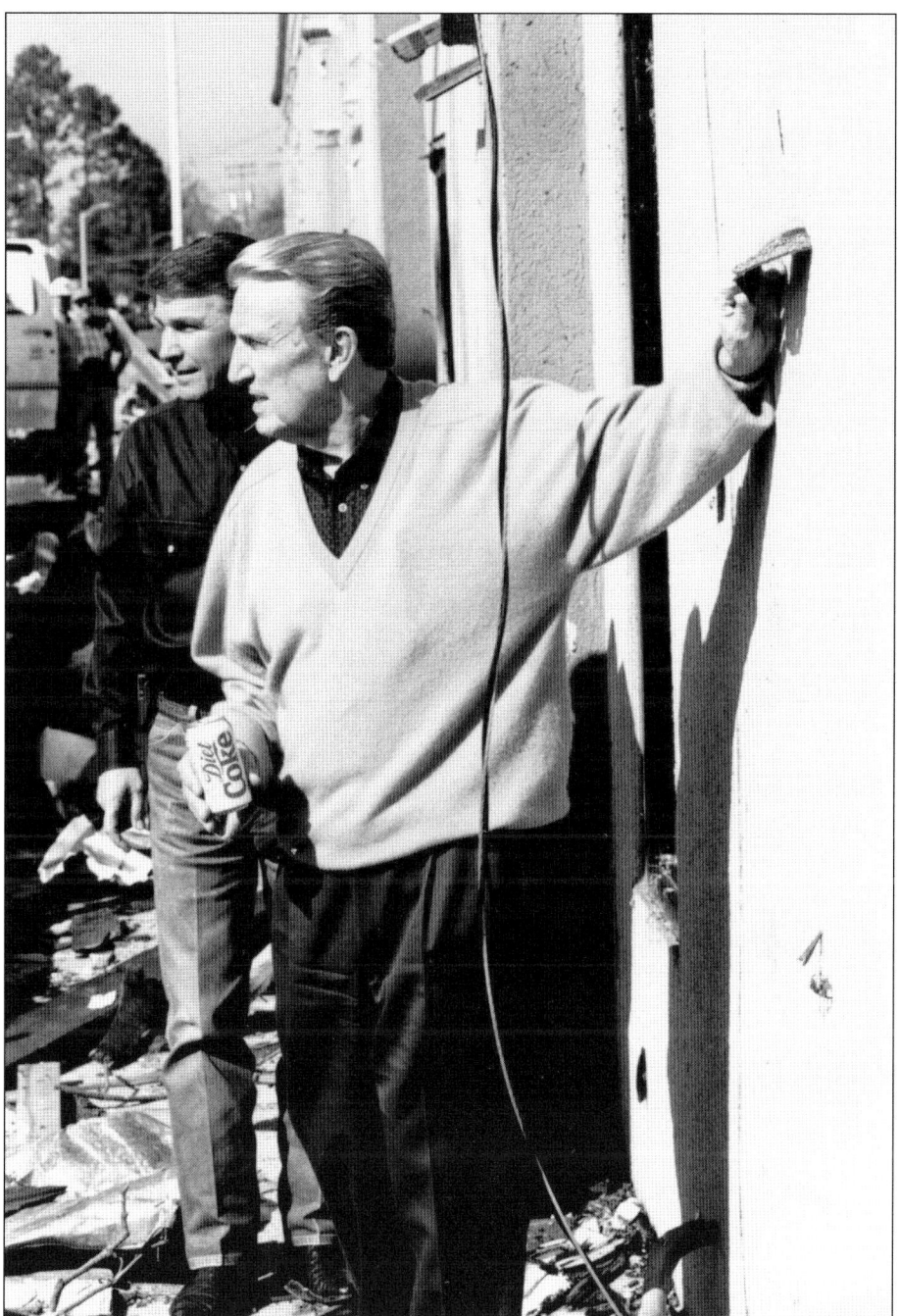

Former Arkansas governor and US senator Dale Bumpers points out a shingle embedded in a wall of Percy Malone's office building on Sixth Street. FEMA director James Lee Witt, a fellow Arkansan, stands beside him. In addition to Senator Bumpers, President Clinton, and Governor Huckabee, a number of state and federal officials visited Arkadelphia in the days immediately following the storm. Among those who visited were US secretary of transportation Rodney Slater, US congressman Jay Dickey of Arkansas, state senator Mike Ross, regional FEMA administrator Buddy Young, and Aida Alvarez, director of the Small Business Administration. (HSU.)

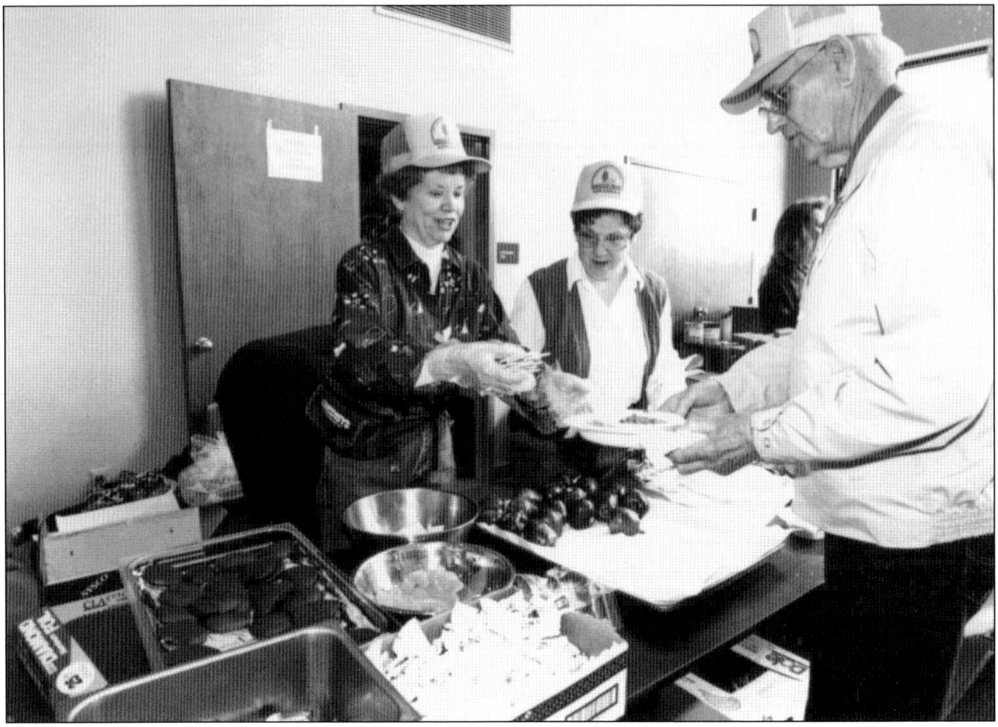

First Baptist Church became a central relief station in the aftermath of the tornado, with the main kitchen serving three meals a day. Third Street Baptist, Park Hill, and First United Methodist Church also provided shelter and meals. Greater Pleasant Hill Missionary Baptist Church distributed food and clothing, as did New Hope Mission. Goza Junior High School collected clothing, and the Arkadelphia Public Schools provided food from their cafeterias for those staying in shelters. Local restaurants and groceries supplied food and meals. The Feed the Children Foundation of Oklahoma sent a truckload of provisions to help Arkadelphia residents in need. (HSU.)

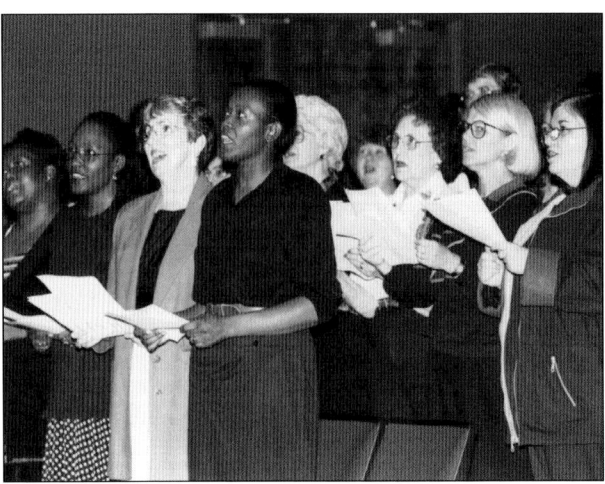

On March 12, two weeks after the tornado, a special worship service for the community was held at Ouachita Baptist University's Jones Performing Arts Center. Gov. Mike Huckabee and local dignitaries spoke, and the Clark County Community Choir sang a selection of "Songs of Solidarity," which included "We Shall Overcome," "The Battle Hymn of the Republic," and "Blessed Be the Tie That Binds." Six ferns in memory of those who lost their lives graced the front of the stage. (HSU.)

ABOUT THE CLARK COUNTY HISTORICAL MUSEUM

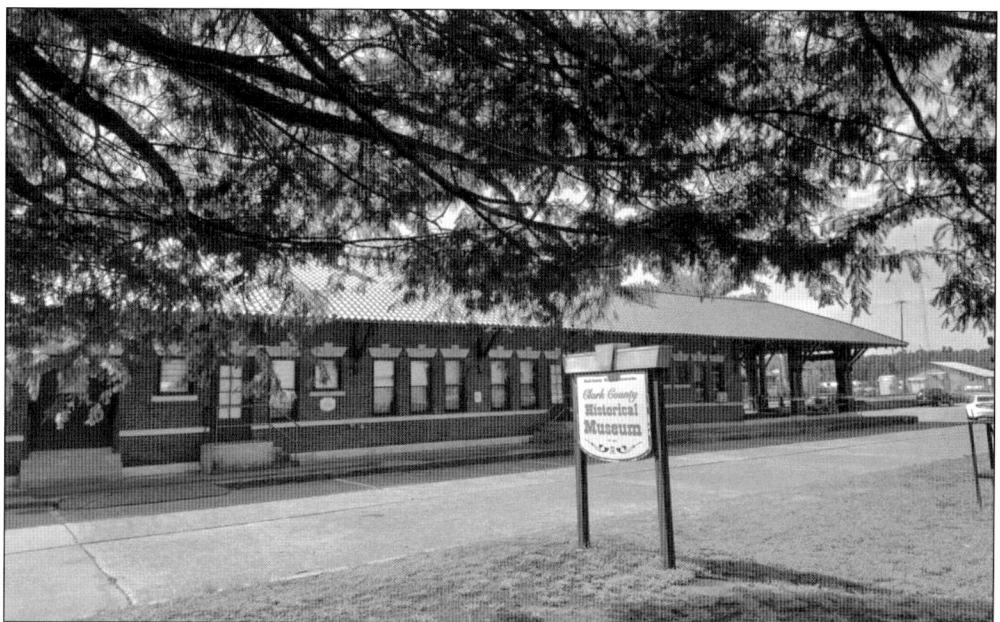

Author royalties from the sales of this book go to the Clark County Historical Museum in Arkadelphia. The Clark County Museum opened in October 2003 in the historical Missouri-Pacific train depot on South Fifth Street. The museum operated continuously under the aegis of the Clark County Historical Association until 2023, when it became an independent nonprofit organization. As the official museum of Clark County, the museum is dedicated to preserving and interpreting the history of all of Clark County's people, places, and events. The museum's collections encompass the history of Clark County from its earliest Native American residents through today. Admission to the museum is free, and visitors of all ages are welcome.

DISCOVER THOUSANDS OF LOCAL HISTORY BOOKS
FEATURING MILLIONS OF VINTAGE IMAGES

Arcadia Publishing, the leading local history publisher in the United States, is committed to making history accessible and meaningful through publishing books that celebrate and preserve the heritage of America's people and places.

Find more books like this at
www.arcadiapublishing.com

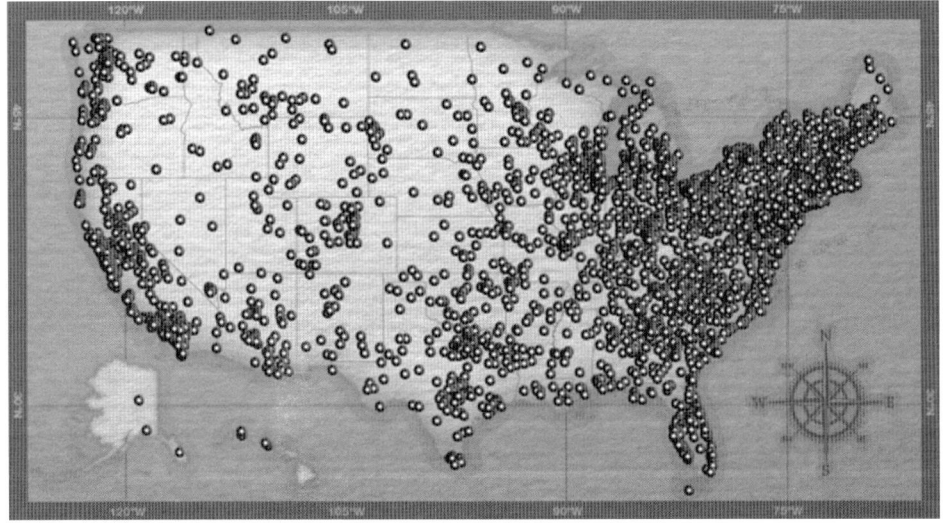

Search for your hometown history, your old stomping grounds, and even your favorite sports team.

Consistent with our mission to preserve history on a local level, this book was printed in South Carolina on American-made paper and manufactured entirely in the United States. Products carrying the accredited Forest Stewardship Council (FSC) label are printed on 100 percent FSC-certified paper.

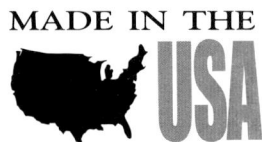

MADE IN THE USA